D1103736

CHARLES PEIRCE'S THEORY OF SCIENTIFIC METHOD

The Orestes Brownson Series

on Contemporary Thought and Affairs

No. 7  1970

CHARLES PEIRCE'S THEORY OF SCIENTIFIC METHOD

FRANCIS E. REILLY, S. J.

FORDHAM UNIVERSITY PRESS

NEW YORK

Library of Congress Catalog Card Number: 79-105527
ISBN 0-8232-0880-X
Printed in the United States of America

ACKNOWLEDGMENT

To Harvard University Press for the *Collected Papers of Charles Sanders Peirce*. Reprinted by permission of the publishers from *Collected Papers of Charles Sanders Peirce,* Vols. I-VIII, Charles Hartshorne, Paul Weiss, and Arthur W. Burks, eds., Cambridge, Mass.: The Belknap Press of Harvard University Press, copyright 1931, 1932, 1933, 1934, 1935, 1958, 1959, 1960, 1961, 1962, 1963 by the President and Fellows of Harvard College.

CONTENTS

to my mother

to Kathleen and Neil

and to the memory of my father

PREFACE

THE PRESENT WORK is an attempt to enter into the thought of Charles Sanders Peirce in the areas which interested him most, scientific method and the philosophical questions it raises. I have organized this book in great measure from Peirce's own writings and have taken account of the chronological setting of his various works where it seemed significant. I have tried at places to point out the close connections of several major themes in his writings, and thereby to show both the rich diversity of his thought and its systematic unity. The major commentators have enlightened my own mind on Peirce's meaning, though my real debt to them may not be obvious from what I have written.

The first chapter is a sketch of Peirce the thinker and writer. Chapters II–V present a study of the spirit and phases of scientific inquiry, and a consideration of its relevance to certain outstanding and overarching philosophical views held by Peirce. This double approach is necessary, I think, because his views on scientific method are interlaced with a profound and elaborate philosophy of the cosmos. He could not, it seems, propose any developed epistemology of inquiry without working out simultaneously a genuine philosophy of the universe and the man who studies it.

I am deeply indebted to Professor James Collins, to my former professors and associates at Saint Louis University, to the administrators of the Loyola House of Studies and of San Jose Seminary, Manila, who gave me the needed leisure to produce this work, and to many friends in the Philippines who helped with certain technical details.

FRANCIS E. REILLY, S.J.

Ateneo de Manila University

Chapter I

CHARLES SANDERS PEIRCE: PHILOSOPHER, SCIENTIST, WRITER

CHARLES SANDERS PEIRCE (1839–1914) was an extraordinary genius in both science and philosophy. His proficiency in the sciences was not limited to the organized studies of physics, chemistry, and geology, but also included an appraisal of the procedures used by those who were successfully advancing knowledge. He claims to have associated with the greatest minds of his day in physical science and to have made some contributions of his own to mathematics, optics, gravimetry, and so forth. In short, as he says, he was completely saturated with the spirit of the physical sciences (1.3).[1]

At the same time his interest in philosophy led him to read and ponder various philosophical systems and to attempt to consider them with empathy as their own adherents did. Peirce's attitude toward philosophy was one of reverence for the great thinkers of the past, and of pioneering originality regarding contemporary issues. As a philosopher he was devoted to profound reflection, and had developed his powers of analysis in those areas of reality which interested him.

As both a philosopher and a scientist Peirce studied the universe, using the work of previous philosophers and the method of the sciences to guide his conjectures about its constitution. For him the method of the sciences was not only a tool employed in examining nature, but was also

[1] The notes for this chapter begin on page 157.

the direct object of his careful study. A lifelong associate of scientists, Peirce says that he devoted thirty or forty years to the study of the methods employed by them.[2] He brought to this study a developed power for philosophical thought on the nature of knowledge and the methods of acquiring it.

His scientific pursuits, together with his philosophical reflection on the way the scientist operates, made him a competent judge of the method of the sciences. For Peirce the study of the scientific method and of the principles which underlie the discovery of scientific truth constitutes the science of logic. "Logic is the doctrine of truth, its nature and the manner in which it is to be discovered" (7.321). Peirce's investigations into mathematical logic and the theory of signs, as well as his formulation and development of the pragmatic method, were directed toward a more thorough understanding of the thought procedures that the scientist uses.[3] Inquiry and its methods were the main objects studied by Peircean logic.[4]

Peirce examined scientific knowledge, as it is open to reflection, analyzed its phases, criticized its results, and worked out several elaborate schemes for classifying the scientific, philosophical, and mathematical disciplines of his day. In a more philosophical spirit, he attributed the success which scientists had in explaining the universe to a certain affinity of the human mind for the ways of nature, a continuity of man with the rest of the cosmos. He studied the extent of the scientific method and contrasted it with unsuitable and unreasonable methods of knowing which men have actually tried to use. He has, then, worked out a philosophy of scientific knowing, an epistemology of the sciences.

The breadth and depth of his studies have led his outstanding commentators to regard him as a light of exceptional brilliance in the history of philosophy. "Some people, indeed, would now claim that the width and depth of his scientific culture and his astonishing combination of critical perseverance with constructive power entitled Peirce to rank as the most original philosopher of the nineteenth century."[5] Philip P. Wiener asserts with good reason that Peirce is "the most versatile, profound, and original philosopher that the United States has ever produced."[6] And yet, impatient of academic routine, he never held a teaching position for long. Dismissed from the newly established Johns Hopkins University after a few years of teaching, for reasons that are still not altogether clear, by ordinary standards a failure, he retired to a town in Pennsylvania in isolation, studying, thinking, and writing at a tremendous pace. But as Morris R. Cohen points out, if the norm of philosophical success is the production of "new and fruitful ideas of radical importance," then Peirce "would easily be the greatest figure in American philosophy." [7]

To a significant extent the interests and the development of this extraordinary genius can be attributed to his home and academic training. He was born on September 10, 1839, "in Cambridge, Massachusetts, in a stone-colored wooden house in Mason Street," the second son of Benjamin and Sarah Peirce (2.663).[8] Being born in Cambridge and being the son of Benjamin Peirce were important in determining what Charles was to become, since Cambridge was the most influential center of American thought, and Benjamin Peirce was among America's foremost scientists in the nineteenth century.[9] A professor of mathematics and natural philosophy, and later of astronomy, at Harvard, the elder Peirce was a scholar of high repute and a teacher of excellent ability. His influence on Charles was deep and lasting, though not altogether beneficial. He was gifted with a mind of exceptional generalizing power and communicated this to Charles in the long walks they used to take and in the formation that he imposed on his son at home. The father supervised his son's education, emphasizing mathematics, philosophy, the experimental sciences and logic, and the development of his son's sensory powers and aesthetic appreciations. Benjamin Peirce was a theist and a Unitarian who believed in a special conformity of the human mind to nature and to nature's God—a theme, as already mentioned, that became prominent in Charles' writing in later years.[10] On the debit side, he seems to have forced the intellectual training of his son and to have neglected a balanced education of the boy in other respects.[11]

Before entering Harvard at the age of 16, Charles had already set up his own chemical laboratory, and had read through Whately's *Logic*. His formal education at Harvard put stress on philosophy and the physical sciences, though he completed his courses there without distinction, being the seventy-first in a class of ninety-one graduates. During his college days he read far beyond the academic requirements, going through Schiller's *Ästhetische Briefe* and beginning a long study of Kant's *Critique of Pure Reason*.

After graduation from Harvard, Peirce "was away surveying in the wilds of Louisiana when Darwin's great work appeared, and though I learned by letters of the immense sensation it had created, I did not return until early in the following summer when I found [Chauncey] Wright all enthusiasm for Darwin, whose doctrines appeared to him as a sort of supplement to those of Mill" (5.64). The influence of Darwin and other theorists of evolution was permanent in Peirce's philosophy.

In the same year he entered the Lawrence Scientific School at Cambridge to study chemistry, was awarded the M.A. degree in 1862, and in 1863 he was the first to receive the Sc.B. in chemistry from Harvard *summa cum laude*. About that time he joined the United States Coast and Geodetic Survey, and retained affiliation with that organization for thirty years. About the same time Peirce studied biological classification under the famous Louis Agassiz, a strong opponent of Darwinian evolution (1.205*n*).

He became interested in the logic of science at an early age, and retained the interest throughout his life. There is evidence that he gave a series of University Lectures at Harvard "On the Logic of Science" during the academic year 1864–65, and another set of twelve lectures on "The Logic of Science and Induction" at the Lowell Institute in the winter of 1866–67.[12]

In the 'seventies he continued scientific work at the Harvard Observatory in the field of astronomy, which resulted in his only book published during his life, *Photometric Researches* (1878). He crossed the Atlantic several times to further the progress of science in Europe. An even more important event during those years was the birth of pragmatism at the "Metaphysical Club" whose members used to meet from time to time in Cambridge. At those informal meetings with Nicholas St. John Green, Wendell Holmes, William James, Chauncey Wright, and occasionally Francis Ellingwood Abbot and John Fiske, Peirce gradually developed his pragmatism, another very prominent theme, which remained a lifelong interest.[13] Peirce was "the one unquestionably great figure in the Pragmatist movement."[14]

Peirce's closest friend throughout his life was William James. It was through James's influence that Peirce was appointed lecturer at Hopkins, and was considered for a similar appointment at Harvard. But

James was clearly aware of Peirce's temperamental troubles. Peirce was "thorny and spinous," and not gifted with social talent. He was ill-at-ease with people, touchy, quick to take offense, suspicious, and arrogant at times.[15] Nevertheless he had "a genuine vein of sentiment and softness running through him, but so narrow a vein it always surprises me when I meet it," as James wrote in a letter to Howison.[16] There was an atmosphere of warm and close friendship between the two, sealed by James's dedication of *The Will to Believe* to his friend, and expressed in his financial help to Peirce during the latter's years of poverty at Milford, Pennsylvania. But at the same time there was an open and admirable frankness in their expressions of disagreement about belief, the pragmatic method and other philosophical questions, as is clear from their many letters. Both Henry and William James were aware of Peirce's abilities, his first-class intellect, his intense and thorough work.[17]

After Peirce's death at Milford on April 19, 1914, Harvard University purchased his manuscripts from his widow. An early collection of important works edited by Morris R. Cohen, *Chance, Love and Logic*, was published in 1923, but the major part of his writings was published by Harvard under the editorship of Charles Hartshorne and Paul Weiss in six volumes of the *Collected Papers of Charles Sanders Peirce* from 1931 to 1935, and in the seventh and eighth volumes under the editorship of Arthur W. Burks in 1958.[18] The eighth volume contains a bibliography of Peirce's writings, a scholarly tool of great value, prepared by Burks. In addition to the standard histories and anthologies of American philosophy, there have been in the last twenty-five years at least eight books of major length on Peirce in both English and Italian. Besides these works there have been a number of handy collections of his writings and numerous articles on particular aspects of his logic and philosophy.

Despite the advantages offered by these bibliographical tools, the student of Peirce's philosophy must face serious problems. There is no single work of Peirce to which the student can turn for a presentation of his philosophy. He did not succeed in publishing a book on any of the important topics which interested him. And although he dreamed of major composition, none of the great topics of interest to him ever received adequate treatment in a single work. What Peirce has left amounts to a large number of reviews, lectures, dictionary articles, random paragraphs, letters to friends, journal articles, unpublished papers, writings for controversy, and a variety of other works. He composed for farmers' journals, for Smithsonian Reports, for technical audiences, for professional philosophers, and these writings ranged over a period of forty years. During this time his style changed considerably. In his youth his style was vigorous and cryptic; but during his later years he composed with brilliance and freedom, and even looseness, with less care for accuracy than during his early days. He himself wrote in a letter to William James in 1898 that his style was brilliant, its brilliance consisting in a mixture of irony and seriousness; indeed the very same views were proposed both ironically and seriously.

The interpreter has the advantage of finding Peirce's main ideas repeatedly presented in this motley variety of writings; it is somewhat easier to judge what his main interests are, since he continually returns to them. But treatments of important topics, which are both unified and adequately thorough, are less easy to find. This makes it necessary to examine numerous texts bearing on a given topic, and to interpret each in the light of the others, remembering that Peirce's literary genres range from the ironic lecture style to the detached accuracy of the dictionary article.

In his later works he repeatedly rethought many of the problems handled in his earlier writings, and while there is unmistakable development in his thought, it is nevertheless true that many of the prominent themes in his philosophy remained fundamentally permanent throughout his life.[19] Since he wrote voluminously and since the recurrence of similar ideas is so frequent, there is no better commentator on Peirce than Peirce himself. For this reason, the present-day commentator should take his "crucial points of departure from statements that Peirce made about Peirce." [20]

There seems to be rather universal agreement—reasonably so—that Peirce was a systematic thinker. Despite the fact that his writings were fragmentary, exposing "rough, cryptic sketches of new fields," the lines of synthesis and system are most obvious.[21] In developing a vocabulary to express his original ideas he was highly creative, and this creativity is an initial, though not final, obstacle to the student of Peirce. As Cohen remarks, Peirce was "a pioneer who lived with new and strange ideas; and he wrote for those willing to think for themselves and find out the truth, not for those who wish philosophy ladled out to them."[22] Continues Peirce: "There are philosophical soup shops at every corner, thank God!" (1.11).

A student of Peirce will learn to appreciate the vigor and brilliance of his new insights into reality as well as the inclusive unity and systematic genius of his thought.[23]

In studying Peirce's theory of scientific method, it should become evident that the many themes discussed are rather tightly unified and interrelated. The systematic thought is there, even though it may take a bit of pondering to detect the synthesis.

Chapter II

THE SCIENTIST'S CONCERN: KNOWLEDGE FOR ITS OWN SAKE

Charles Peirce is not in agreement with the lexicographers' description of science as "systematized knowledge." For Peirce, science is best described as the pursuit carried on by scientific men. Genuine science is a living thing continually growing and developing (1.232). It must not be thought of as a mere collection of established truths. Rather, an intelligent conception of science "as a living historic entity must regard it as the occupation of that peculiar class of men, the scientific men" (1.99).

In the introduction to his projected "History of Science," Peirce asserts that the lexicographer and the non-scientist may regard science as an "organized body of knowledge"; but the genuine scientist regards his pursuit as a "mode of life."[1] And in the course of the same work, he makes another quick reference to the same description of science, and then portrays at length the kind of spirit which should guide the scientist. Science is the pursuit of scientific men, and this pursuit must be motivated by the pure love of knowledge for its own sake.

If we are to define science . . . in the sense of characterizing it as a living historic entity, we must conceive it as that about which such men as I have

[1] The notes for this chapter begin on page 159.

described busy themselves. As such, it does not consist so much in *knowing,* nor even in "organized knowledge," as it does in diligent inquiry into truth for truth's sake, without any sort of axe to grind, nor for the sake of the delight of contemplating it, but from an impulse to penetrate into the reason of things. . . . It is not knowing, but the love of learning, that characterizes the scientific man. . . . If a man burns to learn and sets himself to comparing his ideas with experimental results in order that he may correct those ideas, every scientific man will recognize him as a brother, no matter how small his knowledge may be.

But if a man occupies himself with investigating the truth of some question for some ulterior purpose, such as to make money, or to amend his life, or to benefit his fellows, he may be ever so much better than a scientific man, . . . but he is not a scientific man [1.44f].

An understanding of what science is, therefore, can be achieved only by understanding what the scientist is about. In grasping this it will be unmistakably clear that for Peirce the motive of the scientist is of primary importance: he must be in search of knowledge for its own sake. This, of course, means that the questions asked by the scientist, and the answers which he hopes to find, will be theoretical. Accordingly, the method that he follows will be adapted to the scientist's theoretical questions.

Hence the present chapter will consider scientific inquiry as the pursuit of truth for its own sake. Scientific doubt and belief, and the pragmatic method of scientific inquiry itself, will then appear as theoretical in character.[2] Only in the subsequent chapters will the details of the method be examined.

The divisions of the present chapter are not sharply distinct. Certain considerations occur in both parts, since the chapter has a single topic: the scientist's concern with knowledge for its own sake.

I. THE SCIENTIST'S SPIRIT: THE PURE LOVE OF KNOWLEDGE

The scientist animated by the pure love of truth, pursues knowledge for the sake of knowledge alone.[3] Understanding science as a pursuit of a certain class of men, Peirce points out in an article dealing with the great scientists of the nineteenth century that the distinctive character of men like Darwin, Wallace, Joule, Bernouli, Helmholtz, and Mendeleef was their "devotion to the pursuit of truth for truth's sake." [4] They regarded science, not as something printed in books, or as systematized knowledge, but as a way of life. For men of science achievement is not the primary consideration. What is primary is the spirit that guides the work.[5]

In their pursuit of learning for its own sake scientists are distinguished from other classes of men.[6] For scientists nature is a cosmos, "something great, and beautiful, and sacred, and eternal, and real" (5.589). They are out to learn the truth about the ways of nature, for the sake of learning, and for no other motive. If the quest for truth is motivated by any other purpose than the sheer desire for knowledge, the endeavor cannot belong to the realm of science.

Not only is there a distinction between scientists and practical men, but there is even a certain opposition. The practical man is concerned with action and results. And so, in order to act, he must believe "with all the force of his manhood" that the object of his action is good, and that his plan of action is right.[7] But the scientist is so interested in truth that he is willing to reject his present beliefs if experience demands this. "This is the reason that a good practical man cannot do the best scientific work. The temperaments requisite for the two kinds of business are altogether contrary to one another" (6.3).[8] The practical man cannot hope to understand what the scientist is about, unless he undergoes an intellectual rebirth.[9] He will not give probable reasoning the value that the scientist must give it, and he will tend to regard science as a guide to conduct, and hence will try to find in science the practical certainty that conduct requires.[10] "If a proposition is to be applied to action, it has to be embraced, or believed without reservation. There is no room for doubt, which can only paralyze action. But the scientific spirit requires a man to be at all times ready to dump his whole cartload of beliefs, the moment experience is against them" (1.55). Science, then, is the pursuit of theoretical knowledge, lived by men whose temperament is quite the opposite of that required for practical goals.

In a short passage from a work entitled "On Detached Ideas in General and on Vitally Important Topics," composed around 1898, Peirce explains with vivid clarity the primacy of the theoretical aspects of science, as well as his attitude toward those disciplines that are at once theoretical and practical:

Even if a science be useful—like engineering or surgery—yet if it is useful only in an insignificant degree as those sciences are, it still has a divine spark in which its petty practicality must be forgotten and forgiven. But as soon as a proposition becomes vitally important—then in the first place, it is sunk to the condition of a mere utensil; and in the second place, it ceases altogether to be scientific, because concerning matters of vital importance reasoning is at once an impertinence toward its subject matter and a treason against itself [1.671].

The scientist, therefore, must put his whole person into the pursuit of theoretical knowledge; he cannot serve the two masters, theory and practice, as Peirce says. Rather he must put aside the narrow point of view that practice takes, and let his inquiry be "animated by the true scientific Eros" (1.620).[11] His aim "is simply and solely knowledge of God's truth" (1.239).[12]

The motive and method of the scientist are most intimately related. The man who is animated with a truly scientific love of knowledge for its own sake is bound to come upon the right *method* of proceeding. At first his method may be faulty, but if the genuine scientific *Eros* continues to animate him, he will sooner or later make use of the correct scientific method. In a paper, entitled by Peirce "The Rule of Logic," he speaks of the self-corrective character of an inquiry motivated by the true scientific spirit.

Inquiry of every type, fully carried out, has the vital power of self-correction and of growth. This is a property so deeply saturating its inmost nature that it may truly be said that there is but one thing needful for learning the truth, and that is a hearty and active desire to learn what is true. If you really want to learn the truth, you will, by however devious a path, be surely led into the way of truth, at last. No matter how erroneous your ideas of the method may be at first, you will be forced at length to correct them so long as your activity is moved by that sincere desire [5.582].

An inquirer with the genuine scientific spirit must inevitably adopt the correct method sooner or later; and conversely, if a man approaches an inquiry with an axe to grind, his method will almost inevitably be faulty. The desire to learn must be pure, otherwise the method of inquiry will fail to ask the right questions, or it will give inaccurate replies. A diluted motive almost invariably distorts the method.

In a lecture written in 1898 and entitled "The Logic of Events," Peirce again emphasizes the dependence of scientific method on motive. The spirit of desiring to learn, he implies, is the most necessary requirement of scientific procedure (6.5). But a good intention, though of prime necessity, is not sufficient; the scientist must actually adopt the correct method, and carry on his investigation according to it. "The man who is working *in the right way* to learn something not already known is recognized by all men of science as one of themselves, no matter how little he is informed" (1.235—emphasis added). But if he is following an unsuitable method, through neglect, he is not a scientific man; such neglect may reflect a lack of intelligent sincerity in the seeker's motive. Peirce cannot deny the title of scientist to a man who has an "effective rage to learn the very truth," and who follows the best methods for his time. But the rage to know must be *effective*—that is, the man with a sincere love of learning must make use of the best method of learning.[13]

Since science is a living function of scientific men, it is more an affair of spirit and method than of conclusions.[14] "Mere knowledge, though it be systematized, may be a dead memory; while by science we all habitually mean a living and growing body of truth" (6.428). Peirce even goes so far (but with hesitancy) as to say that content-knowledge may not be necessary for science.

We might even say that knowledge is not necessary to science. The astronomical researches of Ptolemy, though they are in great measure false, must be acknowledged by every modern mathematician who reads them to be truly and genuinely scientific. That which constitutes science, then, is not so much correct conclusions, as it is a correct method. But the method of science is itself a scientific result. It did not spring out of the brain of a beginner: it was a historic attainment and a scientific achievement. So that not even this method ought to be regarded as essential to the beginnings of science. That which is essential however, is the scientific spirit, which is determined not to rest satisfied with existing opinions, but to press on to the real truth of nature [6.428].

It is clear, then, that for Peirce the pure love of truth is an absolutely required characteristic of the scientist. The motive will control the method, which is the life of science. And the results of the inquiry will follow from the proper use of the scientific method. "Science consists in actually drawing the bow on truth with intentness in the eye, with energy in the arm" (1.235). Could "intentness in the eye" refer to the purity of the scientist's motive and "energy in the arm" to the suitability of the method? In any event, science is a living process whose only purpose is "to learn the lesson that the universe has to teach it" (5.589). In a manuscript dated around 1902, Peirce gives an excellent description of science as a way of life which has as its purpose the finding of the truth, which pursues this purpose by a well-considered method founded on scientific results already ascertained by others, and which seeks cooperation in the hope that the truth may ultimately be found, even though not by the present inquirers (7.54).

II. THE THEORETICAL CHARACTER OF DOUBT, BELIEF, AND THE PRAGMATIC METHOD

Consistent with his position on the spirit of scientific inquiry, Peirce maintains that both the questions asked by scientists and the answers proposed by them are theoretical—i.e., they are concerned with the real truth of things, as described above. He repeatedly calls a question doubt, and an answer belief. Although doubt and belief have a wide non-scientific scope, the aim here is to understand what Peirce has to say about scientific doubt and belief, since these mark the beginning and the end of a scientific investigation, a process which he calls inquiry. As will become clearer in subsequent chapters, the method of inquiry in a scientific investigation is pragmatic, a designation which indicates the general upshot of the method but does not specify its details.[15]

An important but imperfect presentation of scientific doubt and belife, and of pragmatic inquiry, is found in two articles written by Peirce before the period of his greatest productivity.[16] The importance of these two articles can be judged from the following facts:[17] 1.) they were the first published enunciation of the importance of doubt and belief, and of the pragmatic maxim;[18] 2.) during his later years he made repeated reference to these two articles, undertook several revisions of them as the editors of the *Collected Papers* testify, repeatedly quoted from them, and continually expanded his understanding of the pragmatic method of sciences, using the two articles as a point of departure.[19]

In "The Fixation of Belief," Peirce attributes the eagerness for learning the truth to the dissatisfaction which doubt causes in a man. In the same article he describes doubt as "an uneasy and dissatisfied state from which we struggle to free ourselves and pass into the state of belief" (5.372). The struggle Peirce terms inquiry, and he asserts that the only purpose of inquiry is the removal of the irritating stimulus of doubt which is the same as the attainment of belief.[20] This state he also describes as "the settlement of opinion" (5.375). Inquiry therefore begins with doubt, and ends with belief (5.375f).

In the second of the two early works, "How to Make Our Ideas Clear," Peirce is somewhat critical of the above.

> It was there noticed ["The Fixation of Belief"] that the action of thought is excited by the irritation of doubt, and ceases when belief is attained; so that the production of belief is the sole function of thought. All these words, however, are too strong for my purpose. It is as if I had described the phenomena as they appear under a mental microscope [5.394].

This is not a serious revision of the views expressed in the earlier article. Doubt and belief are still the start and the resolution of any question (5.394). Thought still has "for its sole motive, idea and function," the production of belief. "Thought in action has for its only possible motive the attainment of thought at rest" (5.396).

What he objects to is the understanding of doubt as an irritant; this is too strong a word for doubt (5.394). And an even more important shortcoming of the first article is the understanding of belief as the close of inquiry. Belief, as the second article explains, is only a "demicadence which closes a musical phrase in the symphony of our intellectual life." Thought relaxes when belief is reached, but the rest is only momentary. Belief is not only a stopping-place; "it is also a new starting-place for thought" (5.397).[21]

Peirce's main interest in the two articles of 1877 is the presentation of the doubt–inquiry–belief procedure in scientific matters. The evidence for this is found chiefly in his presentation of the intellectual and conditional character of the pragmatic maxim and in the description and evaluation of the four methods of fixing belief which have been commonly used.[22]

After brief mention of the genuineness of the doubt which opens a scientific inquiry, I shall explain the theoretical nature of the pragmatic maxim. Although the method is directed toward action—hence the name pragmatic—it is nevertheless theoretical, since its relation to action is decidedly different and even opposed to the relation of practice to action, as will become evident.

Rejecting the spirit of Cartesianism, Peirce makes it clear in "The Fixation of Belief," that inquiry begins with genuine doubt. The scientist must not begin by doubting everything, or by pretending to doubt anything. Rather, doubt must be real and living (5.376).

The same position on the genuineness of doubt recurs in the later writings with no notable development. The scientist's theoretical doubt usually begins with a surprise. A puzzling event occurs which incites the man of science to inquire into its explanation. But, whether surprising or not, the origin of doubt is always external. One cannot simply will to begin to doubt (5.443).[23] A belief-habit that could be broken by will, would not be a genuine belief-habit. The "Critical Commonsensist" (which Peirce claims to be) regards the Cartesian view of supposing that one can doubt at will as an impossibility; only experience can give rise to doubt (5.524).[24] An inquiry inaugurated by a make-believe doubt will be an idle farce (5.376*n*).

Doubts, which arise spontaneously in the curious mind faced with experiences, that are not wholly comprehended, are to be respected, and even anticipated with eagerness. The scientist has a *sacra fames* for real doubt. "Only, his hunger is not to be appeased with paper doubts: he must have the heavy and noble metal, or else belief" (5.514).[25]

Running through the two articles of 1877 and 1878 is the theme that belief, whether scientific or not, is always directed toward action. Doubt leaves a man perplexed and unable to act.[26] But "the essence of belief is the establishment of a habit; and different beliefs are distinguished by the different modes of action to which they give rise" (5.398). Belief involves the establishment of a *rule* of action, which, though not absolutely permanent, is still not completed in a single operation of assent. Some years later, around 1902, he wrote that a habit is a specialization of nature such that a man "will always tend to behave, in a way describable in general terms upon every occasion (or upon a considerable proportion of the occasions) that may present itself of a generally describable character" (5.538).[27] The feeling of satisfaction which accompanies belief indicates more or less surely that a habit which will determine action has been established. One who has reached a state of belief will not necessarily act at once, but will be ready to act when the circumstances which occasioned the doubt arise. "The whole function of thought is to produce habits of action" (5.400).[28]

Although all beliefs are related to action, it would be a serious mistake to interpret Peirce as holding that all belief is practical. There are beliefs which are practical, and beliefs which are theoretical. He distinguishes between practical and theoretical doubt and belief in his article "How to Make Our Ideas Clear." The man who must decide to pay a horsecar fare with five pennies or with a five-cent piece is faced with a practical doubt, however insignificant it may be. The doubt and the decision solving the doubt are practical—that is, they concern an action to be performed.

A more relevant example of doubt and belief is the situation of a man with time to kill in a railroad station. He already knows his destination and train, and presumably has his ticket. In order to amuse himself he compares different routes and trains, "which I never expect to take, merely fancying myself to be in a state of hesitancy." This feigned hesitancy is more like the doubt of science than is the hesitancy of the man paying his carfare. The decision about the fictitious trip is not meant to be useful; it has no practical conclusion. The mere fact that the decision is made *about* an action does not remove it from the realm of theory. A decision made *for* an action, however, is practical.[29] The man in the railroad station contemplating imagined trips is dreaming about actions, but not planning to act. He is carrying on an inquiry, somewhat like the inquiry of the scientist. "Feigned hesitancy, whether feigned for mere amusement or with a lofty purpose, plays a great part in the production of scientific inquiry" (5.394). In solving the doubt, we are trying to find out *how we would act,* not how we will act (5.373*n*).[30]

The character of the imagined action is spelled out in greater detail later in the same article. There, in a context explicitly dealing with belief as the establishment of a habit of action, Peirce explains "imagined action" in two ways. First, the habit of imagined action, in which belief consists, is an acknowledgment of how we would act under certain conditions. "The identity of a habit depends on how it might lead us to act, not merely under such circumstances as are likely to arise, but under such as might possibly occur, no matter how improbable they may be" (5.400). The other understanding of imagined action is more relevant to scientific procedure. It consists in imagining what sensible experiences we would undergo in certain conditions. In other words, we imagine what sensible effects certain things would have on us. And our apprehension of the conceived sensible effects of anything is our whole idea of that thing. "Our idea of anything *is* our idea of its sensible effects" (5.401). In this case our "action" is exclusively related to sensible qualities; it is, as Buchler points out, an experimental term, and not biographical or moral.[31] These two types of conceived action—how we would act and how things would affect our senses—are the only types which can enter into theoretical belief, for, as Peirce explicitly says, our action, habit, belief, and conception have "exclusive reference to what affects the senses" (5.401).[32]

It is important to notice that in both types of imagined action employed in scientific inquiry, a *conditional* resolution is involved.[33]

After a rather rambling presentation of doubt and belief, the article "How to Make Our Ideas Clear," reaches its climax in a tightly constructed rule which the editors have labeled "The Pragmatic Maxim." [34] "Consider what effects that might conceivably have practical bearings, we conceive the object of our conception to have. Then our conception of these effects is the whole of our conception of the object" (5.402). The maxim is an early and crude summary of Peirce's views on the connection between belief and the conceived sensible effects of the objects of belief.

In a letter to William James dated November 25, 1902, Peirce admits the crudity of his understanding of pragmatism in 1877 (8.255). The refinement came later, when he saw that logic is dependent on ethics, and ethics on aesthetics, and that these three normative sciences, as he called them, correspond to his three categories. The inexact identification of meaning with action-reaction, expressed in the 1877 and 1878 papers, is later corrected by the understanding of action-reaction in terms of purpose, which is essentially thought. Vincent Potter correctly sees that "the acknowledgment of the role of ends in action is the insight into the role of the normative sciences, and this acknowledgment brought about Peirce's successive attempts to formulate the pragmatic maxim in a more sophisticated and adequate way." [35]

One such sophistication was the insistence that meaning is intellectual purport, as Peirce wrote in 1906. He refers to his stylistic habit of avoiding repetition of a word; and then he notes that in the maxim's five lines, the word "conception" or a cognate appears five times. This, he says, has two purposes: "One was to show that I was speaking of meaning in no other sense than that of *intellectual purport*. The other was to avoid all danger of being understood as attempting to explain a concept by percepts, images, schemata, or by anything but concepts." Action is the end of thought, not in that it is the purpose of thought, but rather that action is the object of thought: it is that about which the thinker thinks. Thought applies to action exclusively—to *conceived* action, as Peirce emphatically states (5.402*n*3). Thought is not necessarily for action. It is *about* action.

That the pragmatic maxim is designed to clarify intellectual purport is brought out again in the "Issues of Pragmaticism," where Peirce makes reference to the earlier phrasing of the maxim in "How to Make Our Ideas Clear." In the "Issues," he notes that the maxim can be restated in the indicative mood, but with the same stress on theoretical knowledge. "The entire intellectual purport of any symbol consists in the total of all general modes of rational conduct which, conditionally upon all the possible different circumstances and desires, would ensue upon the acceptance of the symbol" (5.438). As Gallie points out, Peirce's proposal to clarify the meaning of a concept by considering *all* its practical consequents is an impossible ideal.[36] However, it is clear that what the pragmaticist is interested in is theoretical knowledge. His pragmaticism is merely an attempt to devise a "method of determining the meanings of intellectual concepts" (5.8f).

The same view of pragmatism is brought out in a letter to William James, written by Peirce in 1902:

> Pragmatism is correct doctrine only in so far as it is recognized that material action is the mere husk of ideas. The brute element exists, and must not be explained away. . . . But the end of thought is action only in so far as the

end of action is another thought. Far better to abandon the word "thought," and talk of "representation," and then *define* what kind of a representation it is that constitutes consciousness.[37]

The true pragmatist is interested in rational meaning, which consists in *experimental phenomena,* in "what *surely will* happen to everybody in the living future who shall fulfill certain conditions," as he wrote in 1905 (5.425). The pragmaticist scientist is interested in certain *kinds* of experimental phenomena. What he tries to imagine in his pragmatic method is something of a certain character. Hence it is a misrepresentation to say that for him rational meaning consists in an experiment. An experiment is a single event. Its individuality is of no interest to the pragmaticist scientist, as it must be to the man of practical action.[38] Thought expects a certain kind of event to occur under given conditions.[39]

Expectation seems to be an important element of Peirce's pragmatism. Knowledge must involve a reference to experience; and this reference is an expectation, an imaginary (in the case of theoretical knowledge) anticipation of experience. "Knowledge which should have no possible bearing upon any future experience—bring no expectation whatever—would be information concerning a dream. But in truth no such thing can be presumed of any knowledge" (5.542). Even the distinction between practical belief and theoretical belief can be explained in terms of expectations. Practical belief is expectant of muscular sensation, and a kind of tension of the striped muscles. Theoretical belief, or, as Peirce calls it here, "an expectation so far as it involves no purpose [or] effort," is expectant of sensation that is not muscular (5.540).

It would be wrong to think that the pragmatic method is merely a way of clarifying meaning independently of any assertion of truth. While a certain amount of pragmatic clarity is a prerequisite to assertion, as Thompson and Murphree point out, the pragmatic method in its fullness is nevertheless a way of grasping truth.[40] In a scientific context, the method is designed, as we shall see in the subsequent chapters, to lead gradually to a knowledge of reality. Understanding the truth in terms of pragmatic meaning is for the man of science a unified process in which clarity of meaning is not divorced from assertions of truth.

The pragmatistic method, therefore, is directed toward theoretical knowledge, intellectual purport. In accordance with this method, conceived actions or experiences are both conditional and general. In other words, the scientist understands reality by representing to himself what type of event would occur under certain conditions (5.528).

It will become more evident in the later chapters that scientific inquiry is pragmatic. What is not so evident, however, is that the method, though adequate to clarify some ideas and to fix some beliefs, can qualify as a general method for unfolding all theoretical meaning. The articles of 1877 and 1878 claim not only to provide a method of intellectual clarification of concepts used in the natural sciences, but also to promote the use of the very same method in any theoretical inquiry. W. B. Gallie detects an ambiguity in Peirce's pragmaticism:

> Either it is a *general maxim* of logic, applicable doubtless in rather special (specially precise) ways to scientific expressions; or else it is that criterion of the distinctness of different scientific expressions, whose applicability distinguishes these expressions as a class or genus from other forms of expression —with the implication that these others, to which Pragmatism does not apply, should be rejected as meaningless or recast to conform to scientific standards.[41]

Peirce recognized the difficulty, Gallie asserts, and preferred, though not exclusively, to adhere to the more restricted application of the pragmatic method. But this was really not a satisfactory solution, because he never gave up the quest for a single, simple method to settle all theoretical doubt. The narrower application of the method to problems in the natural sciences is highly satisfactory, because what a natural scientist—at least in Peirce's day—should seek can be expressed in terms of the conceivable experimental phenomena which the scientific expression would imply. It is especially in this narrower sense—sc., as a procedure of the natural scientist—that Peirce's pragmatic method will be studied in the following pages.

In a lecture written in 1898 Peirce sums up some of the main topics of this chapter. He says of scientific method that it must start from doubt or an interrogation. Such an interrogation is an admission that we do not know something, an implicit desire to know it, and an effort to discover what the truth really is. If that interrogation inspires the seeker, he will examine the instances; if it does not, he will pass them by without attention (5.584).

It is the scientist's motive, the pure love of theoretical knowledge, that makes him different from other men, and that controls his work. His concern for theoretical knowledge will lead him inevitably to choose the best method for attaining such knowledge; this choice is itself a scientific achievement (6.428). The details of the method will be treated in the chapters which follow.

Chapter III

THE STAGES OF THE METHOD (*i*): EXPERIENCE AND HYPOTHESIS

THE SCIENTIST'S LOVE OF KNOWLEDGE for its own sake must direct his inquiry according to the method that will best suit his eagerness for the truth. His rage to learn must be effective—that is, it must be accompanied by a method that will satisfy his interest in the truth most reasonably. This chapter will begin to describe the characteristics of the method which Peirce judges most adapted to the needs of scientific inquiry.

Historically there have been several ways that men have followed to advance toward the truth.[1] The poorest of these is the method of tenacity, as Peirce calls it, by which one maintains a rigid steadfastness in the beliefs that he already holds. Such an attitude may give a man peace of mind. His beliefs are satisfactory because they are his, and he will not undertake any inquiry that may disturb his calm belief. But discussion with other men will show him that their opinions differ from his, and his confidence may be shaken. Tenacity fixes the individual's belief, but it does not fix the community's belief. For this reason its effect on the individual's mind may be only temporary (5.377f).

The shortcomings of the method of tenacity are met by the method of authority. According to the latter method, Peirce says, an institution teaches the people to believe what it would have them believe, and

[1] The notes for this chapter begin on page 164.

punishes those who refuse to believe. Such a method, however, discourages thinking and forbids private investigation; it is too public, and the strength of the institution tends to keep its members in intellectual slavery. But not all the slaves are docile. Doubts begin to arise in the minds of some and their belief in the official teachings is weakened. They come to know of doctrines other than their own, and they suspect that perhaps there may be better reasons for accepting the opinions of others (5.379–381).

According to a third method, natural preferences are unimpeded by any external authority. A man adopts views that he finds agreeable to his reason, independently, perhaps, of observed facts. This is the a priori method and is more respectable than the other two, Peirce asserts, although its failures have been more manifest, since it makes inquiry a matter of taste. What a person believes is largely determined by accident. "The opinions which today seem most unshakable are found tomorrow to be out of fashion. They are really far more changeable than they appear to a hasty reader to be" (5.382*n*; also 5.382f).

The most satisfactory way of fixing belief, which is the enterprise of the scientist, is to investigate the external world.[2] Let nature answer the questions that the scientist asks. This is a scientific inquiry, and is basically a question put to nature.[3] The scientific method is, as Murphree says, "inquiry proper, inquiry in its eulogistic sense."[4] The doubts that rise in the scientist's mind should be answered "by some external permanency—by something upon which our thinking has no effect" (5.384). This method which appeals to nature, both real and public, should lead every inquirer to the same conclusion. Peirce describes the fundamental hypothesis of this method as follows:

> There are Real things, whose characters are entirely independent of our opinions about them; those Reals affect our senses according to regular laws, and, though our sensations are as different as are our relations to the objects, yet, by taking advantage of the laws of perception, we can ascertain by reasoning how things really and truly are; and any man, if he have sufficient experience and he reason enough about it, will be led to the one True conclusion [5.384].

A man, then, so long as he follows the method of tenacity, will not ask any questions; the subject of authority will look to the authority for the answers to his questions; the apriorist will answer his doubts according to his taste. But only the man of science will ask nature for an answer. The inquirer who turns to nature for answers to his doubts will necessarily rely on experience. Experience will be the occasion for wonder about nature, and nature herself will ultimately supply the answer to his wonder. The genuine man of science, however, must somehow go beyond experience; he must look for explanations, even unexperienced explanations of what he has experienced. But, finally, his explanations will have to be tried before the court of experience, where nature will evaluate the scientist's explanations.[5]

Two of the stages of the scientific method will be treated in this chapter. The following chapter will attempt to explain the remaining steps of the method. The present chapter will deal with the experience which precedes the formation of the explanatory hypothesis, and with the formation of that hypothesis. Regarding the formation of the hypothesis, I shall treat Peirce's basic teaching on this phase of the method, as well as some of the requirements for choosing an hypothesis, and certain relevant theoretical questions.

I. EXPERIENCE WHICH PRECEDES THE FORMATION OF THE EXPLANATORY HYPOTHESIS

The inquirer who follows the method of the sciences advocated by Peirce will look to nature for an answer to his questions. The answer will be given to him through his observation of nature. Experience is the necessary beginning for all of our knowledge, since there is no human knowledge that is not based on observed facts.[6] "All knowledge whatever comes from observation" (1.238; also 6.522, 5.392, 5.611). Although observation which precedes the hypothesis may not be a part of the scientific method in the strict sense, still it is an absolutely necessary prerequisite, and deserves adequate treatment here. The present section is therefore an attempt to study the important features of the observational phase of the scientific method.

Some of these features are contained in a short sentence found in Peirce's article on the reality of God. "Every inquiry whatsoever takes its rise in the observation . . . of some surprising phenomenon, some experience which either disappoints an expectation, or breaks in upon some habit of expectation of the *inquisiturus*" (6.469). The short quotation mentions the *inquisiturus,* the person who is beginning a scientific investigation, and the habits of mind which he brings to the project. This is an important topic, and deserving of careful consideration, because of the valuable insights it affords into the nature of observation. The inquirer begins his scientific work with a background of experience. The longer he has lived the life of a scientist, the more experience he has accumulated; the expectations that he brings to his project are more refined, more accurate than when he first began to do scientific work. Similarly, the man who has just become a scientist is nevertheless equipped with some habits of expectation, less developed and less exact than those of the veteran. But, veteran or not, the scientific *inquisiturus* has some background of experience which acts as part of the context for his next experience.

The above-quoted text also speaks of observation which "breaks in" on the investigator. Since the experience is forceful, there must be an observer who experiences; there must be the inertia of past experience, which resists the current forceful event. "Experience . . . is the cognitive resultant of our past lives," and the past has its own inertia, the force against which new phenomena strike (2.84). The inquirer comes to his work of observing, with the advantage of an operative cognitive background.

Therefore, although Peirce underlines the necessity of experience as the basis of science, he still insists that this is not a purely passive, mechanical reception of data. The inquirer's mind does not function like a seismograph record. It is a mind already refined and developed, a mind that has a definite question that it wants nature to answer. In an early lecture delivered at Harvard,[7] Peirce mentions the importance of observation, but stresses that this is much more than a vacant stare at nature.

> Modern students of science have been successful because they have spent their lives not in their libraries and museums but in their laboratories and in the field; and while in their laboratories and in the field they have been not gazing on nature with a vacant eye, that is, in passive perception unassisted by thought, but have been *observing*—that is, perceiving by the aid of analysis—and testing suggestions of theories. The cause of their success has

been that the motive which has carried them to the laboratory and the field has been a craving to know how things really were, and an interest in finding out whether or not general propositions actually held good—which has overbalanced all prejudice, all vanity, and all passion [1.34].

The important theme here is the nature of the scientist's observation. It is not pure sensation. The observer is a man, "an experimenter of flesh and blood," with an habituated, trained, and expectant mind (5.424). In his scientific observations, he must be expected to act as an intelligent agent.

Peirce approves of Whewell's view in this regard, "Progress in science depends upon the observation of the right facts by minds *furnished with appropriate ideas*" (6.604). Observation is perception with thought and analysis. Science begins with wonder, with a doubt of some sort, and with a "pondering of these phenomena in all their aspects, in the search of some point of view whence the wonder shall be resolved" (6.469). Both the wonder, and the examination of reality intended to be the beginning of the resolution of wonder, are acts involving active and purposive intelligence.[8]

In a very brief reference to Ernst Mach, Peirce expresses his position very clearly and crisply. While Mach "allows thought no other value than that of economizing experiences," Peirce places the greatest emphasis on thought, and considers sensation valueless, except as a vehicle of thought (5.601).[9]

Reason,[10] then, is not confined to the formation of the explanatory hypothesis. But it pervades the whole operation of scientific inquiry. Research is "conversation with nature," and conversation requires intelligence on the part of the investigator who asks questions of an intelligibly structured nature, and expects replies from the same through his intelligent scrutiny of nature's ways. And the conversation continues, as Peirce says, "till the *mind* is in tune with nature" (6.568, emphasis added). These words are found in an article "Logic and Spiritualism," composed about 1905, and intended for publication. In this article he repeats the theme which I have been emphasizing: science must join experience with reasoning, even in the initial observation phase. For example, he says that when the chemist sets up his retort and begins his experiment, "he trusts that what happens once happens always; nature follows general laws, in other words, has a reason. . . . Experimentation is strictly appeal to reason" (6.568).[11]

In an article on observation in Baldwin's *Dictionary* Peirce writes that observation is "an act of voluntary attentive experience, usually with some, often with great, effort." And in explaining what experience is, he says: "Experience supposes that its object reacts upon us with some strength, much or little, so that it has a certain grade of reality or independence of our cognitive exertion" (2.605).[12] The carefully worded description of observation brings out the intellectual character of scientific observation. The inquirer is observing voluntarily and with an effort at cognitive exertion.[13] Scientific observation must be more than purely passive sensation.

It should be brought out here, that for Peirce the starting-point of a reasonable inquiry is the percept and not the sense-impression, understanding sense-impression as Karl Pearson describes it.[14] According to Pearson, Peirce says, a knower is like a telephone operator, cut off from the world, except for the reports of it which come into the switchboard. For Peirce, however, we are not cut off from the world, and we do not depend on such indirect reports. We observe the external world directly, and it is only after some experience of this sort that we come to know ourselves.

It is the external world that we directly observe. What passes within we only know as it is mirrored in external objects. In a certain sense, there is such a thing as introspection; but it consists in an interpretation of phenomena presenting themselves as external percepts. We first see blue and red things. It is quite a discovery when we find the eye has anything to do with them, and a discovery still more recondite when we learn that there is an *ego* behind the eye, to which these qualities properly belong. Our logically initial data are percepts [8.144].[15]

The same brief note also treats the resistance which external objects offer to the knower, and how the repeated resistance of an inkstand, for example, is an indication of its reality. The inkstand is there, and continues to be really there, in spite of the observer.[16]

The problem of deciding what percepts represent the real world as opposed to the world of dreams is not quite the same as the problem of the reality of generals. The latter question will be discussed in a later chapter. Peirce has proposed three tests in his "Minute Logic" to distinguish the real, perceptually presented, from an hallucination: a voluntary attempt to dismiss the percept, the opinion of the bystanders, and a prediction that if the percept represents the real, a certain experience must result, like Macbeth's attempt to clutch the dagger (2.142).

At the beginning of this section I quoted a short selection in which Peirce states that inquiry begins with the observation of a surprising event which is somewhat contrary to the inquirer's expectation. Peirce refers to the forceful shock of surprise in observation as "brutal inroads of ideas from without. I call such forcible modification of our ways of thinking the influence of the world of fact or *experience*" (1.321).[17]

Reflection on this experience of shock which a change of experience causes, leads Peirce to assert that therefore[18] there must be a kind of resistance or effort in the observer, against which the shocking change strikes. His former experience has set up a certain inertia which resists the new experience.

> It is the compulsion, the absolute constraint upon us to think otherwise than we have been thinking that constitutes experience. Now constraint and compulsion cannot exist without resistance, and resistance is effort opposing change. Therefore there must be an element of effort in experience; and it is this which gives it its peculiar character [1.336].[19]

The word "experience," then, is more especially suited to changes and contrasts involving resistance.

However, the surprising aspect of the observed event which initiates a scientific inquiry is not necessarily something unique or extraordinary in nature. It may only be as surprising as is any experience which excites scientific curiosity. The scientist asks explanatory questions of nature, both of the ordinary workings of nature, and of the artificial control which he may exert on nature. It is the uniformity of nature that demands explaining, and an event which the curious mind wants explained is for him a surprising event. "A uniformity, or law, is *par excellence,* the thing that requires explanation" (6.612). The scientist finds the uniformity of nature surprising in the sense that his curiosity is insatiable. He is driven on to inquire about the explanations of even the most ordinary events of nature.

Understanding an unexpected event as one which arouses the scientist's curiosity, whether it be extraordinary or not, it can be said that it is the contrast between a habit of experience and an unexpected event that gives rise to scientific doubt, and then to inquiry. Peirce develops this in a work composed about 1901, in which he takes issue with the opinion of Paul Carus that the irregularity of a surprising event makes it a proper subject for scientific inquiry. This is an error, he says, since "mere irregularity, where no definite regularity is expected, creates no surprise nor excites any curiosity" (7.189).[20] The type of experience that calls for an explanation is that which breaks a habit of expectation. In other words, a phenomenon presents itself which, if there were no special explanation, would not have been expected (7.194). Certain experiences build up habits of expectation in the observer, and when this habit is broken in upon by some unexpected event, the mind changes from belief to doubt, and should undertake a process of inquiry to explain the unexpected fact (7.198; 7.200). The function of an explanation, therefore, is "to supply a proposition which, if it had been known to be true before the phenomenon presented itself, would have rendered that phenomenon predictable" (7.192).

In summary, then, experience is a cognitive operation. It involves the awareness of an external object, and it has an element of force. The observation with which scientific inquiry begins contains something unexpected, and it is the unexpected character that makes us forcefully aware of the externality of the object, and which moves the inquirer to search for an explanation. "*Experience* means nothing but just that of a cognitive nature which the history of our lives has forced upon us" (5.539).

II. THE FORMATION OF THE EXPLANATORY HYPOTHESIS

Scientific inquiry properly begins with a hypothesis, a conjecture which will attempt to explain the phenomena (6.469). In his projected "History of Science," Peirce refers to science as a diligent inquiry into truth "from an impulse to penetrate into the reason of things" (1.44). The scientist cannot be satisfied with a mere acquaintance with phenomena; nor can a complicated correlation of data be regarded as genuine science. There must be some penetration beyond the data. A scientist is a man who "burns to learn and sets himself to comparing his ideas with experimental results in order that he may correct those ideas" (1.44). The ideas which the scientist tests are first suggested to him in a tentative hypothesis. This mental process is the subject of the present section.

"Abduction" is the term which Peirce uses to designate the mental activity by which a hypothesis is formed. He also calls this activity retroduction, presumption, and hypothesis (i.e., hypothesizing).[21] This is a living process occurring in the minds of scientists.[22]

The two main functions of science are the framing and the testing of conjectures. The scientist puts questions to nature, attempts an answer, and then examines nature to see how closely the conjectured answer agrees with nature. "Science itself, the living process, is busied mainly with conjectures, which are either getting framed or getting tested" (1.234). It is, therefore, distinct from the thoroughly established truths, which a scientist may use or apply.

Peirce brings out with emphasis the importance of abduction in science, in a piece of writing until recently unpublished, entitled "The Laws of Nature and Hume's Argument Against Miracles."[23] In opposition to Hume, Peirce emphasizes that our knowledge is not derived from experience alone. In fact, "every item of science came originally from conjecture, which has only been pruned down by experience. . . . The entire matter of our works of solid science consists of conjectures checked by experience."[24]

The scientist in forming his conjectures is dependent upon experience somehow, taking experience to mean the operation, explained in the previous section, not divorced from reason. Despite the possible overstatement, Peirce does make it clear that abduction is a vital function in science.

The method is described in greater detail in an article which Peirce wrote on "Reasoning" in Baldwin's *Dictionary*.[25] "Abduction . . . furnishes the reasoner with the problematic theory which induction verifies" (2.776).

This section will treat the framing of the explanatory hypothesis, or abduction; the process of verification will be described in the next chapter. The treatment of abduction will be divided into three sub-sections: Peirce's basic teaching on abduction, some requirements for choosing hypotheses, and some theoretical considerations.

a) *Peirce's Basic Teaching on Abduction*—In 1893 Peirce brought together and revised some of his previously published essays and prepared them for a projected book, "Search for a Method." Some of the essays for the proposed book had been written as early as 1867. His views on abduction in this collection of essays exhibit a gradual development in that the later works present a review of the earlier positions, along with new insights into the function of abduction. The mere fact that the early essays were intended for publication in 1893 is a clear indication that Peirce did not repudiate the earlier doctrine.[26]

My presentation of Peirce's basic teaching on abduction will begin with the gradual evolution of his position found in the projected book, and will afterwards rely mostly on works originally written after 1890, in which his maturer views on this most important mental process are contained.

His article of 1867 "On the Natural Classification of Arguments" presents abduction as a type of inference, and compares it with deduction and induction.[27] Accordingly the presentation is largely that of formal logic, with comparative examples of inductive, deductive, and abductive syllogisms. The word *abduction* does not yet occur, but the type of argument is called *hypothesis* in these early articles. The process is described as "an argument which assumes that a term which necessarily involves a certain number of characters, which have been lighted upon as they occurred, and have not been picked out, may be predicated of any object which has all these characters" (2.515). There is therefore a movement from a manifold of characters to a unified character.

"Some Consequences of Four Incapacities" was published in the following year, and contains the same view of hypothesis.[28] Both these articles present induction and hypothesis as inversions of the deductive syllogism. The selection quoted above and the examples given in the first article indicate that hypothesis involves a reduction of many predicates to one, or at least to fewer than before. But the second article makes this more explicit, and also shows the relation of deduction to hypothesis-forming. After repeating the description given above almost verbatim, he writes:

The function of hypothesis is to substitute for a great series of predicates forming no unity in themselves, a single one (or small number) which involves them all, together (perhaps) with an indefinite number of others. It is, therefore, also a reduction of a manifold to unity. Every deductive syllogism may be put into the form

If A, then B;
But A:
∴ B.

And as the minor premiss in this form appears as antecedent or reason of a hypothetical proposition hypothetic inference may be called reasoning from consequent to antecedent [5.276].[29]

These first two articles, therefore, in addition to the considerations proper to formal logic, propose hypothetic inference as a unifying operation. When we know that some character invariably involves others, and that a given object has the latter, we may conclude tentatively that such an object also has the former character. This is an instance of hypothesis-forming. Similarly, when we know that a class of objects has a certain set of characteristics and that a given single object also has the same characteristics, we can conclude that the given object probably belongs to that class. In either case there is an advance in knowledge (provided that the hypothesis survives the verification process), a decrease in the number of predicates, a reduction of a manifold of predicates to unity.[30]

Ten years later Peirce's article, "Deduction, Induction, and Hypothesis," was published, in which hypothesis and induction are still explained as inversions of a deductive syllogism.[31] "All inference may be reduced in some way to Barbara" (2.620). But the inversion of this form will not manifest the distinctive characters of non-deductive reasoning.[32] Deduction, induction, and abduction are alike in that they each contain a proposition which is a *rule,* another which is a *case,* and a third which is a *result.* In deduction, rule, case, and result are respectively the major and minor premises, and the conclusion. Abduction concludes with a case, inferred from a known rule and a known result (2.619–623). In other words, we draw a hypothesis when we explain a curious circumstance by supposing it to be a case of a general rule. There is no perfectly certain conclusion here, no formal necessity to form such a hypothesis. The hypothesis is proposed as a possible, even likely, explanation of experience.

It is this explanatory function of hypothesis that marks a clear advance over the two earlier essays. But apparently Peirce was not yet aware of the importance of his new insight into hypothetic inference, since the explanatory role of this type of inference is not stressed; it is merely mentioned (2.625, 628). Another very important understanding of abduction that is mentioned but not developed is that it infers facts not capable of direct observation (2.642).[33]

It was only in later articles that Peirce realized the importance of these two aspects of abduction. The emphasis on the explanatory function of hypothesis appears in "A Theory of Probable Inference," originally published in 1883, and later intended as the last essay of "Search for a Method." The essay describes the formal and statistical aspects of hypothetic inference, as the previous articles also do. But it stresses the explaining role of hypothetical inference. This stress remained permanent in Peirce's subsequent writings on abduction. "We have seen that Inductions and Hypotheses are inferences from the conclusion and one premiss of a statistical syllogism to the other premiss. In the case of hypothesis, this syllogism is called the *explanation*. . . . The hypothesis is adopted *for the sake* of the explanation" (2.716f).[34]

It is clear, therefore, that the essays intended for the projected "Search for a Method" exhibit a gradual development in Peirce's views of abduction. There is progress from a purely logical understanding of this type of inference to its role in scientific inquiry. In the earlier writings it is compared with deduction and induction. Then the considerations of these three types of inference take on a statistical character, preparing them for use in scientific procedures. Finally the explanatory function of abduction appears, and begins to be emphasized far above the merely logical considerations of the earlier works.[35] The reduction of the manifold of predicates to unity accomplished by abduction has come to mean that the unified predicate must explain why the object or class has the manifold of predicates.[36] In fact in the writings composed after 1890, the explanation which abductive inference proposes for observed events is its *only* justification (1.89). Abduction from being a type of inference has become the first step—the explanatory phase—of scientific inquiry.

In dealing with the explanatory function of abductive inference, I will rely mostly on the works which Peirce composed after 1890. The previous section of this chapter has already indicated that what stirs a man of scientific interest to the process of inquiry is the surprising aspect of some observed event. This gives rise to doubt or wonder, and he begins to look for explanations of the event that will solve the doubt. Abduction suggests a hypothesis, perhaps in the form of a question, which would serve as an explanation of the observed facts (2.776).

The scientific explanation suggested by abduction has two characteristics that must be pointed out now (along with others that will be dealt with later): 1.) an explanatory hypothesis renders the observed facts necessary or highly probable; 2.) an explanatory hypothesis deals with facts which are different from the facts to be explained, and are frequently not capable of being directly observed.

That a scientific explanation renders the observed facts necessary is the explicit teaching of Peirce's article on reasoning in Baldwin's *Dictionary*:

> Upon finding himself confronted with a phenomenon unlike what he would have expected under the circumstances, he looks over its features and notices some remarkable character or relation among them, which he at once recognizes as being characteristic of some conception with which his mind is already stored, so that a theory is suggested which would *explain* (that is, render necessary) that which is surprising in the phenomena [2.776].[37]

Peirce asserts that the suggested theory *would* explain or render necessary, because its truth is not yet known, nor can its approximation to the truth become known except as a result of the verification process. At present the explanation is only a conjecture, hardly more than a question. But even before its truth or falsity becomes known, its logical connection with the observed facts must be recognized. The scientist must know that if the explanation is correct, then the observed facts necessarily or very probably follow.

A rather important piece of writing, published for the first time in the *Collected Papers,* proposes substantially the same teaching on abduction as the article in Baldwin's *Dictionary*. However, he adds that the hypothesis may render the observed facts necessary, *or at least highly probable* (7.202).[38] Since the hypothesis is itself no more than probable before it has been tested, it can, prior to the verification phase, be no more than a probable explanation. But the text seems also to indicate that the connection between the proposed explanation and the facts to be explained may at times be no more than very probable. To render necessary, therefore, as an explanation attempts to do, is not always to posit an infallible connection between the explanatory hypothesis and the observed facts.[39]

A second characteristic of Peircean abduction which must be discussed at present is its antipositivistic spirit. One of the distinguishing marks of the Comtean positivists with which Peirce takes issue is their attitude toward hypotheses. For them a general requirement for a legitimate hypothesis is that it be capable of direct verification (2.511*n*; see also 7.91).[40]

But Peirce argues that such a narrow restriction is by no means implied in the proof of the validity of hypothetic inference. That validity is established by the fact that the observed facts are rendered necessary or very probable by the hypothesis, and that the instances used to test the hypothesis are chosen at random, a requirement which will be investigated in the next chapter.

The explanatory hypothesis must be sensibly verifiable but its verifiability need not consist in its own direct observability. It must explain the observed event and be sensibly verifiable somehow. A hypothesis explaining an observed event may be not merely about the observed fact, but may also be any other supposed truth from which the observed event would result (6.525). For Peirce, a theory is an inference from the observed to the unobserved. The pragmaticist speaks of possible future experience. And if the predicted experience actually materializes, then its premise in the present has now ceased to be observable. For the pragmaticist, the premise of hypothetical inference and its conclusion cannot both be observed together. One of them must be unobservable. This, Peirce says, "is the conclusive objection to Positivism." The positivist himself, according to Peirce, cannot justify by direct observation his insistence on direct observation. "The logical rule, therefore, which is the whole basis of Positivism appears to me to be entirely false."[41]

The progress that science has made must be attributed to the power of the human intellect, fed with the facts of experience, to introduce new ideas. "Experience is our only teacher. . . . There manifestly is not one drop of principle in the whole vast reservoir of established scientific theory that has sprung from any other source than the power of the human mind to *originate* ideas that are true" (5.50).

The scientific method, accordingly, must combine experience with original thought.[42]

It is difficult for anyone to give any further description of the process that a scientist goes through when he hits upon an explanatory theory. Deductive processes can be easily described, and, as we shall see, scientific induction has its rules too. But abduction has no such strict rules of procedure, though there are certain requirements for it.

Peirce attributes the originating and explanatory phase of the scientific method to the inquirer's "imagination." In his projected "History of Science" he writes:

> When a man desires ardently to know the truth, his first effort will be to imagine what that truth can be. . . . It remains true that there is, after all, nothing but imagination that can ever supply him an inkling of the truth. He can stare stupidly at phenomena; but in the absence of imagination they will not connect themselves together in any rational way [1.46].[43]

In the same work, Peirce narrows down his meaning of imagination to a careful focus: "The scientific imagination dreams of explanations and laws" (1.48). This power somehow depends on the goad of experience, but goes beyond the present and the past to a plausibility that need not itself be directly experienced.

Scientific imagination progresses by leaps. Its operation is free and brilliant, and not altogether secure. No unassailable reason can be given for the hypothesis at the time of its formation. It is an act of imagination, that may in a particular case never lead to truth. But it is by the explaining imagination that science progresses (1.109).

Although a vigorous and even undisciplined imagination is often a useful prelude to science, the scientist must still guide and direct this most necessary power, since, if it is allowed to run unbridled, it may mislead the investigator. It must be carefully guided by experience, since observation triggers the imaginative leap, the abductive inference. Some new experience, or novel way of regarding experience, or a previously unperceived relation between facts, gives rise to the explanatory hypothesis.[44] Abduction, for which imagination is so indispensable, cannot perform the critical and evaluating function that belongs to induction. Abduction only suggests that something *may be* the case. But it is by such suggestions alone that the inquirer understands; it is the only operation of the mind that contributes any new idea. "If we are ever to learn anything or to understand phenomena at all, it must be by abduction that this is to be brought about" (5.171). "All the ideas of science come to it by the way of Abduction" (5.145).

Abduction alone gives us an understanding of things. At first, it is only a weak argument, a mere surmise, but every step in the development of vague ideas into present-day science began as a weak conjecture. Although observation prompts the inquirer to suggest an explanatory hypothesis, and predicted experience strengthens the hypothesis, it is still the hypothesis itself that makes the real contribution to the progress of science (2.625; 2.640–642; 2.755; 2.777).

b) Some Requirements for Choosing Hypotheses—Even though scientific abduction is an operation that is free and brilliant, there are still some requirements that must be met with if the abductory phase of inquiry is to progress successfully. There are in addition certain procedures for choosing the more apt of several suggested hypotheses.

The most important requirement which a hypothesis must meet is that it be verifiable experimentally.[45]

Economy is a practical requirement of some importance though it also has its theoretical aspects. For the sake of completeness I will treat both the practical and the theoretical aspects of economy here.[46] Since the inquirer is possessed with a passion for knowing the truth, he must be able to evaluate the proposed explanatory theories and eliminate unsuitable hypotheses right at the start, without testing them. Economy of money, time, and energy is, therefore, a consideration of some importance in the abductive phase. Peirce goes so far as to say that economy "would override every other consideration even if there were any other considerations. In fact there are no others" (5.602; see also 7.220*n*18).[47]

Although the value of knowledge is absolute in one sense, there are still certain necessary economic considerations. Knowledge—even the negative knowledge gained by rejecting hypotheses proven false—becomes more valuable by being an avenue through which more knowledge can be reached (7.51). Furthermore, since science is the pursuit of scientific men, the scientist's situation must be considered. He is a man, subject to financial and temporal limitations, despite his burning eagerness to learn, as Peirce says in his projected "History of Science."[48]

Hence, when several possible hypotheses present themselves to the inquirer's mind, it is a question of necessary economy which he will test first. There may be some critical test that will halve the number of suggestions. If so, economy would urge the investigator to make use of such an experiment (7.220). Similarly, when two hypotheses occur to the mind of the inquirer, one of which could be tested in two or three days, while the other would take a month to test, the former should be tried first, even if its apparent likelihood is less. Clearly it is a question of the economical use of time (5.598). Furthermore, a good hypothesis for testing is one, which, if false, can be proven false with ease. "The best hypothesis, in the sense of the one most recommending itself to the inquirer, is the one which can be the most readily refuted if it is false" (1.120; see also 6.528–530).

In addition to the question of cost Peirce proposes two other factors of economy in abduction: the effect of a given hypothesis on other scientific projects, and the value of the hypothesis in itself.

The relation of the proposed hypothesis to other projects Peirce regards as especially important in the choice of an explanatory hypothesis for testing. He writes that this aspect of economy demands caution in the scientist. He does not tackle the matter directly, but compares the cautious scientist to a man skilled in the game of "twenty questions," who by no more than twenty carefully chosen questions can learn what two hundred thousand foolish questions might fail to reach. "The secret of the business lies in the caution which breaks a hypothesis up into its smallest logical components, and only risks one of them at a time" (7.220).

At the same time the scientist must search for a hypothesis that is broad and inclusive. "Correlative to the quality of caution is that of breadth" (7.221). If a hypothesis that includes several types of phenomena within its scope can be formed, then, other things being equal, it is good economy to test such a hypothesis in preference to others (7.221).

Caution and breadth in the choice of an explanatory hypothesis will lead the scientist to favor those theories that will benefit science whether they survive the testing process or not. The attempt to test hypotheses chosen with caution and breadth will afford the scientist a type of knowledge that will be the background for further progress. The entirely satisfactory hypothesis is very rare, but even the carefully chosen hypothesis which turns out to be unsatisfactory can be helpful to the progress of science. The chosen hypothesis may not fit the facts, but "the comparison with the facts may be instructive with reference to the next hypothesis" (7.221).

It is here that the value of the fruitful hypothesis can be seen. The theory that can lead to the prediction of many crucial testable consequences can be more thoroughly tested and hence is more helpful to the progress of science, whether it actually survives the verification phase or not. Peirce calls this the "idealistic" character of a hypothesis. The mere fact that an idea is more fruitful of consequences gives some indication that it may be true. Verifiable thought for Peirce is a sign; this means that it "translates itself into another sign in which it is more fully developed. . . . The valuable idea must be eminently fruitful in special applications, while at the same time it is always growing to wider and wider alliances" (5.594f; see also 5.598). If in ignorance about which hypothesis is the more probable, it is better "to adopt a hypothesis which leaves open the greatest field of possibility" (1.170). In this way the inquirer may make a more striking contribution to the progress of knowledge. This economic aspect of the chosen hypothesis Peirce compares to the billiard player's "leave" (7.221).

When dealing with the value of the hypothesis in itself, Peirce endeavors to explain why the scientist expects a given hypothesis not only to be suitable for testing but more especially to be proven true by surviving the test. The expectation may be either reasoned or instinctive (7.220).

A reasoned expectation that a hypothesis may be in accord with the facts is based on our preconceived ideas. Since these are presumably derived from experience, there is some reason to expect that a hypothesis in agreement with them may be true. But the presumption may be erroneous, and our preconceived ideas may be only the fruit of a priori speculation so thoroughly discredited by Peirce. Reasoned expectation is sometimes called likelihood, and, as experience shows, "likelihoods are treacherous guides" (7.220; see also 1.120).

Nothing has caused so much waste of time and means, in all sorts of researches, as inquirers' becoming so wedded to certain likelihoods as to forget all the other factors of the economy of research; so that, unless it be very solidly grounded, likelihood is far better disregarded, or nearly so; and even when it seems solidly grounded, it should be proceeded upon with a cautious tread, with an eye to other considerations, and a recollection of the disasters it has caused [7.220].

This attitude is in perfect agreement with Peirce's fear of the a priori, and his reliance on knowledge derived from experience.

The hypothesis that is in accord with instinct is far superior to the reasoned or likely hypothesis. Peirce urges investigators to trust the power of the mind to hit instinctively on the right explanation of observed facts (6.530). It is through instinct that the scientist dismisses as irrelevant the configuration of the planets, the actions of the dowager empress, the color of his daughter's dress, at the time of experimentation. Even though these events could lead to experimentally verifiable consequences, they are still unsuitable explanations, as the scientist instinctively knows (7.220; 5.591). It is most important for the progress of science that investigators be able to dismiss testable but erroneous explanations without spending time and money on useless experimentation. And it is through the skillful use of instinct that scientists have as a matter of fact been able to eliminate foolish explanations and to test the right hypotheses rather early in the inquiry.

In a more theoretical approach to the role of instinct in abduction, Peirce attributes the success of scientists in guessing the explanations of the universe to the kinship of man's mind with the rest of the cosmos. The phenomena which inaugurate the scientific inquiry *can* be explained by the human mind; they are, as Peirce puts it, open to rationalization by us.

We are therefore bound to hope that, although the possible explanations of our facts may be strictly innumerable, yet our mind will be able, in some finite number of guesses, to guess the sole true explanation of them. . . . Animated by that hope, we are to proceed to the construction of a hypothesis [7.219].

The basis for this hope, as he points out in the next paragraph, is the conviction "that the human mind is akin to the truth" (7.220).[49]

There is some further clarification of the meaning of instinct in his Lowell Lecture "How to Theorize" (5.603). Instinct is a mind adapted to man's requirements. It is like the instinct of animals which enables them to feed themselves and survive individually, and to reproduce their kind and to secure its survival. Like the animals, man has a mind adapted to his requirements. In the same paragraph, Peirce also refers to instinct as certain natural beliefs that are true. The acquisition of these true natural beliefs is not entirely shrouded in mystery. The human mind is a part of the universe. Throughout the universe certain uniformities prevail, and extend also to human nature. Since man's mind is continuous with the rest of the cosmos, it is to be expected that there will be an agreement between the ideas which present themselves to the human mind and those which exist in the laws of nature. Man's mind has developed under the influence of highly pervasive laws that extend to the whole cosmos. Hence we must expect that man should have a "*natural light,* or *light of nature,* or *instinctive insight,* or genius," that will guide him to a correct or nearly correct conjecture about those laws (5.604; 1.81).

Peirce was thoroughly convinced that "science is nothing but a development of our natural instincts" (6.604). Even granting that this may be an oversimplification, it still cannot be denied that it agrees with his other positions on the role of imagination in forming hypotheses, and on the key doctrine that all progress in science lies in abductive inference. In his projected "History of Science," Peirce writes that we are struck by the importance which the great physicists of history have given to instinctive judgments.[50]

> Galileo appeals to *il lume naturale* at the most critical stages of his reasoning. Kepler, Gilbert, and Harvey—not to speak of Copernicus—substantially rely upon an inward power, not sufficient to reach the truth by itself, but yet supplying an essential factor to the influences carrying their minds to the truth [1.80].

This is a description of the process of abduction, as Peirce declares in the next paragraph, where he writes that abduction bases its hope of reaching the truth on this natural tendency of the mind (1.81).

Peirce notes that there are two classes of subjects concerning which an "instinctive scent for the truth" seems to be proved. We seem to move toward truth instinctively when we are dealing with the mechanical forces of bodies, and with our estimate of how human beings think and feel. Our sciences of physics and psychics have grown from naturally successful guesswork applied to these two fields, under the control of inductive testing. Peirce compares man's power of guessing at the truth with the instincts of animals which guide their activities of feeding and breeding. Feeding, as it turns out, is an instinctive application of physics (mechanics), while breeding is an instance of psychics. One might judge this a far-fetched connection, were it not for the fact that it is frequently repeated in Peirce's different works. Since the comparison is so oft-repeated, we must take it as representative of his genuine position (6.500; 6.531; 6.497).

There is evidence that man's power of penetrating the secrets of nature depends on this [instinct at guessing the truth], in fact that all the successful sciences have been either mechanical in respect to their theories or psychological. Now, some notions of mechanics are needed by all animals to enable them to get food, and are needed most by man; while correct ideas of what passes in his neighbors' minds are needed for the existence of society, and therefore, for the propagation of his kind [6.491].

A few years earlier he wrote that "all science is nothing but an outgrowth from these two instincts [about feeding and breeding]" (6.500).

And in "How to Theorize," he brings together the basis of instinct (the kinship of the human mind with the cosmos) with the pre-eminent success of hypotheses concerning physics and psychics. The history of science, he says, reveals that

Man's mind has a natural adaptation to imagining correct theories about forces, without some glimmer of which he could not form social ties and consequently could not reproduce his kind. . . . It is somehow more than a mere figure of speech to say that nature fecundates the mind of man with ideas which, when those ideas grow up, will resemble their father, Nature [5.591].

It would, however, be erroneous to exaggerate the power of instinct in guessing the right explanation. It is not true to say that the instinctive guess is right more often than wrong but it is not likely to be many times more wrong than right (5.173).

Again, the aid derived from instinct becomes less and less as the inquirer progresses into a science. Still there will be no further progress in science without the infinite saving in money and time afforded by giving an early test to those hypotheses recommended by instinct (7.220).

In his famous article "A Neglected Argument for the Reality of God," he asserts that the explanation suggested by instinct is what he means by the "simpler" explanation. This is a revision of an earlier understanding of the meaning of the simpler of two hypotheses. In the earlier writings he maintained that the simpler hypothesis was the explanation with the fewest elements. Such an explanation, according to this view, should be tested ahead of the more complicated theories (4.35; 5.60; 4.1; 7.92f).[51]

But in the "Neglected Argument," composed in 1908, he admits that the earlier view was erroneous.[52] He confesses that he tried to twist Galileo's prescription that "of two hypotheses, the *simpler* is to be preferred," to mean that the *logically* simpler hypothesis should be adopted, i.e., the hypothesis which adds the least to what has been observed.[53] He submits to Galileo's own interpretation: the simpler hypothesis is the more natural and facile, the one suggested by instinct. To choose the simpler hypothesis, as Peirce advises, is to rely on Galileo's *il lume naturale* (6.477).

The simpler hypothesis is the one suggested by common sense with which Peirce identifies instinct. There is no doubt that in speaking of the beliefs proposed by instinct and common sense he includes the operations of speculative knowledge. The whole context is a clear indication of this.[54] But the instinctive type of knowledge operation is not the same as the operation performed by "reason." Certain instinctive beliefs are far more trustworthy than the results of science that have been rendered precise by reason, he wrote in 1906 (6.496).

Reasoning is a controlled and criticized operation, which understands itself as "one of a general class of possible inferences on the same model and all equally valid" (6.497). But an instinctive, common-sense operation of knowledge cannot be classified in the same way. We are compelled to think as we do, without being able to provide any premise leading to the instinctive belief. There are no premises or principles to go back to in instinctive beliefs, as there are in genuine reasoning processes. It is because of this that reasoning is a controlled and criticized operation, but the instinctive belief is not.

This, of course, does not mean that explanatory hypotheses chosen by instinct are to *remain* uncriticized. It means merely that they are formed and chosen for testing by the common-sense operation of instinct, and are not the result of, or chosen for testing by, a controlled and critical process. The control and criticism necessarily come in a subsequent step in the scientific inquiry—in the verification process. Instinct is the tool of science only at the moment when the hypothesis to be tested is chosen from among several suggested hypotheses.[55] In making such a choice, instinct is a surer instrument than reason (5.445; 6.530).

He returns to the frequently repeated theme mentioned above, in asserting that instinct is the source of all knowledge and wisdom, since all the triumphs of science have been confined to two general areas, physics and psychics, which are elaborations of our common sense. Because of this the men who have attempted to overthrow common sense and be perfectly reasonable have ended with ridiculous positions (6.500).

What Peirce is proposing, then, is a "critical common-sensism," as he explicitly calls it. It respects both the common-sense indubitable presentations of experience combined with the brilliant and free leaps of imagination and instinct, and the carefully controlled criticisms of the verification process (1.129).[56] In the second chapter I explained the role of genuine doubt in a scientific inquiry, along with the importance of those beliefs which are indubitable as long as they are not called into question by the shock of experience. And in the next chapter the process of verification, which is a controlled critique of suggested explanations, will be described. Both these phases of Peirce's theory of method must be taken into consideration if he is to be understood rightly.[57]

Peirce's pragmatic philosophy, his critical common-sensism, and his theory of scientific inquiry are closely interrelated, and one cannot be studied apart from the others (5.439). The sections which follow may help to enlighten some of these relations.

c) *Two Theoretical Aspects of Abduction*—The study of the role of instinct in abduction, as is clear from the above, is largely theoretical. Further theoretical knowledge of abduction can be gained by showing how it is related to the perceptual judgment, and by associating it with Peircean pragmatism, two considerations which will constitute the final section of this chapter.

The close connection between abduction and the perceptual judgment is brought out in the last of his seven lectures on pragmatism, composed in 1903.[58] "Abductive inference shades into perceptual judgment without any sharp line of demarcation; or, in other words, our first premisses, the perceptual judgments, are to be regarded as an extreme case of abductive inferences, from which they differ by being absolutely beyond criticism" (5.181).[59] And in a work published in 1906, another indication of the close relation between abduction and the perceptual judgment is given.[60] After remarking that a knower is under compulsion to make those perceptual judgments which he actually makes, and that an exercise of compulsion is what he means by existence, he goes on to write that

> Whatever feature of the percept is brought into relief by some association and thus attains a logical position like that of the observational premiss of an explaining Abduction, the attribution of Existence to it in the Perceptual Judgment is virtually and in an extended sense, a logical Abductive Inference nearly approximating to necessary inference [4.541].

In both of these texts he is asserting that the perceptual judgment is quite like an abductive inference. For this reason there is some value in studying the points of comparison and of difference between the two. The main source of information for this section is the series of six or seven lectures on pragmatism which he delivered at Harvard in the spring of 1903.

The perceptual judgment is the formation of a mental proposition, an assent, concerned with the sense experience of the person who makes the judgment. The knower judges what it is that he perceives. This is "a judgment asserting in propositional form what a character of a percept directly present to the mind is" (5.54). Meaning originates in the perceptual judgment. Hence this act of the mind is the premise of all critical thinking and all mental control. It itself is not subject to control or criticism, since there is no meaning beyond it which could serve as a norm of criticism and control. The meanings which are understood of the perceived objects are general, and for this reason the perceptual judgments are said to contain general elements. Finally a perceptual judgment is an interpretation of a perceived object, and though there are several interpretations possible, the one actually adopted seems forced upon us.

These characteristics of the perceptual judgment will become more clearly understood in the following points of comparison between it and abductive inference. There are four important similarities between the perceptual judgment and the abductive hypothesis. First, they both contain elements of generality. Right at the beginning of his sixth lecture on pragmatism Peirce emphasizes that perceptual judgments involve generality. Immediately asking what the general is, he answers with Aristotle's definition: "It is *quod aptum natum est praedicari de pluribus*. . . . If there be any perceptual judgment, or proposition directly expressive of and resulting from the quality of a present percept, or sense-image, that judgment must involve generality in its predicate" (5.151). There must be generality at least in the predicate of the perceptual judgment. But in the seventh lecture, after stating as his second cotary proposition that perceptual judgments involve generality, he goes on to say that, because of this, universal propositions can be inferred from them, indicating, without explicitly saying so, that science is built up from perceptual judgments (5.181).

Toward the end of the sixth lecture he explicitly deals with the perceptual judgment as gaining a knowledge of the general elements of the world. It is important to note that he compares the explanatory hypothesis to the perceptual judgment on this precise point, and asserts that the two belong to the same type of intellectual operation. Asking how scientists have been so successful in devising the correct explanations of phenomena, he writes:

> However man may have acquired his faculty of divining the ways of Nature, it has certainly not been by a self-controlled and critical logic. Even now he cannot give any exact reason for his best guesses. It appears to me that the clearest statement we can make of the logical situation—the freest from all questionable admixture—is to say that man has a certain Insight, not strong enough to be oftener right than wrong, but strong enough not to

be overwhelmingly more often wrong than right, into the Thirdnesses, the general elements, of Nature. An Insight, I call it, because it is to be referred to the same general class of operations to which Perceptive Judgments belong. This Faculty is at the same time of the general nature of Instinct [5.173].

It is clear that this paragraph brings together several themes already mentioned: the generality of both abductive inferences and perceptual judgments, the instinctive character of abduction, and the absence of control and criticism in the abductive process.

The generality of abduction can be better understood by remembering that, as was explained before, Peirce regards abduction as the inference of a case. The conclusion of the process of abductive inference is a proposition which places an individual in a class, or a less extensive class in a more extensive class. The abductive process concludes with a proposition which resembles in form the minor premise of a deductive syllogism in Barbara, as Peirce would put it. By this he means that the hypothesis (or the minor of a deductive syllogism in Barbara) asserts that an individual case, or class of cases, is included in the more general class represented by the predicate of the major premise of the deductive syllogism. An explanatory hypothesis is a conjectured understanding of the real, and the understanding is necessarily general, just like the predicate of the perceptual judgment.

Secondly, abduction and the perceptual judgment are also similar in that each is in some aspect beyond the control of reason, in that neither judgment is the necessary conclusion of an inference.

The perceptual judgment is forced upon the knower and for that reason is beyond the control of reason. In the sixth lecture Peirce writes: "All that I can mean by a perceptual judgment is a judgment absolutely forced upon my acceptance, and that by a process which I am utterly unable to control and consequently am unable to criticize" (5.157; see also 5.55; 5.115f; 5.181; 5.212). The latter are not subject to criticism, but they constitute the basis for criticizing all other judgments.

Somewhat similarly the abductive hypothesis is beyond the control of reason in its formation. Above we saw that the explanatory hypothesis is formed by imagination, as Peirce says, and is not exclusively the result of controlled and critical reasoning. Furthermore when several testable explanations occur to the inquirer, he must rely on instinct, in order to make an economical and helpful choice of one for testing. But instinct operates independently of the control of reason, and is therefore not directly subject to criticism.

The explanatory hypothesis, therefore, is like the perceptual judgment, inasmuch as it is found in a flash of insight, by the use of imagination, somewhat outside the influence of reason, and is chosen for testing by an instinctive selection also independently of the deliberate control of reason.

In their relation to the *ultimate* control of reason, however, the two are dissimilar. The explanatory hypothesis, generated by instinct, is subject to criticism. Indeed it must be criticized and tested by reason; and its validity rests in its subjectability to testing. The perceptual judgment, on the other hand, is not subject to criticism, since it is the basis of criticism, the final court of appeals for all criticism. It is the ultimate premise for reason and for the criticism which reason guides. The explanatory hypothesis may fail to survive the verification process, but "we cannot form the least conception of what it would be to deny the perceptual judgment" (5.186; 5.181).[61]

Thirdly, there is a newness or originality about an explanatory hypothesis, which is also found in the perceptual judgment. Peirce makes use of the traditional dictum *Nihil est in intellectu quod non prius fuerit in sensu* as a motto for his position regarding the originality of the perceptual judgment. Adapted to the present question, the dictum comes to mean that there is no meaning except what originates in the perceptual judgment. This is his first cotary proposition, given in the seventh lecture on pragmatism in 1903. It is for this reason that the perceptual judgment is beyond criticism; there is no basis of meaning more fundamental than the perceptual judgment and the reality known thereby.

The character of originality that is proper to abductive inference has already been treated. Abduction is the only form of reason that contributes ideas to science. Abduction terminates with a suggested hypothesis, not hitherto seen, or at least not seen in quite this way, which will explain the observed facts.

Here too, there is an obvious difference, similar to the one mentioned above, between the two: abduction merely conjectures in an original way, what the explanation for the phenomena might be. But the perceptual judgment has immediate contact with the fact which it asserts.

Fourthly, abductive inference and the perceptual judgment are similar in that they are both interpretative.[62]

> If the percept of perceptual judgment were of a nature entirely unrelated to abduction, one would expect that the percept would be entirely free from any characters that are proper to interpretations, while it can hardly fail to have such characters if it be merely a continuous series of what, discretely and consciously performed, would be abductions [5.184].

From reading the text it is not perfectly obvious what Peirce means by interpretative character of abduction. But from a careful scrutiny of interpretation as applied to the perceptual judgment, we may succeed in designating abductive inference as interpretative in some sense.

Interpretation occurs in widely differing ways in the perceptual judgment. "We perceive what we are adjusted for interpreting," even though it be less perceptible than that for which we are less adjusted (5.185). And conversely, we fail to perceive the more perceptible, because we are not adjusted for interpreting it. We may interpret a drawing now as a serpentine line, now as a stone wall. An optical illusion will be interpreted as steps ascending, and a moment later as steps decending.

> Some unconscious part of the mind seems to tire of putting that construction upon it [the optical illusion, seen as steps from above] and suddenly we seem to see the steps from below, and so the perceptive judgment, and the percept itself, seems to keep shifting from one general aspect to the other and back again. . . . The most striking thing [in optical illusions] is that a certain theory of interpretation has all the appearance of being given in perception [5.183].[63]

The perceptual judgment is interpretative because it is abstract. That is, it represents one or more features of the known object without exhausting the meaning of the object. The knowable aspect which is grasped in the perceptual judgment is only one of several (7.198). Nonetheless the perceptual judgment is true in the sense that "it is impossible to correct it, and in the fact that it only professes to consider one aspect of the percept" (5.568). It is for this reason that the interpretation made in the perceptual judgment is not the only one possible, and the aspect represented in it is really as given as it appears so forcefully to be.

In abduction the observer's keenness is called into play, since the value of his choice of a class depends on his imagination and the sharpness of his insight.[64] An experienced observer will hit upon the right hypothesis sooner than the inexperienced observer, other things being equal. Similarly the scientist with keener insight and more agile imagination will be the more successful. The inquirer's ability and experience make important contributions to the way he interprets the observations. His own personal background as well as the history of the science concerned are important parts of the adjustment. Interpretation in this view, then, occurs at the point of classification of the phenomena. It is materially the same as classifying the events observed.

While both the perceptual judgment and the explanatory hypothesis are interpretative in the sense that both types of proposition classify according to the observer's point of view, the interpretation which the explanatory hypothesis proposes is still tentative, and often erroneous, while on the contrary the interpretation which the perceptual judgment asserts is certain and undeniable, however dependent it may be on the observer's point of view. In imposing an interpretation on observed data, the observer may shift from one point of view or one sort of adjustment to another, and so come up with various interpretations. No one interpretation can be called the unique and only possible interpretation. Adjustment is dependent on the observer. It is controllable, and somehow voluntary. But, given a definite adjustment, the corresponding interpretation is given as an objective character of the phenomenon.[65]

The scientist at the abductive stage, however, while he can adjust his point of view at will, is still faced with a choice of several possible explanations. Abductive classification, i.e. interpretation, is not wholly given in the phenomena. The scientific inquirer must still make the imaginative leap toward an interpretation which he expects *may* explain what he has observed.

Peirce in the seventh lecture of 1903 asserts that the interpretation proposed in an abductive inference must be given in experience. It must precede the formation of the hypothesis. This position seems to contradict what was already said, namely that abduction adds new and original ideas, and is really the only source of growth in science. How can these two seemingly contradictory positions be reconciled? [66]

Peirce is of the opinion that "every general element of every hypothesis, however wild or sophisticated it may be [is] given somewhere in perception, . . . every general *form* of putting concepts together is, in its elements, given in perception" (5.186).[67] Explaining this position, he says that the entire logical matter of a conclusion of any type of inference must be contained in the premises (5.194). Remarking that abduction is designed to explain observed events, Peirce explicates the form of abductive reasoning thus:

> The surprising fact, c, is observed; But if A were true, c would be a matter of course, Hence there is reason to suspect that A is true. Thus, A cannot be abductively inferred or if you prefer the expression, cannot be abductively conjectured until its entire content is already present in the premiss, "If A were true, c would be a matter of course" [5.189].

Hence the premises in the process of abductive inference are the proposition which asserts the experience and the conditional premise which shows the explaining function performed by the hypothesis. And, as in any inference, the conclusion, which is here the explanatory hypothesis, depends on the premises. The logical matter, then, of the abductive conclusion must be contained in the premises. One can conclude that, if this analysis is true, the fact that abductions have been mistaken for perceptual judgments does not then necessarily mean that the logical matter of the hypothesis originates in the hypothesis itself. Even though hypotheses and perceptual judgments are easily confused, and even though meaning-content originates in the perceptual judgment, it does not necessarily follow that abductive conclusions are sources of meaning. Rather the meaning-content, i.e., the general elements of the hypothesis, must be given somewhere in perception.

Merely *explaining* a perception is not a sufficiently close link with perception. The general element, or, in logical terms, the predicate of the hypothesis, must have been discovered ultimately in perception. In the above reasoning process, the hypothesis A is a proposal that something may belong to a general class. Yet in abduction, before we can place an item within a general class, we must previously know that general class. Such knowledge comes ultimately from experience, perhaps of other items within the class.

We must still ask where the originality of abduction occurs. It remains a difficulty to ascertain how Peirce can maintain that abduction is a source of progress and new ideas in science. The newness and originality seem to be in the predication, in asserting that an object or an event may possibly belong to a known class of objects or events. The classification that abduction imposes is admittedly a fallible interpretation. The fallibility of the predication is more obvious when several possible classifications, i.e., several possible hypotheses, present themselves.

But the point to emphasize is that the class, the general element, is already known before the abductive inference is drawn. The hypothesis does not present itself whole and entire in perception, as Peirce expressly remarks (5.193). Rather, although the elements of the hypothesis are in our minds beforehand, "It is the idea of putting together what we had never before dreamed of putting together which flashes the new suggestion before our contemplation" (5.181). The originality of the hypothesis does not consist in the discovery of a new class, but in seeing that the object of perception may be a member of a known class (5.193).[68]

The similarities and dissimilarities between the abductive judgment and the judgment of perception, explained above, should make it clear that it is not quite accurate to *identify* the two. The perceptual judgment can be described as "an extreme case of abductive inference" or as belonging to the same general class as the latter; but to maintain that the perceptual judgment is abductive, as Murphey does, is open to question.[69] At least the perceptual judgment cannot be identified with the abductive judgment made use of in a scientific inquiry.

Murphey states correctly, however, that the role of the perceptual judgment is basic in Peirce's epistemology. These judgments are the starting points of all knowledge, and they constitute the ultimate criterion with which all explanatory hypotheses must be checked (5.116).[70] This is true for Peirce since there is no meaning, no understanding of the universe, except what can be derived in some way from experience.

The question of meaning is linked with the second theoretical aspect of abductive inference, sc. Peirce's pragmaticism, because, as has been explained above, meaning must be pragmatic. "From the pragmatical principle, which I still regard as highly useful, although not as the ultimate principle, a different conception of the function of hypothesis and of the logic of hypothesis necessarily results." [71] The second section of the seventh lecture of 1903 points out and explains how pragmaticism is the logic of abduction. In this context the pragmaticist maxim is concerned with the admissibility of hypotheses; in fact it is the only requirement for the eligibility of suggested hypotheses. As it is understood in logic, furthermore, this is the only thing that the maxim pretends to do. These teachings bring out the close relationship of Peircean pragmaticism to his views on abduction. There are, then, three propositions summarizing his position on pragmaticism and abduction: 1.) pragmaticism proposes a maxim about the admissibility of hypotheses; 2.) this is a sufficient maxim, rendering all others needless; 3.) in logic, this is all that the maxim of pragmaticism pretends to do.

The first proposition regards a hypothesis as a suggested explanation of phenomena. As we have seen, sensible verifiability, either direct or indirect, is the norm of admissibility for hypotheses. But here we find a new approach to the question of the acceptability of hypotheses. A hypothesis may be judged admissible if it is in accord with the pragmatic maxim.[72] Close examination of the maxim reveals that conceptions are not said to differ because they lead to different results in conduct. The criterion of distinction lies rather within the order of the mind. One concept is said to differ from another in virtue of a modification-of-conduct that *might be conceivable*. The criterion of admissibility, therefore, speaks not of conduct, pure and simple, but of thought about conduct.[73] According to this view, therefore, to be eligible as a possible explanatory hypothesis, a conjecture must open the possibility for a conceivable change of conduct.[74]

It must be understood, however, that the pragmaticist maxim is not as rigid a restriction on the extent of hypotheses as it may seem at first to be. Pragmaticism makes conception go far beyond the practical; it demands that the abductive process refer ultimately to a possible practical effect.

If pragmatism is the doctrine that every conception is a conception of conceivable practical effects, it makes conception reach far beyond the practical. It allows any flight of imagination, provided this imagination ultimately alights upon a possible practical effect; and thus many hypotheses may seem at first glance to be excluded by the pragmatical maxim that are not really so excluded [5.196].

Is it true to say, therefore, that sensible verifiability is the same as a conceivable modification of practical conduct? It would seem so. Peirce's pragmatic maxim as it functions within the logic of science is an expression of the verifiability-requirement for explanatory hypotheses. According to this opinion, when Peirce speaks of practice, of practical conduct, and the like, he is referring to experimental verifiability. Both the practical, as here understood, and the verifiable are related to the observable; both the requirement of verifiability and the pragmatic maxim demand that the conceptions under consideration be observable, at least indirectly. My interpretation is borne out in the same lecture when Peirce says that, barring reasons to the contrary, any hypothesis may be admissible which is capable of experimental verification. "This," he says, "is approximately the doctrine of pragmatism" (5.197).[75]

Another basic point is that the pragmatic maxim is sufficient as a rule governing the admissibility of hypotheses, and rendering all others needless. It seems that this proposition can only be justified by supposing that the pragmatic maxim as applied to abduction is the same as the requirement of verifiability. Without this supposition, the reasons offered to justify this position cannot stand up. At best they only assert tautologically that the pragmatic maxim permits all admissible hypotheses, and excludes all inadmissible hypotheses.

In logic the pragmatic maxim is a judge of the admissibility of hypotheses, and has no other function. It cannot interfere with induction, since induction teaches us what to expect experimentally, and "any expectation *may* conceivably concern practical conduct" (5.196). And it affects deduction only consequently to its effect upon abduction.

Chapter IV

THE STAGES OF THE METHOD (*ii*): DEDUCTION AND INDUCTION

AT THE BEGINNING OF THE SECTION ON ABDUCTION, I made mention of Peirce's description of science as a living process, busied mainly with conjectures that are being framed or tested (1.234). Systematized items of knowledge may become subject to scientific inquiry only when they are brought down from the shelves to be purified or transformed. It is then that they enter the dynamic process again. But the process itself is one of framing and testing conjectured explanations of phenomena. Science progresses by means of the brilliant imaginative leaps of abduction coupled with carefully controlled evaluation in the verification phase.

There are two main steps in the process of scientific verification of hypotheses: deduction and induction. In order to get a clearer understanding of the whole movement of verification, a general picture of this process will be drawn before the steps are treated separately. In addition the ability of the inductive phase to converge on the truth must be discussed, since this is the guarantee of the whole process of inquiry. The divisions of the fourth chapter, therefore, are the following: 1.) a general picture of the verification process; 2.) the deductive phase; 3.) the inductive phase; 4.) two requirements for scientific induction; 5.) the parts of induction; 6.) the convergence on truth.

I. A GENERAL PICTURE OF THE VERIFICATION PROCESS

In a lecture delivered at Harvard in 1869 Peirce makes mention of the important contributions to science which the testing process has made. He will not go quite so far as to say with George Henry Lewes, a Comtean of sorts, that the true cause of the success of modern science is verification.[1] Rather a combination of the observation of nature, theorizing, and verification has led to the triumphs of science. Scientists, at work in the laboratory and field, "have been observing—that is, perceiving by the aid of analysis—and testing suggestions of theories" (1.34). This short sentence is obviously not intended to be a carefully chiseled definition of the scientific method. Yet it makes reference to the chief stages of the method: observation, abduction, and verification.

In the verification stage, the scientist is trying to see how close to the truth his hypothesis comes. He draws certain experiential conclusions from the hypothesis, and then tries to see whether the predicted conclusions actually occur.[2] The hypothesis must be fruitful of some predictions, which under certain specified conditions should be observable. After making these predictions, the scientist must fulfill the conditions and see whether his predictions come true (2.755).[3]

The same steps are again listed in a set of rules designed to test the probability of a hypothesis:

1. The hypothesis should be distinctly put as a question, before making the observations which are to test its truth. In other words, we must try to see what the result of predictions from the hypothesis will be.
2. The respect in regard to which the resemblances are noted must be taken at random. We must not take a particular kind of predictions for which the hypothesis is known to be good.
3. The failures as well as the successes of the predictions must be honestly noted. The whole proceeding must be fair and unbiased [2.634].

This quotation points out some of the requirements for verification, but the important thing to note here is that science demands that its hypotheses be verified, and that the verification process be carried out according to reasonable rules. The inquirer must be so detached from

[1] The notes for this chapter begin on page 172.

his hypothesis as to make repeated attempts to refute it. An ascetical detachment from his suggested explanations, together with a reasonable method of testing these explanations, must characterize his activity. With such an attitude the scientist will be able to propose his hypothesis, if verified, as a genuine step forward in the progress of science (6.216).

Instinct may suggest the correct choice right at the beginning of the process of abduction, but this does not exempt the suggested explanation from testing. Instinct has frequently erred. Similarly no antecedent likelihood of a hypothesis can be regarded as safe. Likelihoods are mostly subjective, and so are of little value in directing us toward the truth. "Every hypothesis should be put to the test by forcing it to make verifiable predictions," independently of its subjective likelihood (5.599).

II. THE DEDUCTIVE PHASE

The testing begins with an examination of the hypothesis, and with a gathering of experiential consequences which would follow from its truth.[4] This step, Peirce asserts, is a process of deduction (6.470).[5]

After an explanatory hypothesis capable of being tested experimentally has been chosen, the investigator deduces experiential predictions from it, and watches for the predictions to come true. By deduction he draws virtual predictions of possible experiments from his hypothesis. A "virtual prediction," Peirce explains, is an experiential consequence, deduced from the hypothesis, and selected as a consequence independently of whether or not the inquirer knows its truth. He must not prejudice the issue in his favor by selecting predictions which he knows will turn out in virtue of that knowledge. Rather he should select a prediction of whose truth he is ignorant; or at least he must not make a selection which he would not have made, had he been so ignorant (2.96; 2.784).

In a paper entitled "Hume on Miracles," composed about 1901, Peirce discusses the testing of hypotheses. As an illustration of abduction and verification he chooses the hypothesis: this man believes in the infallibility of the pope. If the hypothesis is true, the same man most likely will also believe other doctrines commonly held by Catholics, and will engage in Catholic devotional practices. Furthermore the members of his family will most likely do the same. These propositions, reached by deduction, are predictions which can be put to the test, in order to verify the hypothesis. Granted that this is a poor example of a scientific hypothesis, and granted that the predictions are to be fulfilled mostly by asking the man concerned (although partly by observing his conduct); still, by making the proper adjustments, we can see what Peirce is getting at when he speaks of the predictions which a scientific hypothesis should lead to, and of the deductive character of forming these predictions (6.527).

A more informative statement of Peirce's position can be found in his article entitled "A Neglected Argument for the Reality of God," where he treats the process of inquiry at some length. After describing the observation phase and the formation of the hypothesis, he writes:

> Retroduction does not afford security. The hypothesis must be tested.
>
> This testing, to be logically valid, must honestly start, not as Retroduction starts, with scrutiny of the phenomena, but with examination of the hypothesis, and a muster of all sorts of conditional experiential consequences which would follow from its truth. This constitutes the Second Stage of Inquiry. For its characteristic form of reasoning our language has, for two centuries, been happily provided with the name Deduction [6.470].

Deduction, then, is an unfolding of experiential consequents from the explanatory hypothesis. Its main function is to explicate the hypothesis, by drawing experiential consequences from it.

Although Peirce is careful in his earlier logical works to show that deduction is the inference of a result from a rule, he still does not give any clear explanation of how the explication of consequents from a hypothesis constitutes an instance of deduction. However, there may be some value in attempting such an explanation from what Peirce says elsewhere.

It has already been noted that an explanatory hypothesis is a predication of generality. It classifies an event, or it places a class of events under a more general class. At least the predicate of the hypothesis, like the perceptual judgment, conveys a meaning. The text most recently under examination stated that in a scientific inquiry deduction explicates meaning, by collecting experiential consequences of the hypothesis

(6.469–475).[6] The problem is to show how the prediction of experiential consequences from a hypothesis deserves the name deduction.

One might answer that for Peirce an abduction concludes with a case. The typical example of deduction for Peirce is the syllogism in Barbara with a rule for a major premise, a case for a minor, and a result for a conclusion (2.620). Using the same terms, an abduction concludes with a case, i.e., a predication of a class about an object or event, or about a less inclusive class. In the process of generating verifiable predictions from the hypothesis, then, the investigator may concentrate on the meaning of the predicate of the hypothesis. In explicating the hypothesis, he may analyze the class, and draw out into clear view the characteristics of the class. This would be a process of rendering the hypothesis clear and understandable. However, for this analysis to rank as a phase of the verification process, the characteristics which the investigator chooses for checking must be experimentally verifiable. It is a real deduction, in which the hypothesis functions as a minor premise. For example: All the members of class B have observable characteristics *x*, *y*, and *z*. But event A may belong to class B. Therefore, event A should have observable characteristics *x*, *y*, and *z*.

The conclusion or result of this inference has no more certainty by virtue of the deduction than the minor premise. The minor in this inference is the hypothesis, whose value is being tested. It is only a tentative explanation of observed phenomena, and is therefore proposed only as a question—or, at best, as a plausible suggestion. What Peirce would call the result of the deductive inference is, by virtue of the inference, only plausible, only a question. It is, however, a question put to nature, an interrogation which nature is expected to answer. The characteristics predicated in the result must be observable. Hence the truth of the result is reached, not by a reasoning process, but by *experience*. This deductive step must generate *observable* predictions from the hypothesis. If the predictions turn out as expected, then we have reason for placing some trust in the hypothesis; in this case nature has answered our question by saying that we have some ground for thinking that event A belongs to class B. The hypothesis has been verified at least partially.

The deductive process in a scientific inquiry must terminate with genuine predictions of the "if–would" variety. This means that at this stage, the results of testing must be unknown, or virtually unknown.[7]

The scientist asks nature whether event A has observable characteristics *x*, *y*, and *z*. And, in ignorance, he waits for an answer from nature. If the hypothesis is right, the predictions will come true. But before observing the results of his experiments, he is still in doubt about the truth of the hypothesis. Peirce asserts that in calling the consequents of the hypothesis "predictions" he does not mean that they must be future events. They are predictions only in the sense that they antecede the investigator's *knowledge* of their truth (2.759). As was mentioned above, this may be only a virtual antecedence, but it must be at least this.[8]

The deductive phase, therefore, of a scientist's investigation terminates with observable predictions which have been drawn from the explanatory hypothesis. The scientist must now see whether or not the predictions come true. This is the inductive phase of scientific inquiry.

III. THE INDUCTIVE PHASE

After the scientist has deductively inferred observable predictions from his explanatory hypothesis, he begins to test the predictions by a process of induction. Peirce notes that it is not the fact predicted by deduction that necessitates the truth of the hypothesis; but it is "the fact that it has been predicted successfully and that it is a haphazard specimen of all the predictions which might be based on the hypothesis and which constitutes its practical truth" (6.527). The success of the prediction is evaluated by the inductive phase of the scientific method.

Induction, therefore, is the process by which the inquirer scrutinizes nature to see whether the predicted observable consequences of the hypothesis actually occur; he then judges the hypothesis according to its success in predicting; and from this evaluation he proceeds to adopt, adjust, modify, or reject the hypothesis.

In Baldwin's *Dictionary* Peirce presents a carefully constructed description of induction and its role in inquiry, under the heading "Reasoning."

Induction takes place when the reasoner already holds a theory more or less problematically (ranging from a pure interrogative apprehension to a strong leaning mixed with ever so little doubt); and having reflected that if that theory be true, then under certain conditions certain phenomena ought to appear (the stranger and less antecedently credible the better), proceeds to *experiment*, that is, to realize those conditions and watch for the predicted phenomena. Upon their appearance he accepts the theory with a modality which recognizes it provisionally as approximately true. The logical warrant for this is that this method persistently applied to the problem must in the long run produce a convergence (though irregular) to the truth; for the truth of a theory consists very largely in this, that every perceptual deduction from it is verified. It is of the essence of induction that the consequence of the theory should be drawn first in regard to the unknown, or virtually unknown, result of experiment; and that this should virtually be only ascertained afterward [2.775].[9]

The article is a brief outline of scientific method, with emphasis placed on the inductive phase.

Both here and in the fifth of the lecture series on pragmatism delivered at Cambridge, Massachusetts, in the spring of 1903, he mentions the justification of inductive testing of explanatory hypotheses. The justification is that induction, if perseveringly followed, must converge on the truth. Induction can evaluate the proximity of the theory to the facts and can then, if necessary, serve as a basis for a more satisfactory theory. In this way, induction gradually closes in on truth. Verification, therefore, in addition to its evaluative judgment, also has a corrective function, such that continual application of the inductive method affects a gradual convergence of the hypothesis on truth.

But this ability of induction to approach the truth will be considered at length later. The primary aim here is to present the fundamental aspects of induction in scientific inquiry.

These can be found in the fifth and sixth lectures of the series just mentioned. In the course of the fifth lecture, Peirce lists the three types of reasoning: abduction, induction, and deduction. Induction, he says, is "the experimental testing of a theory" (5.145). It presupposes that a hypothesis has already been adopted, and then it proceeds to measure the concordance of the consequences of that hypothesis with fact.

In the sixth lecture of the same series, Peirce again states that induction is a course of experimental reasoning. It is a question put to nature, based on a supposition (5.168).[10]

The same lecture outlines in brief the whole process of verification, and then goes on to point out the generalizing character of the inductive phase of verification. "Induction consists in starting from a theory, deducing from it predictions of phenomena, and observing those phenomena in order to see *how nearly* they agree with the theory" (5.170).[11]

In a selection which his editors have called "The Varieties and Validity of Induction," Peirce presents some of the possible evaluations that the investigator may place upon his hypothesis.[12] After examining the predictions drawn from the hypothesis, the scientific inquirer

> goes on to judge of the combined value of the evidence, and to decide whether the hypothesis should be regarded as proved, or as well on the way toward being proved, or as unworthy of further attention, or whether it ought to receive a definite modification in the light of the new experiments and be inductively re-examined *ab ovo*, or whether finally, that while not true it probably presents some analogy to the truth, and that the results of the induction may help to suggest a better hypothesis [2.759].

It is very likely, then, that a scientific inquiry will not come to a halt as soon as the first hypothesis is framed and tested. Most probably the hypothesis will have to be modified somewhat to meet the recommendations of the testing. A modified hypothesis results from the testing and from a new abduction. The modified hypothesis will then have to submit to the same sort of testing as its predecessor.

Both the positive and the negative results of the verification help the progress of science. A hypothesis that fails can be fruitful and economical in the sense that its testing can cut off a large number of useless areas, and highlight the still useful possibilities. Verification, whether it accepts or rejects the conjectured hypothesis, helps the forward progress of science by pointing to more fruitful areas for future conjectures, by closing off certain useless avenues previously open, by furnishing new observations for the next abduction, and by increasing both the experience and the skill of the observer.

> If Nature replies "No!" the experimenter has gained an important piece of knowledge. If Nature says "Yes," the experimenter's ideas remain just as they were, only somewhat more deeply engrained. If Nature says "Yes" to the first twenty questions, although they were so devised as to render that answer as surprising as possible, the experimenter will be confident that he is on the right track [5.168].

The inquirer is supposed to make an economical use of any experience gained in testing his hypothesis.

IV. TWO REQUIREMENTS FOR SCIENTIFIC INDUCTION

Before explaining the details of the inductive phase of scientific inquiry, the two principal requirements for any scientific induction should be treated. The main source for this will be "A Theory of Probable Inference," an essay which Peirce contributed to a book which he edited, The Johns Hopkins *Studies in Logic*.[13] The two requirements are these: the character for which the objects are being tested must be predesignated, and the instances for testing must be drawn fairly.[14]

Peirce repeatedly insists that the character for which objects or events are inductively tested be predesignated.[15] The investigator must determine what he is testing for, before he begins to test. In the inductive phase of the scientific method, if the inquirer decides to examine the objects for common characteristics which he has not previously designated, his results are liable to be disastrous.

The general context of the pertinent section of the *Studies in Logic* is his treatment of probable inference. One of the premises of a probable inference expresses a ratio, and the conclusion repeats the ratio with probability. When the inference is deductive, the form is:

> The proportion r of the M's are P's,
> S', S'', S''', etc. are a *numerous* set, taken at random from among the M's;
> Hence, *probably* and *approximately*, the proportion r of the S's are P's [2.700].

Peirce insists that the predicate P must be known before instances of the M's are drawn, i.e., before we know whether S', S'', etc. are really P's or not.

> But if we draw the instances of the M's first, and after the examination of them decide what we will select for the predicate of our major premiss, the inference will generally be completely fallacious. In short, we have the rule that the major term P must be decided upon in advance of the examination of the sample [2.736].

Peirce is here concerned with deductive inference. But he immediately applies the same rule to induction. "The same rule follows us into the logic of induction and hypothesis" (2.737). If the predicate *P* has not been designated before the investigation, there is serious danger that the investigator may find some recondite character, common to the objects chosen, but not found in any other members of that class. This requirement is closely linked with the deductive stage of inquiry, the operation that predicts observable phenomena from the hypothesis, since prediction involves a predesignation. One cannot merely be content with asserting that, if his hypothesis is true, a given class of objects should then be characterized by *some* observable quality. The observable quality must be named, and not merely left vague. Otherwise, an investigator could find, with sufficient ingenuity, some characteristics common to the few chosen instances, but not at all common to the class.[16]

Peirce's position here is not that the *ratio* of successful predictions to cases tried must be predesignated. It is only the *character*, or the predicate of the prediction, that must be specified beforehand. The inductive process may conclude with a ratio, but it must be given a predicate to seek, before it begins to function (2.739).[17]

The same position on predesignation of the character in an inductive process is found in several articles composed by Peirce for Baldwin's *Dictionary*. Under the heading of "Predesignate," Peirce writes that the word is applied "to relations, characters, and objects, which, in compliance with the principles of the theory of probability, are in probable reasonings specified in advance of, or, at least, quite independently of, any examination of the facts" (2.789). Quantitative induction is an instance of the probable inference to which Peirce makes reference.

Under the heading "Reasoning" in Baldwin's *Dictionary*, Peirce states that "it is of the essence of induction that the consequence of the theory should be drawn first in regard to the unknown, or virtually unknown, result of experiment; and that this should virtually be only ascertained afterward" (2.775).[18] The predictions which flow from an explanatory hypothesis should be drawn deductively before the investigator tests and learns whether or not they are true. If we make use of the opposite procedure and scrutinize the phenomena to find agreements with our hypothesis, "it is a mere question of ingenuity and industry how many we shall find" (2.775). But in this case we would not be really testing the hypothesis.[19]

As is frequently the case with Peirce, he repeats his basic teachings in numerous writings. I shall cite only one more work in which he speaks of the necessity of predesignating the character in question in a process of induction. The text occurs in "Hume on Miracles," in which he again says that a hypothesis must be tested by experience, by drawing consequences from it with *certain results*, and then noting how frequently the predictions come true. He then goes on to say that induction is an inference that, in a whole class, about the same ratio of a certain characteristic will exist as has been found in a random sample, "provided the nature of the ratio for which the sample is to be examined is specified (or virtually specified) in advance of the examination" (6.526).

The reference to the random sample introduces the next requirement for induction in a scientific inquiry. Besides predesignating the character for which he will test, the investigator must also honestly pledge that the instances examined constitute a *fair sample* of the class of instances under question. The principle of statistical inference, whether deductive or inductive, is that a representative sample selected for testing probably exhibits a given characteristic in about the same ratio as the whole class from which the sample was drawn. Hence the scientist, in testing his hypothesis, must collect a fair sample of the objects under examination,

> taking due account, in doing so, of the intention of using its proportion of members that possess the predesignated character . . . and [he will presume] . . . that the value of the proportion . . . probably approximates, within a certain limit of approximation, to the value of the real probability in question [2.758; also 2.702; 2.515].[20]

It is important to realize that there is a double restriction here, on the value of knowledge gained through such an induction. First, the ratio reached through examination of instances only approximates the ratio of the whole class. Secondly, even this is only a probable approximation.[21] But, in order to achieve as close an approximation as possible, the inquirer must do what he can to secure a representative cross-section of the class for experimental testing.

In one of his descriptions of quantitative induction, Peirce makes reference to "scientific principles," according to which the random sample should be chosen.[22] He does not list the principles in the same work. However, by a careful study of his other remarks on sampling we can gather together the main rules which should govern the selection of instances for testing. In general, the process of sampling must be fair and honest. It must not be so random and so unregulated as to be absolutely free from any control. The investigator, it must be remembered, is carrying on a disinterested pursuit of the truth, and must be guided more by his love for truth than by any enthusiasm for his explanatory hypothesis. Hence some control on the testing process is necessary (2.757f).

Peirce gives a clear picture of what random sampling amounts to, in an article "The Laws of Nature and Hume's Argument Against Miracles." At the beginning of this article he answers the question: what is a law of nature? And in reply he mentions that a law of nature is a generalization formed from the results of observation. The observations must be made so as to conform to outward conditions. In other words the instances observed must represent the whole class as far as possible. They must not be chosen with an eye to finding the character sought for. The inquirer must not prejudice the verification process by looking for instances which will confirm the theory; instead, the testing must be fair, unbiased, and representative.[23]

Obviously the instances chosen must be of the class to be tested. Peirce in a discussion of probable deduction, whose rules can be applied with equal force to induction, says that the particular instances chosen for inspection must belong to the subject-class[24] under examination, but the investigator must "not allow his will to act in any way that might tend to settle what particular [instance] is taken, but should leave that to the operation of chance" (2.696). His interest is in the kind, not in the individual. Naturally, testing can only function on individuals; but even granted that each individual tested has its own peculiar determinations, the inquirer must not select it for testing on the basis of its individual traits (2.727).

The method of fair sampling must be such that it will lead closer and closer to the truth (2.696; 2.730). This method of selecting individual instances is the basis of induction.

Synthetic inference is founded upon a classification of facts, not according to their characters, but according to the manner of obtaining them. Its rule is, that a number of facts obtained in a given way will in general more or less resemble other facts obtained in the same way; or, *experiences whose conditions are the same will have the same general characters* [2.692].[25]

As Peirce points out in the next paragraph, the scientific inquirer knows the trustworthiness of his procedure. Since synthetic inference (abduction and induction) is the only type of inference achieving new ideas, Peirce concludes that human certainty amounts merely to a knowledge that the processes of deriving knowledge have in general led to true conclusions. And the process of inductive knowledge depends on the representative character of the individuals chosen for testing (2.693).[26]

Finally, we are dealing with *probabilities* in quantitative inductions, and "probability is wholly an affair of approximate, not at all of exact, measurement" (2.733). The inductive conclusion will reach the approximate evaluation of a ratio drawn from a limited sample, and applied to a whole class. However, with all the requirements, restrictions and regulations, it still remains true that "sampling is . . . a real art, well deserving an extended study by itself: to enlarge upon it here would lead us aside from our main purpose" (2.727).

V. THE PARTS OF INDUCTION

A more precise understanding of induction can be gained from considering the three parts or phases of this process. In "A Neglected Argument for the Reality of God," Peirce mentions and briefly describes classification, probation, and the sentential part of induction.

The mind, engaged in induction, performs first of all an operation of classification. "[Induction] must begin with Classification, which is an Inductive, Non-argumentational kind of Argument, by which general Ideas are attached to objects of Experience; or rather by which the latter are subordinated to the former" (6.472). The scientific inquirer tests his hypothesis by judging how accurately it generates observable predictions, and a prediction is a tentative classification. The singular experience, when it takes place, will present itself to the observer as something meaningful, and meaning is always general. In predicting, the scientist has not yet experienced the individual predicted events; yet he knows what *sort* of thing he should find if the hypothesis is true (2.515; 2.710–712; 2.784).

When the inquirer does fulfill the conditions of his prediction, he is performing what Peirce calls the operation of inductive *probation*. What is required at this step is that the inquirer should observe the number of times that the hypothesis has predicted successfully as related to the total number of times that the conditions of the prediction were fulfilled. In some cases, this will amount to a mere counting of instances of equal value, an operation which Peirce has called *quantitative* induction. At other times, simple counting will not be enough; in addition an estimate of the importance of the various characteristics of the subject-class under investigation will be required. This he calls *qualitative* induction. Peirce gives a clear but quite unscientific example of what he means when he says that, in testing the hypothesis that a certain man is a Catholic priest, the inquirer should put more value on the man's role in ceremonial functions than on the style of clothing that he wears.

Quantitative and qualitative induction are similar in that they both lead to probable conclusions, and they both effect a closer and closer convergence on truth but never quite attain full certitude.

"The whole [scientific] inquiry will be wound up with the Sentential part of the Third Stage, which, by Inductive reasonings, appraises the different Probations singly, then their combinations, then makes self-appraisal of these very appraisals themselves, and passes final judgment on the whole result" (6.472).[27] This sentence written in 1908 is a clear expression of the evaluative function of induction.

Earlier in his literary career, Peirce stressed the generalizing movement of induction without strong emphasis on its function in a scientific inquiry. In 1867 he defined induction as an "argument which assumes that a whole collection, from which a number of instances have been taken at random, has all the common characters of those instances" (2.515). About ten years later (1878), the notion of an inductive inference of a ratio appeared in his writings, accompanied by the generalization:

Induction is where we generalize from a number of cases of which something is true, and infer that the same thing is true of a whole class. Or, where we find a certain thing to be true of a certain proportion of cases and infer that it is true of the same proportion of the whole class [2.624].

In 1883, although he is concerned with probabilities and ratios, he nevertheless retains the generalizing movement of induction. We can learn by experience the ratio of a certain characteristic among a sample, and from this infer the ratio to be found in the whole class. The two ratios, he says, are "probably and approximately equal" (2.702; see also 2.732).

In his later writings Peirce did not reject what he wrote earlier but stressed that induction is the process which verifies hypotheses by testing the consequences deduced from them. In "The Varieties and Validity of Induction," he writes:

The only sound procedure for induction, whose business consists in testing a hypothesis already recommended by the retroductive procedure, is to receive its suggestions from the hypothesis first, to take up the predictions of experience which it conditionally makes, and then try the experiment and see whether it turns out as it was virtually predicted in the hypothesis that it would. Throughout an investigation it is well to bear prominently in mind just what it is that we are trying to accomplish in the particular stage of the work at which we have arrived. Now when we get to the inductive stage what we are about is finding out how much like the truth our hypothesis is, that is, what proportion of its anticipations will be verified [2.755].

It is important to note in this selection that the inductive process asks how closely the hypothesis corresponds with truth—that is, *it investigates what proportion of the consequences generated by the hypothesis will be verified.*[28] Induction is both a generalizing movement and an evaluative judgment.

The inductive conclusion that, for example, the *predictions* of a hypothesis are probably about 90 percent correct is the basis for affirming that the *hypothesis itself* is about 90 percent correct. Peirce's article in Baldwin's *Dictionary* on "Reasoning" presents induction both as a generalizing inference and as the means of testing hypotheses (2.775).

Through induction, the inquirer should be able to pass sentence on his explanatory hypothesis: it may be regarded as proved, partially proved, unworthy of further investigation, in need of modification, still highly dubious, and so forth. These are the various modalities of acceptance to which Peirce refers when he says, writing of induction in Baldwin's *Dictionary,* that upon the appearance of the predicted phenomena the reasoner "accepts the theory with a modality which recognizes it provisionally as approximately true" (2.775).

Finally, in a section of his "Minute Logic" composed about 1902, Peirce says that through induction the inquirer "concludes that the hypothesis is true in the measure in which those predictions are verified, this conclusion, however, being held subject to probable modification to suit future experiments" (2.96). The author, of course, is again presenting the same teaching about the evaluation which an investigator places on his theory, through induction. But there is an addition: reference is made to probable modifications of the hypothesis. The theory can be changed so as to come closer to the truth. Such changes and modifications constitute the final topic in our consideration of induction.

VI. THE CONVERGENCE ON TRUTH

One of the striking things about induction is that, besides leading to a proper appraisal of hypotheses, it also is a method of making indefinite progress toward the truth. In a scientific inquiry the process of verification is more than an umpire judging hypotheses; it also corrects them.[29] In a work composed about 1903 Peirce says that induction is a method[30] that "will in the long run yield the truth, or an indefinite approximation to the truth, in regard to every question" (2.269). And in another work written about 1905 he asserts that quantitative induction "always makes a gradual approach to the truth" (2.770). Similarly, qualitative induction either confirms the theory, or shows the need of some alterations in it. Even though the required alteration be small, some progress toward the truth, no matter how insignificant, is achieved (2.771). These texts and others like them do not define sharply how induction gradually closes in on the truth. Like many others, they merely assert that induction, if pursued long enough, comes closer and closer to a knowledge of the way things really are.[31]

There are two ways by which induction leads to an increasingly better knowledge of reality. First, if the process of sampling is protracted, the knowledge of the true ratio within the class will be sharpened. It is not that we ever come near to exhausting the instances, but we do come closer to a knowledge of the true ratio by knowing more instances.

The topic under discussion here is closely related to Peirce's treatment of the leading principle or guiding principle of inference. In general a leading principle is a habit of thought controlling and validating inference from premise to conclusion (2.462–465; 2.588f; 3.160–168; 4.69; 5.365–369). In the case of induction the leading principle is the scientific attitude that a random sample of a class represents the whole class, and that the significance of the sample grows in strength as the testing process goes on, leading toward an increasing approximation to the truth in the long run (5.275; 5.349; 7.131–134).

Peirce's work on probable inference to which I have already referred asserts that it is the "constant tendency of the inductive process to correct itself." He then goes on to explain that "the probability of its [induction's] conclusion only consists in the fact that if the true value of the ratio sought has not been reached, an extension of the inductive process will lead to a closer approximation" (2.729). An inference based on a limited number of instances may well be erroneous; but when the sample tested is enlarged, the ratio begins to approximate the truth, as Peirce says earlier in the same work (2.709). If the inquirer prolongs his testing of individual instances of a class he will achieve an increasingly accurate expression of the truth.

> It is mathematically certain that the general character of a limited experience will, as that experience is prolonged, approximate to the character of what will be true in the long run, if anything is true in the long run. Now all that induction infers is what would be found true in the usual course of experience, if it were indefinitely prolonged. Since the method of induction must generally approximate to that truth, that is a sufficient justification for the use of that method, although no definite probability attaches to the inductive conclusion [6.100].

This kind of convergence on truth is attained by the method of prolongation of experiences.

This is clearly brought out in several of Peirce's articles in Baldwin's

Dictionary. For example, in the article on "Probable Inference" he writes:

> The general character of the whole endless succession of similar events in the course of experience will be approximately of the character observed. . . . Therefore, if the character manifested by the series up to a certain point is not that character which the entire series possesses, still, as the series goes on, it must eventually tend, however irregularly, towards becoming so; and all the rest of the reasoner's life will be a continuation of this inferential process [2.784].

The same view of the corrective character of induction is also found in the *Dictionary* article on "Reasoning." He writes there that "induction is justified as a method which must in the long run lead up to the truth, and that by a gradual modification of the actual conclusions" (2.777).

Again, in an article on "Validity" Peirce repeats the same view. He asserts that what induction does is "to commence a proceeding which must in the long run approximate to the truth" (2.780). The context reveals that Peirce is writing this with great care, distinguishing finely between what others have claimed induction does, and what it really does. In the very nature of things, he insists, the method which induction follows must lead to results which approximate the truth indefinitely (2.781).[32] There is no postulate here that future samplings will be the same or nearly the same as those already examined. But if the sampling process is prolonged, the ratio discovered will be increasingly representative of the true ratio in all possible experiences of the class under consideration (6.39–42).

This characteristic of the method, as he repeatedly says, is the justification for its use in the experimental testing of a theory. It may at first lead to error, but sufficient persistence in the inductive method will gradually diminish the error (5.145; 6.474; 2.781; 6.100).[33]

There is, however, *a second sense* in which induction contributes to progress in knowledge. It advances our knowledge of scientific hypotheses, not only by evaluating them, but also by aiding in their correction. The experience gained in the process of testing the predictions can be used as a basis for forming a revised hypothesis. Even though the revised hypothesis is formed by a new abductive inference, the experience on which the new abduction is formed is still gained in testing the consequences of the old hypothesis.[34] After one hypothesis is tested and found imperfect, the inquirer has at his command a greater wealth of experience since the knowledge now comprehends not only the experiences from which the original hypothesis sprang, but also the new experiences gained in testing the observable consequences of that hypothesis. The inquirer, then, is in a much better position to form abductively a more correct hypothesis, because the experiences which he can use to guide him are much richer.

His revised hypothesis will be closer to the truth also because of the evaluation that he has placed on the previous hypothesis. The careful method of evaluating his first hypothesis not only has increased his experience, but has also sharpened his sense of values. His "feel" for the ways of nature has become more accurate. His instinct, the faculty of selecting the most suitable of the suggested explanations, has acquired a more extensive background, not only of sense-experience, but of experience in selecting. Instinct, of course, is not a blind faculty; it depends on the inquirer's knowledge of nature and his experience. What is said here of the individual inquirer is also true of the community of inquirers. The enterprise of aiding in the progress of science is necessarily a community undertaking, in which the successes and failures of one or another member are of value for the whole scientific community.

> Coming down to the more immediate and more pertinent causes of the triumph of modern science, the considerable numbers of the workers, and the singleness of heart with which . . . they cast their whole being into the service of science lead, of course, to their unreserved discussions with one another, to each being fully informed about the work of his neighbour, and availing himself of that neighbour's results; and thus in storming the stronghold of truth one mounts upon the shoulders of another who has to ordinary apprehension failed, but has in truth succeeded by virtue of the lessons of his failure [7.51].

The testing of a hypothesis, therefore, whether successful or not, aids the progress of science in two ways. The new experiences of phenomena in the testing process function as the basis for a new, more accurate hypothesis. And the investigator becomes more qualified to select a better hypothesis, because of his more adequate background.[35] The new abductive inference is formed by a mind enlivened by increased experience, and sharpened by a more accurate instinct for the truth. Selective instinct has been perfected by an increased fund of observation, and by the even more important addition of evaluative experience. This, perhaps, is what Peirce refers to when he says that induction is really ampliative reasoning; although abduction is the only process of inference which is genuinely additive of ideas, the inductive process prepares the scientist for making new abductions.

As was briefly mentioned above, the convergence on truth which the inductive process is able to achieve is the justification for the validity of this process.[36] Around 1905 Peirce wrote: "the true guarantee of the validity of induction is that it is a method of reaching conclusions which, if it be persisted in long enough, will assuredly correct any error concerning future experience into which it may temporarily lead us" (2.769).

Although it is true that scientific inquiry makes a gradual approach to the truth by forming and testing increasingly better hypotheses, the key step in the process of improvement is the strictly inductive phase of generalizing from a limited and random sample, since it is the sampling of real instances that puts the scientist in touch with the universe he is endeavoring to understand, and enables him to track down the secrets of that universe. Of course the cleverness of the observer is very important; but that cleverness has been developed by empirical contact with real individual events, and by forming and testing explanatory conjectures about the experienced reality. Furthermore the exercise of the observer's skill is dependent on those experiences of the universe which he gains largely in testing explanations through generalizing on instances chosen at random.

It is for this reason that Peirce can say that the validity of induction depends on *"the manner in which these* [instances] *were brought to the inquirer's attention"* (2.763). The instances must be chosen in such a way as to be as representative as possible of the class to which they belong.[37] As I indicated in the section on random sampling, induction is based on the manner of obtaining the facts from which it constructs its general propositions (2.692f).

In discussing these problems Peirce is clearly trying to refute the opinion of John Stuart Mill that induction is really a process of deduction with a major premise asserting the uniformity of the universe and a minor reporting the observed events. Peirce rejects this explanation of induction by denying that induction is so dependent on deduction, and refusing to accept the absolute uniformity of nature.

About 1905 he listed five reasons, and asserted that there were others besides, for rejecting Mill's opinion. In addition to stating that induction must go beyond its premises, while syllogistic deduction must not, he asserts that induction rests not only on the facts observed, but on the "manner in which those facts have been collected" (2.766). The facts observed must be representative, and therefore they have to be chosen in a corresponding manner.

A proposition stating the uniformity of nature Peirce regards as an assumption, and he maintains that inductive inference "does not depend upon any assumption that the series will be endless, or that the future will be like the past, or that nature is uniform, nor upon any material assumption whatever" (2.784; 2.102).[38]

It would be a serious mistake to think that Peirce is eliminating uniformity from the universe. What he is objecting to is the use of a proposition asserting uniformity as the major premise in an inductive inference, and the understanding of such a proposition as an assumption. Actually the scientist depends on the uniformity of the universe, which for Peirce is closely linked with its intelligibility. He explicitly states that induction is "manifestly adequate, with the aid of retroduction and of deductions from retroductive suggestions, to discovering any *regularity* there may be among experiences" (2.769). No series of experiences, he says, can be so lacking in uniformity as to be outside the reach of induction. Regularity is a feature of the universe, and it is because science studies the real, characterized by regularity, that it can gradually converge on the truth. "Reality is only the object of the final opinion to which sufficient investigation would lead" (2.693; 5.345).

The next chapter will develop at length the ideas of Peirce on the regularity of the universe, and other important topics related to the value and limits of the scientific method.

Chapter V

THE MODERATE FALLIBILISM OF SCIENCE

IN STUDYING PEIRCE'S VIEWS ON SCIENTIFIC METHOD, one is inclined to ask how valuable scientific knowledge is, and how certain and permanent is the knowledge gained through this method.

The answers to these and similar questions are not easy. In fact Peirce's views on these topics are tightly intertwined, and whoever attempts to answer one of these questions adequately is almost inevitably forced to branch off into the other questions. Peirce himself admits that his opinions form "a very snarl of twine" (6.184). Throughout this chapter, therefore, I shall try to pick out a few strands of the snarl, relevant to the topic, and shall attempt to explain them in their own import. In addition, some of the connections between strands will have to be explained.[1] Peirce's thought is unusually close-knit, and his difficulty as a writer lies in his inability to achieve a partial focus without bringing into view numerous connections and relations with the whole picture of reality.[2]

The different themes are so intertwined, that they must be clarified through an imposition of order. Two main themes will be selected, and the others will be grouped around these two. The present chapter has been named from the stronger of the two themes: the moderate fallibil-

[1] The notes for this chapter begin on page 177.

ism of science. The other main theme is the parallel that exists between scientific knowledge and its object.

Peirce repeatedly and firmly asserts that scientific knowledge is not a completely certain and adequate representation of its object. Science never achieves the final and absolute formulation of the universe. The acknowledgment of this necessary limitation of scientific knowledge Peirce has called "fallibilism." It is an attitude of reserve toward science, a deliberate withholding of a complete and final commitment toward the achievements of the scientific method. At the same time, there is a spirit of confidence in science, and an assurance that science really does converge on the truth. Peircean fallibilism, then, is not a complete distrust of scientific knowledge. Rather it is tempered by the reasoned conviction that scientific knowledge is the best knowledge we have, and that the method of the sciences is the only reliable method of settling opinion. Hence I have called his attitude a moderate fallibilism.

The moderate fallibilism of science will be considered as a consequent of the method of the sciences, and of the object which the sciences study, namely, the universe. I shall examine the main characters of the universe, as Peirce views it, and then show how these characters are also found in the mind, effecting a parallel between the mind and nature.

The sections, then, will be the following: 1.) the method of the sciences and fallibilism; 2.) the object of the sciences and fallibilism; 3.) the evolution and continuity of knowledge; 4.) the affinity of mind and nature.

I. THE METHOD OF THE SCIENCES AND FALLIBILISM

The method of the sciences produces a fallible result. Knowledge gained through a scientific inquiry cannot be absolutely exact, absolutely universal, or absolutely certain (6.607). While the scientific method gradually converges on truth, it never really achieves a final and completely certain formulation of the truth.[3] There should always be some hesitancy in the inquirer's mind about the value of his results. Inquiry begins with doubt, but the "settled opinion" which the investigation finally reaches does not afford an absolutely perfect security to the inquirer's mind.[4]

Despite the fact that the scientist makes use of a method which, if continued, will gradually converge on truth, he must never rest content with what he has achieved. It must be obvious to the reader that, as Nagel says, "the substance of his [Peirce's] discussion of scientific method centers around his perception that science is more sure of the correctness of the general procedures it employs than it is of any specific result achieved by them."[5] Any particular settlement of opinion at which inquiry aims is not the final terminus of the inquiry process. It is only a rest. Belief is the "demi-cadence which closes a musical phrase in the symphony of our intellectual life" (5.397). The closure is not final; genuine doubt may open the same question again, and inaugurate a new process of inquiry. There is always the possibility of error in the process.

The acknowledgment of this limitation is the check which fallibilism places on the optimism of the inquirer. But the optimism continues, Peirce tells us, since belief is also a resting-place in the sense of forming a basis for further inquiries. It may open new doubts and new areas of investigation for the searching mind. Belief, as a habit of thought, perfects the mind of the inquirer and influences his thinking in future inquiries. Belief is both a stopping-place and a "new starting-place for thought" (5.397). No single opinion can be regarded as completely settled, nor can any opinion act as an isolated position, cut off completely from all possibility of influencing other inquiries.

While there is a convergence on the truth, then, there is no final grasp of the ultimate and exact state of reality. This fallibilism arises from the nature of scientific inquiry as explained in the last chapter: a hypothesis is tested by seeing how well its experiential predictions are verified. Part of the testing process is inductive reasoning, i.e., a judging of the ratio of something in a whole collection by the ratio found experimentally in a sample. Despite the fact that this process can grow in accuracy, it is nevertheless open to error continually. The sample selected, as Peirce says, may be completely unlike the rest of the collection. Hence "we cannot be absolutely certain that our conclusions are even approximately true" (1.141f).

More fundamental still is the fallibility of the perceptual judgment, the starting point and the ultimate appeal in scientific inquiry. While the perceptual judgment is beyond criticism, as explained before, it does not seem in Peirce's opinion to be absolutely certain. This does not mean that every perceptual judgment can be doubted, since doubt must be genuine in the sense that it must arise on the occasion of a surprising experience which disappoints our expectations (5.443). The perceptual judgment is indubitable inasmuch as it is the response which nature gives with some forcefulness to the questions which the inquirer poses, or it is a cognitive experience, again with forcefulness, that sends an inquirer searching for explanations (5.157). But we can doubt only when there is a positive reason to doubt (5.376; 5.514; 5.524). However, a belief-habit, which arises after a long series of uniform perceptual judgments, may later yield to doubt on the occasion of a new perceptual judgment which disappoints the expectations of the habit. What Peirce seems to be driving at, as Buchler explains at length, is that the perceptual judgment, though not dubitable at will, is nevertheless reformable;[6] no series of perceptual judgments can be regarded as absolutely certain and completely beyond further change. "*Any* of our beliefs *may* turn out to be false."[7] All beliefs are subject to correction.[8]

Knowledge gained through the sciences, while it is of far more value than that achieved by the methods of tenacity, authority and preconceived ideas, is still subject to error and always open to further perfection. The path of inquiry must be kept open, in order to reduce the error. But there is no hope of finally eliminating all error. "There are three things to which we can never hope to attain by reasoning, namely, absolute certainty, absolute exactitude, absolute universality" (1.141). And if these "three things" cannot be achieved by reasoning, they cannot be achieved at all.[9]

The best knowledge which we possess is uncertain and inexact. What is one day acknowledged as indubitable may on the next be proved false. "We can never be absolutely sure of anything, nor can we with any probability ascertain the exact value of any measure or general ratio" (1.147). This is a vigorous position, untenable for men not given to philosophical reflection and for minds developed in the direction of action. But among men with the spirit of science, "the doctrine of fallibilism will find supporters" (1.148; also 5.514; 5.587).

Besides being limited by the fallible character of its results, science is also confined to a *narrow range of inquiry.* Scientific questions have de facto been rather exclusively limited to the development of the two disciplines of mechanics and psychics.[10] There is a recurring theme in Peirce's writings which asserts that the animal instincts needed for nutrition and reproduction have directed the lines of hypothesizing which our inquiries into nature have followed. The former set of instincts has led us to develop the science of mechanics, and to select quite spontaneously mechanical hypotheses as explanations of observed phenomena. The latter set of instincts has done the same for psychics. But these are very narrow restrictions. "There may for aught we know be a thousand other kinds of relationship which have as much to do with connecting phenomena and leading from one to another, as dynamical and social relationships have" (5.586).

Fallibilism, then, is incorporated into Peirce's theory of scientific method. But it is also an obvious mental characteristic of Peirce as a person. Peirce proposes his "contrite fallibilism" as one of the sources of his philosophy.[11] It is an attitude of mind which characterizes both the beginning and the end, or demi-cadence, of inquiry. "I used for myself to collect my ideas under the designation *fallibilism*; and indeed the first step toward *finding out* is to acknowledge you do not satisfactorily know already" (1.13). A desire to learn the truth of things, and a humble confession of ignorance must inaugurate the inquiry. "Out of a contrite fallibilism, combined with a high faith in the reality of knowledge, and an intense desire to find things out, all my philosophy has always seemed to me to grow." A contrite fallibilism must also characterize the demi-cadence of inquiry. Peirce relates that the greatest pleasure he ever derived from praise came from a remark intended as a rebuke. His critic claimed that Peirce did not seem to be absolutely sure of his conclusions. Meant for blame, it was really the highest praise (1.10).

Toward the end of his life, Peirce composed another autobiographical note on his mental habits, and his cautious regard for the opinions of other thinkers.

There is one intellectual habit which I have laboured very seriously to cultivate, and of which I have a number of times experienced advantages enough, each one of them, to repay all the work I have done toward acquiring it: I mean the habit, when I have been upon the point of assenting, in my own mind, to some conclusion, [and when] I knew that some other mind (whose ways of thinking were very unlike my own, but whom I had known to have reached, in his way, truths not easy to reach) had considered the matter and had reached a conclusion inconsistent with the one that was recommending itself to me, of pausing, endeavoring to put myself in that other's point of view, reconsidering more minutely my whole reasoning, seeking to weld it to other reasonings and reflexions which all sound thinkers would approve, and doing my best to find weak points in the reasoning I came so near to embracing [6.181].

Fallibilism, then, is built into Peirce's theory of the method of sciences, and is also a ruling principle of his own intellectual life. But fallibilism is also based on the nature of the object of knowledge. The objects, which the scientist comes to know, are of such a nature, that any suitable knowledge of them must be subject to error.

II. THE OBJECT OF THE SCIENCES AND FALLIBILISM

The object of the sciences is such that any knowledge of it is necessarily fallible. In considering the object of scientific knowledge, we shall see that it is both real and changing. The real is entirely cognizable; hence the scientist goes about his work with a spirit of hope. But the real is outside the mind, independent of the mind's activity, and subject to chance variations; and for this reason the investigator can never be absolutely certain of his knowledge of the real. Our consideration of the fallible character of knowledge arising from the object of knowledge will be divided as follows: *a*) the reality of the object; *b*) the evolution of the object; *c*) law and chance in nature; *d*) the element of continuity.

a) *The Reality of the Object*—There are at least two places in Peirce's later writings on realism in which he asserts that he never revised his early views on realism. In the third of the Lowell Lectures of 1903 he mentions his review of Fraser's *Berkeley* wherein he declared himself a realist, and claimed that science, despite a superficial resemblance to nominalism, has been and must be realistic at heart (1.20).[12] Again in

1905 in an article in *The Monist* he refers back with approval to the review of Fraser's *Berkeley* and to his famous "How to Make Our Ideas Clear," originally composed in 1877 (5.453).[13] On this basis we can safely use his early works on realism as representative of a fundamental position which he never abandoned.

In all these works, both early and late, we find that he presents a consistent view about the object of the sciences. This view comprises a theory of the world as related to mind, and a defense of real "generals." Both these major themes, in addition to others, will have to be discussed with some fulness. But in the present section I shall deal mainly with the first of these themes. A theory of the world as related to mind is for Peirce a theory of the *reality* of the object.

Besides the review of *Berkeley,* two other early anti-Cartesian articles contain his basic theory of the reality of the object. These were published in the new *Journal of Speculative Philosophy* in 1868, and were entitled "Questions Concerning Certain Faculties Claimed for Man," and "Some Consequences of Four Incapacities." Peirce's criticisms of Descartes, found mainly in these writings, are, as Gallie attests, "as important as those made by Spinoza or Leibniz, Hume or Kant," and their importance lies in the fact that Peirce questions the basis, the presuppositions, and premises of Cartesianism.[14] These three works are most important in studying Peirce's thought, since they contain, perhaps in an undeveloped condition, almost every basic theme of his philosophy.[15] In "Some Consequences," as well as in the review of *Berkeley,* three main characteristics of the object as real stand out prominently: the real is independent of the individual mind; the real is cognizable; and for these two reasons the real is a public object (5.211; 8.12–17). I shall attempt a partial isolation of each of these three themes for better understanding; but a complete isolation is neither desirable nor possible. In Peirce they are closely wrapped together, and no attempt should be made to unwind the cable completely.

The real is independent of the individual mind. Peirce insists that the inquirer seeks to know something apart from his thoughts. "My philosophy may be described as the attempt of a physicist to make such conjecture as to the constitution of the universe as the method of science may permit" (1.7). The scientist is trying to learn the lesson which the universe has to teach him and for this reason he must be attentive to the lessons which nature gives. It is nature which starts the scientist on his inquiry by showing him facts which rouse his curiosity and send him looking for explanatory theories. And it is nature which closes the inquiry by passing judgment on the theories devised. Science has always been, and must be, realistic at heart.

Such is the method of science. Its fundamental hypothesis, restated in more familiar language, is this: There are Real things, whose characters are entirely independent of our opinions about them; those Reals affect our senses according to regular laws, and, though our sensations are as different as are our relations to the objects, yet, by taking advantage of the laws of perception, we can ascertain by reasoning how things really and truly are; and any man, if he have sufficient experience and he reason enough about it, will be led to the one True conclusion. The new conception here involved is that of Reality [5.384].[16]

A scientist must form his opinion of nature, not merely because it is "agreeable to reason," nor merely because it has been held, nor because a group of men has declared it the orthodox view. Rather, the method to be followed is one which bases its opinions on "some external permanency . . . , something upon which our thinking has no effect" (5.384; 5.589; 1.20).

The method of the sciences, therefore, is concerned with real things which exist outside the mind, and are independent of any individual's knowledge of them.[17] In a carefully constructed article for Baldwin's *Dictionary,* Peirce describes reality as "that mode of being by virtue of which the real thing is as it is, irrespectively of what any mind or any definite collection of minds may represent it to be" (5.565).[18] Cognition does not affect its object. Scientific inquiry investigates nature and cannot make any progress apart from its dependence on the reality which it studies.

Men may change reality by acting on it, but not by thinking or inquiring about it.

I define the *real* as that which holds its characters on such a tenure that it makes not the slightest difference what any man or men may have *thought* them to be, or ever will have *thought* them to be, here using thought to include, imagining, opining, and willing (as long as forcible *means* are not used); but the real thing's characters will remain absolutely untouched [6.495].

Thought, then, depends on the real, but the real is independent of thought, and is the measure of thought.[19] Truth, Peirce says, "consists in a conformity to something independent of [a man's] *thinking it to be so,* or of any man's opinion on that subject" (5.211).[20] The real is the goal toward which scientific investigation is continually moving. Nevertheless everything is related to the mind, in the sense that it can be known, as we shall see immediately. But the real is not constituted by the mind. It is these real independent facts that a man must learn to respect, before he can be considered a scientist. He must not trifle with facts (1.110).[21]

The object of thought, however, must obviously not be so independent of thought as to be unrelated to it. The reality which the scientist investigates must be cognizable. Peirce says that the object of experience must affect the knower. "Experience supposes that its object reacts upon us with some strength, much or little, so that it has a certain grade of reality or independence of our cognitive exertion" (2.605). In this short quotation Peirce brings out both the independence of the object known and the influence which it has on the knower.

A large section of Peirce's "Some Consequences of Four Incapacities" [22] undertakes the refutation of the so-called Cartesian position that "the very realities of things can never be known in the least" (5.310).[23] For Peirce, as for Hegel, reality is knowable. In fact, cognizability and being are synonymous terms. There must be no despairing block placed in the path of inquiry. There is nothing to prevent our knowing things as they are. However, in accordance with his spirit of fallibilism Peirce warns us that, although we most likely do know things as they really are in numberless cases, we can still never be absolutely certain of such knowledge in any special instance (5.257; 5.311).

Both the knowability of reality and its independence of the mind are positions essential for the understanding of science. If reality were not independent of thought, there would be no scientific method, as Peirce has described it. To know a purely dependent reality, one would merely have to think his own thoughts, apart from any forceful experience from without. A scientist in a universe dependent on thought would not have to take cognizance of the views of others, whether contemporary or past. There would be no room for doubt, no inquiry. Opinion would never gradually settle; there would be no careful computation of ratios, no shaky hypotheses to test. Knowledge would not gradually converge on truth. The mind would know the truth merely by thinking, no matter what its judgments might be. "Reality" would not prompt the inquirer to begin thinking. Such a "reality" would be purely a result of thought, and knowledge would be a dream. This, of course, is an impossible situation.

On the other hand, if reality were so unrelated to thought as to be incognizable, then all our scientific endeavors would be useless. Inquiry would achieve nothing but its own imaginings. The way of inquiry would be forever blocked; in fact there would be no way at all. Nothing would prompt the potential knower to undertake an investigation. Nothing would be open to his mind. There would be no check on the pertinence of his hypotheses, if indeed he could form hypotheses in the strict sense—i.e., judgments referable to reality. All his thoughts would be dreams, absolutely unrelated to reality.

On the contrary, "the reality of things consists in their persistent forcing themselves upon our recognition. . . . Reality, then, is persistence, is regularity" (1.175). Peirce must maintain that the objects of scientific endeavors are independent of thought, and yet related with a certain persistence to thought.[24] Otherwise there can be no science such as he describes.

For Peirce, the real is a public object. In "Some Consequences" Peirce presents his view of the real by contrasting it with the unreal, and by relating both the real and the unreal to the social character of knowledge. We must first have had a conception of the real, Peirce says, when we discovered that there was an unreal, an illusion. When we first corrected ourselves, we knew the difference between the real and the unreal. Self-correction, an awareness of the difference between the real and the unreal, logically calls for a distinction between something that will stand under long and public investigation, and "something" which is related solely to the private, inward life of the individual knower. The real is independent of what individuals may think of it, but it is that which public information and cooperative reasoning will finally reach. It is what the community of knowers affirms.[25]

> The real, then, is that which, sooner or later, information and reasoning would finally result in, and which is therefore independent of the vagaries of me and you. Thus, the very origin of the conception of reality shows that this conception essentially involves the notion of a COMMUNITY, without definite limits, and capable of a definite increase of knowledge. And so those two series of cognition—the real and the unreal—consist of those which, at a time sufficiently future, the community will always continue to re-affirm; and of those which under the same conditions, will ever after be denied [5.311].

If the ideal state of complete knowledge of the real were ever reached, that knowledge would be a perfect representation of the real. The real, then, can be described as what it would be known to be in the ideal state of perfect knowledge. And true knowledge must have some reference to the real, as an object of *public* inquiry. The perfect knowledge of the real, then, is what the community would agree on. This, it seems, is the meaning of Peirce's conclusion:

> Finally, as what anything really is, is what it may finally come to be known to be in the ideal state of complete information, so that reality depends on the ultimate decision of the community; so thought is what it is, only by virtue of its addressing a future thought which is in its value as thought identical with it, though more developed. In this way, the existence of thought now depends on what is to be hereafter; so that it has only a potential existence, dependent on the future thought of the community [5.316].

This view is the direct opposite of the Cartesian teaching that the individual consciousness is the ultimate test of certainty. In the sciences, as Peirce states in the introduction to "Some Consequences," a theory is on probation until scientists reach agreement on it. Once this agreement has been reached, no one doubts it, and so the question of its certainty is idle. The agreement of scientists is an important consideration, because, as has been mentioned, the object of science is intersubjective and public. It is not only the vastness of nature that calls for cooperation among inquirers; the objectivity of nature will make the author of a theory doubt its value if trained minds refuse to accept it (5.264f).[26]

In treating the real as a public object Peirce is proposing what amounts to a pragmatic description of the real. In other words when he asserts that the real is that which would be the object of ultimate public agreement, that on which opinion would finally settle, he is indicating, at least partially, what the *meaning* of the real is. In addition he is proposing a verification test for the real: if a proposed reality is truly real, investigators would agree on it ultimately.[27] As a source of pragmatic meaning, then, the question of the actuality of infinite inquiry and ultimate agreement is no more relevant than actual action is in any pragmatic investigation. What is sought is pragmatic meaning, and this is *about* some sensibly verifiable object or process. The condition "if public agreement is ultimately reached" is counterfactual —that is, it is intellectually meaningful whether or not the condition is actually fulfilled.[28]

While the general meaning of the real can be readily formulated pragmatically, the question of proposed individual reals is a rather different matter. In attempting to reach a true settlement of opinion on matters of fact and explanation, the investigator's mind is moderately fallible. "We cannot be quite sure that the community ever will settle down to an unalterable conclusion upon any given question." Nor can we hope for any overwhelming consensus. "All that we are entitled to assume is in the form of a *hope* that such conclusion may be substantially reached concerning the particular questions with which our inquiries are busied" (6.610).

In a lengthy rejoinder to Paul Carus, editor of *The Monist*, Peirce gives a very brief definition of reality. After insisting that real facts, as distinguished from dreams, call for explanations, he proceeds to answer a possible objection from Carus. He pictures Carus as objecting that "being in general" is beyond explanation. Such an opinion expresses a certain skepticism regarding the possibility of philosophy, Peirce asserts. "In a certain sense, my theory of reality, namely that reality is the dynamical reaction of certain forms upon the mind of the community, is a proposed explanation of being in general" (6.612). As we shall see later, Peirce regards the universe as growing in regularity and law; this is also a growth in reasonableness and intelligibility, because what knowledge of things we have is a knowledge of generality. But he also refers to this growth as a gradual development of existence. The world evolves from non-existence to existence. The real, then, is intelligible, and, in a certain sense for Peirce, reality is intelligibility. But intelligibility is not a relation of the real to individual minds. Rather it is a relation to the "mind of the community." The real is public and is publicly knowable.[29]

That a realistic philosophy is the basis for the social character of knowledge is also presented in Peirce's "How to Make Our Ideas Clear." Reality is again described in terms of its opposition to fiction. A fiction, he says, possesses only those characters which thought gives it. In contrast with this, Peirce defines the real "as that whose characters are independent of what anybody may think them to be" (5.405). This definition is followed by a further clarification. "The only effect which real things have is to cause belief" (5.406). Belief in the real is true belief, while belief in the unreal is false belief. The pragmatic overtones of this description become clear when he writes that the truth or falsity of a belief is determined by the experiential method presented in "The Fixation of Belief." That experiential method is the scientific and pragmatic method described at length in the previous chapters.

Furthermore, in explaining how belief in the real is distinguished from belief in the unreal, Peirce appeals to the social character of scientific knowledge. After discrediting once again the methods of tenacity and authority as inadequate for fixing belief, Peirce takes up the criticism of the a priori approach. The man who follows the a priori approach to knowledge will regard cognition as an exclusively private affair. His own opinion, as long as it is consistent with his preconceived ideas, will be true. Another man's opinion may be quite different, and an argument will follow on disagreement. But conflict for the apriorist is a permanent thing. Belief is never to be settled, disputation will never cease. This individual character of opinion is altogether different from the social character of scientific knowledge.[30]

For the scientist, investigation will eventually give one solution; if pushed far enough, scientific inquiry will result in a position agreed upon by scientists, and enjoying a relative security. A dozen ways of measuring the velocity of light, if they are accurate, will eventually yield the same result, because the object which different scientists study, perhaps by different kinds of inquiry, is one, and is independent of the vagaries of individual men (7.335). Scientists are carried along toward a foreordained goal. The opinion which is destined to be finally agreed to by all is the truth, Peirce says. And "the object represented in this opinion is the real" (5.407).

Peirce admits that it seems paradoxical to say that "the object of final belief which exists only in consequence of the belief, should itself produce the belief." But this is his genuine position. He does not mean that the object begins to exist only when the belief begins to exist. What he does mean is that the object exists "only by virtue of a condition, that something will happen under certain circumstances; . . . [and] it will exist though the circumstances should never happen to arise" (7.340f). The condition that he refers to here is that inquiry, animated by the scientific spirit, and carried out according to the scientific method, may reach a final settled opinion, a true belief. If such a condition is met with, the object of that true opinion is the reality (8.16). There is no assurance, of course, that such settled opinion on all realities will be reached. The condition may or may not be fulfilled, and herein again lies the fallibilism of human knowledge (7.344). What is sure, however, is that the method of the sciences is capable of leading to a settled belief, which is true, and whose object is the real (5.408; 7.335; 8.16; 8.153).

It may happen that some false propositions be held as true for many generations, but such ignorance "can not affect what would be the result of sufficient experience and reasoning. And this it is which is meant by the final settled opinion, . . . and it directly satisfies the definition of reality" (7.336*n*). In other words, investigation is destined to reach a relatively ultimate assertion agreed upon by the community of scientists, and that assertion is the settlement of opinion, however temporary it may be. The object which the opinion represents is the real.

In a letter to Lady Welby written at the end of 1908, he connects together his view of truth, the public character of knowledge, and a strong insistence on fallibilism:

Unless truth be recognized as *public*—as that of which *any* person would come to be convinced if he carried his inquiry, his sincere search for immovable belief, far enough—then there will be nothing to prevent each one of us from adopting an utterly futile belief of his own which all the rest will disbelieve. . . . But if Truth be something public, it must mean that to the acceptance of which as a basis of conduct any person you please would ultimately come if he pursued his inquiries far enough—yes, every rational being, however prejudiced he might be at the outset. . . . I do not say that it is infallibly true that there is any belief to which a person would come if he were to carry his inquiries far enough. I only say that that alone is what I call Truth. I cannot infallibly know that there *is* any Truth.[31]

The real is not the result of investigation, but is the object which investigation continually strives to represent.

b) *The Evolution of the Object of Scientific Knowledge*—Any adequate treatment of the evolution of the object of scientific knowledge should emphasize two important themes. First, the object of scientific knowledge is changing, and therefore whatever accurate knowledge of it may have been achieved must fade somewhat as the object evolves and moves away from the given intelligent formulation of it. Secondly, the object nevertheless evolves toward an increased regularity and improved intelligibility. For these reasons, any instance of scientific knowledge is fallible, but there is hope for an even better understanding of the universe, provided that the march of inquiry continues generation after generation.

For the sake of clarity I shall first consider the generality of evolution, and then in the two following sections I shall consider evolution from the standpoint of law, chance, and continuity. In the course of these divisions, the main themes will be noted.

Evolution is, for Peirce, one of the leading conceptions of science (1.154).[32] Something of an explanation of this high regard for evolution is set forth in his projected "History of Science," in which he asserts the importance of the theory of evolution for understanding history, particularly the history of science—both its public history and its development in individual minds. On the other hand, "as great a light is thrown upon the theory of evolution in general by the evolution of history, especially that of science—whether public or private" (1.103). An understanding of one will further an understanding of the other.[33] In this section Peirce is speaking primarily of the evolution of organic species, and the theories which he treats are those of Darwin, Lamarck, and Clarence King.[34] It is likely, he says, that all three types of evolution have acted,[35] but the last has been the most effective.

King's theory includes the changing environment as one of its essential elements. Organic species change because their surroundings undergo sudden cataclysmic changes. And it is to the altered environment that the organisms become adapted. Obviously then, Peirce does not confine evolution to the development of organic species,[36] since the environment itself changes (2.86).

Even in science and other cognitional operations, a change can occur in accepted views, perhaps by a fortuitous modification of a judgment (Darwin), or by a continual modification of an opinion in the effort to adjust that opinion to observed facts (Lamarck). But science progresses mainly by leaps (King), by a new method of observing, or a new way of regarding what we have observed (1.107–109).[37]

That Peirce considered evolution to be a general character of reality can be seen also in the closing paragraph of a manuscript which his editors have entitled "Fallibilism, Continuity and Evolution." Fallibilism cannot be appreciated in its true significance without first considering evolution. But "evolution means nothing but *growth* in the widest sense of that word" (1.173f). And, agreeing with Spencer, Peirce goes on to say that diversification, the passage from homogeneity to heterogeneity, is an important factor of growth (1.174).

An inquirer who accepts the principle of continuity (which I shall treat later) will not be content with any explanation of things except that they *grew,* as Peirce says, although he does not say how early in his scientific life the inquirer should hit upon the evolutionary hypothesis. Since he holds that a man who has a genuine ἔρως to learn the truth will sooner or later adopt the scientific method of inquiry, and that this inductive method, if persisted in, will reach the truth in the long run, it would be according to Peirce's mind to say that the inquirer in our age would sooner or later choose the evolutionary hypothesis as one of the general explanations of nature.

Another text indicating the general extent of evolution is found in the second chapter of Peirce's proposed "Minute Logic." In a discussion of the existence of natural classes he writes that, if there were no final causes in nature, "natural selection, and every form of evolution, would be false. For evolution is nothing more or less than the working out of a definite end" (1.204). Evolution, then, has a rather wide meaning for Peirce, since it has many forms.[38]

It is easy to see, therefore, how the scientific knowledge of nature must be fallible. No matter how closely its formulations may approximate the truth, its focus is destined to blur as nature moves away in its course of development. The settlement of opinion which inquiry achieves can be nothing more than a demi-cadence, since the object of inquiry is gradually evolving.

But the scientist who really understands this general evolutionary character of the universe will realize that while his knowledge of the universe will never be perfectly accurate, the universe is still becoming progressively more knowable. Nature evolves, but its evolution is in the direction of greater knowability. The universe through evolution acquires more regularity, and increased regularity means increased intelligibility. The inquirer faces his work with a humble acknowledgment of the fallibility of his knowledge, but this fallibilism is tempered by a reasoned assurance of the increasing intelligibility of nature. This is brought out in the following text.

> If all things are continuous, the universe must be undergoing a continuous growth from non-existence to existence. There is no difficulty in conceiving existence as a matter of degree. The reality of things consists in their persistent forcing themselves upon our recognition. If a thing has no such persistence, it is a mere dream. Reality, then, is persistence, is regularity. In the original chaos, there was no regularity, there was no existence. It was all a confused dream. This we may suppose was in the infinitely distant past. But as things are getting more regular, more persistent, they are getting less dreamy and more real [1.175].

The universe is continually growing in reality, in "existence," which in the present context means in persistence and in regularity.[39]

There is a rough equivalence among these for Peirce. In the infinitely distant past there was far less "existence," reality, persistence, regularity, than there is now. And, similarly, in the infinitely distant future there will be far more. The universe becomes more and more ruled by law, less and less indeterminate.[40] In view of this increase in law and regularity, the universe becomes more knowable, more open to scientific inquiry, since the scientist depends on the regularity, the general characters of the universe. Because the universe is gradually becoming more and more knowable by scientific knowledge, no block must be placed in the way of scientific progress; no one may say that the final scientific formulation of the universe has been achieved. The universe is on the march, and a realistic science must march in pursuit of it.

There is, then, not merely *change* in the universe; *there is change in the direction of knowability.* The regularity of the universe toward which nature evolves is the object of scientific investigation. Its persistence is what forces the intellect to recognize it as real, and to look for a suitable explanation. Paradoxically, as the universe moves further away from a given phase of scientific knowledge, it becomes more knowable. This is why science must continually move forward. Hence, if science ever comes to a full stop at any point and professes to have reached the final scientific formulation for nature, it is not only divorcing itself from nature, but blinding itself to the increasing light of nature's knowability.

As nature progresses, it moves away, in a sense, from existing knowledge; but in an even more important sense it approaches knowledge, since its scientific knowability increases. An inquiry which ceases, then, has two defects: 1.) it no longer represents reality, which is changing; 2.) it has cut itself off from reality which is more deserving of being known. The completely settled opinion has ceased to seek the prize, and the prize has become more worth seeking.

The scientist, therefore, must pursue nature with an awareness of the fallibility of his results. But this fallibilism must be moderated by a realization that nature evolves in the direction of increased intelligibility. Our next section will treat at greater length the movement of the universe toward greater regularity and law.

c) Law and Chance in Nature—Nature, the object of scientific knowledge, evolves in the direction of increasing law and regularity. There is a conformity of things to law, even though such conformity "exists only within a limited range of events, and even there is not perfect" (1.407).[41] But, no matter how limited the regularity of the universe may be, it is nevertheless true that what little understanding of it we have gained has come to us through the regularities which we have observed.

In a philosophical spirit, Peirce is searching for an explanation of these regularities. He is attempting to explain the law of laws. While the devotees of the special sciences confine their inquiries to certain narrow uniformities, the philosopher goes beyond the limited regularities of idioscopy and inquiries about uniformity in general.[42] These topics are somewhat involved, and so, in order to achieve some clarity, I shall divide the matter into two themes: 1.) law for the scientist and the philosopher; 2.) law as developed from chance.

For both the scientist and the philosopher, nature is subject to law and for this reason it is capable of being understood. For both of them the observed uniformities of the universe are open to reason. Not only is uniformity capable of being understood, but it is precisely in virtue of its uniformity that the universe can be known by the scientist and philosopher. Even though uniformity is not completely universal, it is the type of thing which must be accounted for.[43] "Law is *par excellence* the thing that wants a reason" (6.12). The chemist is interested in testing this particular piece of matter, not because it is its own singular individual self, but because it is a sample representing its kind. The common uniform behavior of members of a class is what calls for explanation (4.530).

The same idea is brought out also in Peirce's work "What Pragmatism Is."[44] The focus is somewhat different, since Peirce is primarily interested in explaining his pragmatism. A pragmatist of Peirce's sort holds that rational meaning consists in *experimental* phenomena and not in *an experiment.* Experimental phenomena are not past particular events. Rather they are what surely *will* happen to people who fulfill certain conditions. "The phenomenon consists in the fact that when an experimentalist shall come to *act* according to a certain scheme that he has in mind, then will something else happen" (5.425). The pragmatic maxim does not say anything about single experimental phenomena. It speaks only of what will happen conditionally and in the future; and such events cannot be singular. The maxim "only speaks of *general kinds* of experimental phenomena" (5.426). The pragmatist treats of these general objects as real, Peirce says, because whatever is true represents the real, and the laws of nature are true.[45] The scientist is trying to observe uniformities in nature, and to explain the uniformities. A universe of things which are completely singular and characterized by no uniformity whatsoever is radically unintelligible, and there can be no science about such a chaos (5.424–427; 1.26).

In a similar way the philosopher is concerned with regularity. In this way he is like the idioscopic scientist; but his interest is more general, since he endeavors to understand the generality of uniformity. Peirce, the philosopher, is seeking for an explanation, not of particular laws, but of law in general, and this explanation is given in evolutionary terms. "Conformity with law is a fact requiring to be explained; and since law in general cannot be explained by any law in particular, the explanation must consist in showing how law is developed out of pure chance, irregularity, and indeterminacy" (1.407).

As was mentioned above, in "The Architecture of Theories," Peirce brings out both the evolutionary character of law, and its development from an element of chance. This theory of evolution is proposed as the only possible explanation of the presence of law in nature, and it also accounts for the imperfect cogency of law (6.13). In the same place and elsewhere Peirce asserts that our mistakes may be due not only to defects of observation, but more especially to the swerving of facts from law. There is a lawlessness running through nature which accounts in part for the spirit of hesitancy which a devotee of fallibilism must cultivate (1.132; 1.402). This serves as an introduction to our next topic.

Law has developed from chance. In other words, the chance variations, which introduce novelty into the universe, gradually submit to law and become stabilized into regular patterns, open to understanding. And it is by continuity that things and events, which originally arose by chance variations, become stabilized and gradually reach the status of law.

The explanation of law must consist in showing how it has evolved from a state of irregularity and chance. The universe has developed from chance to its present state; and it will continue to develop and increase in the direction of law and regularity. This is a continual movement toward greater perfection.[46] From the indeterminacy and chance of the past, the world is developing and growing in the direction of law, persistence, and regularity. This is a passage from non-existence to existence, since for Peirce "the existence of things consists in their regular behavior" (1.411; also 1.407, 409).

How, therefore, have the laws of nature come about? We can answer this question only by following the steps of the scientific method. Obviously there is no possibility of observing the gradual emergence of regularity from the original chaos, but there is room for conjecture and verification. Peirce, therefore, says: "I will begin the work with this guess. Uniformities in the modes of action of things have come about by their taking habits" (1.409). All things have the tendency to form habits. It is more likely that things will in the future act as in the past rather than otherwise. This tendency continually increases. Not only is there a tendency to act as before, and thus form a regular mode of action, but "this tendency itself constitutes a regularity, and is continually on the increase. . . . Its own essential nature is to grow" (1.409). An action once performed tends to be repeated, and thus a habit grows. Habit gradually strengthens itself into a law. And in the indefinitely distant future, what began as a tiny germ of a tendency toward repetition will develop into "absolute laws regulating the action of all things" (1.409). The same idea is repeated in the "Rejoinder to Dr. Carus," in which he says that the habit-taking tendency is itself a habit, and therefore has a tendency to grow. For this reason only the "slightest germ" of such a tendency is required. And this germ was produced by chance (6.14; 6.612).[47]

Toward the end of "The Architecture of Theories" we read that "a chaos of unpersonalized feeling" preceded the chance origin of the habit-taking tendency. This feeling was without regularity—hence, was without existence, as Peirce understands it.

This feeling, sporting here and there in pure arbitrariness, would have started the germ of a generalizing tendency [which] . . . would have a growing virtue. Thus, the tendency to habit would be started; and from this, with the other principles of evolution, all the regularities of the universe would be evolved. At any time, however, an element of pure chance survives and will remain until the world becomes an absolutely perfect, rational, and symmetrical system, in which mind is at least crystallized in the infinitely distant future [6.33].

Peirce proposes the habit-taking tendency of the universe as a hypothesis,[48] to explain the gradual evolution of the world from indeterminacy to law. This hypothesis, he says, "is our guess of the secret of the sphynx," making a quick reference back to the title of the proposed work (1.410).

To give the hypothesis any value, consequences must be deduced from it which can be tested by observation, according to the method described in detail above. This process must depend on a method of deducing the characters of the laws which would gradually evolve through the action of habit-formation on chance occurrences, and on a method of learning, through observation, whether or not the predicted characters belong to the actual laws of nature (1.410).

In explaining his hypothesis, Peirce presents a description of how habits were first formed, how "flashes" first occurred. He calls a "flash" that first something which came forth before time from the womb of indeterminacy, by the principle of firstness. By the principle of habit, which he is apparently trying to prove here, there would have been a second flash resulting from the first, then more flashes, more and more closely connected. Thus the habit would have gradually increased. The habit-taking tendency would have kept growing "until the events would have been bound together in something like a continuous flow" (1.412). Independent flashes might have started independent streams of habits, unrelated to each other. It would be the tendency of habit-formation to set up an increasing separation between streams long separated, and to bind together in increasing union streams long associated. The completely separated streams might result in "so many different worlds which would know nothing of one another" (1.412).[49]

The above description of the origin of things is not an observable prediction. Rather it is an explication of the hypothesis. In other words, if the hypothesis is true, then something like the above must have occurred at the beginning. And the very general tendencies, operative at the beginning of the universe, must still be operative now, in a way not wholly different from their original activities. The latter is the observable consequence, although it is admittedly very vague and general. The verification is unusually brief: "The effect would be *just* what we actually observe" (1.412, emphasis added).

With the development of time, states will be formed from the flashes.

The states themselves will form habits, and bunches of habits will be substances, things. By chance, some states will form habits of persistence and be strengthened in existence; others will fall away to nothingness (1.414).

In fact, habits, from their mode of formation necessarily consist in the permanence of some relation, and therefore, on this theory, each law of nature would consist in some permanence, such as the permanence of mass, momentum, and energy. In this respect, the theory suits the facts admirably [1.415].

Here is another group of consequences predicted from the hypothesis, and a rapid assertion of the truth of the predictions.

In addition, at the end of "The Architecture of Theories," after proposing the same hypothesis about the origin of the universe, Peirce asserts that the hypothesis explains many of the dominant elements of the cosmos, and that it can be verified in greater detail than he himself attempts.

That idea has been worked out by me with elaboration. It accounts for the main features of the universe as we know it—the characters of time, space, matter, force, gravitation, electricity, etc. It predicts many more things which new observations can alone bring to the test. May some future student go over this ground again, and have the leisure to give his results to the world [6.34].

"The universe as we know it" is an obvious reference to the observer and the present state of his knowledge of the general characters of the universe. In order to appreciate the attributes of the universe which Peirce speaks of, an observer would have to train himself to consider highly generalized formulations of phenomena. The same kind of phenomena and the same sort of observer are spoken of also in a quotation just cited: "The effect would be just what we actually observe" (1.412).

It can hardly be doubted that the description of the break from chaos is meant to show how habit-taking, as well as spontaneity and law, operated as elements in the earliest stages of the world's evolution. "Three elements are active in the world: first, chance; second, law; and third, habit-taking" (1.409).[50]

We have, then, a brief summary of how the laws of nature came into being, proposed as a hypothesis. The hypothesis itself is quite vague and general, and the verification, as proposed, is also vague and general.

Peirce is not unaware of the vagueness of this position. Furthermore he considers his description *figurative*. We must not interpret this as an assertion that what really first arose from the darkness of the original chaos was a flash of light as we know it. Peirce is careful to express his hypothesis with rigid restrictions.

Our conceptions of the first stages of development, before time yet existed, must be as *vague* and *figurative* as the expressions of the first chapter of Genesis. Out of the womb of indeterminacy we must say that there would have come something, by the principle of Firstness, which we may call a flash [1.412, emphasis added].

The use of "something" and "we may call" does not commit him to a strict interpretation. Similarly his "vague and figurative" and the "womb of indeterminacy" indicate that Peirce is merely trying to give his reader some inkling of the general character of the origin of things. The passage must be interpreted as a metaphorical description of the ἀρχή.

Peirce fully realizes the inadequacies of language in dealing with topics of this sort. The words "before" and "after" have a temporal meaning; but time itself supposes the existence of something in the universe, and is itself "an organized something, having its law or regularity." But the discussion concerns a state of "things," "before" the universe was organized. It is Peirce's intention, therefore, to speak of a sequence of some kind, though not of a temporal sequence (6.214).[51]

Since chance for Peirce is such an important element of the universe, before turning to a discussion of continuity, I shall attempt to present a fuller treatment of those aspects of Peircean tychism which are more relevant for our purposes (6.201).[52] I shall organize the matter under two headings: *i*) the evidences for the chance-hypothesis; *ii*) the increasing uniformity and variety of the world.

In his "Rejoinder to Dr. Carus," Peirce points out that his doctrine of chance is a hypothesis, designed to explain certain phenomena.[53] Its hypothetical character, however, does not prevent it from being established with a high degree of certainty (6.606). There are two main evidences for this hypothesis, which we shall consider: the imperfect observance of law, and the obvious fact of diversity.[54] The sciences which have been developed have all depended on observed regularities. "It is by means of regularities that we understand what little we do understand of the world" (1.406). The gradual development of the cosmos to increased regularity has been a growth of reasonableness in nature. Conformity to law is not complete; it exists "only within a limited range of events and even there is not perfect, for an element of pure spontaneity or lawless originality mingles, or at least must be supposed to mingle, with law everywhere" (1.407).

The arguments which the mechanists adduce to prove a completely necessary regularity in the universe prove only that there is an *element* of regularity, and not that regularity is full and universal. No law of nature holds with complete exactitude on every occasion, as observation shows (6.46). This is one of the reasons why our knowledge of nature is always subject to error. Fallibilism rests partially on this element of lawlessness. Arbitrary chance is the explanation proposed for this deficiency, and hence the deviations from regularity are understood as instances of chance.

Another evidence for chance, not entirely different from the first, is the existence of diversity in nature. "All the diversity and specificalness of events is attributable to chance" (6.53).[55] The catalogues and classifications of the many sciences and non-scientific disciplines indicate to some degree the extent of variety in the world. Now, variety, the hypothesis proposes, owes its existence to chance. Variety, merely as the unlikenesses between things, will not send us seeking an explanation, but it is the generality of variety, "the manifold diversity or specificalness, in general, which we see whenever and wherever we open our eyes," that wants an explanation (6.613). Peirce's explanation in this place is quite general: "To say [that] the diversity is the result of a general tendency to diversification is a perfectly logical probable inference" (6.613). And the hypothetical explanation leads to verified consequents: we do find a high degree of diversity in nature. Admittedly the hypothesis does not explain specific cases of diversities, or any individual facts.[56] Similarly the hypothesis of chance explains only the general phenomenon of irregularity, and not individual lawless events (6.60).

Although the habit-taking tendency of things is responsible for the continuation in existence of those varieties which do in fact continue to exist, the original appearance of novelties in the world is still the result of chance. Novelties arise spontaneously (6.30). When an observer notes diversification in the universe, he can infer that the chance element of the universe is operative; conversely, when he sees that uniformity is increasing, he can attribute this to the functioning of habit. What diversification he observes is the vestige, as Peirce says, of chance (6.267).

The chance which Peirce proposes to explain irregularity and diversity is absolute chance. "There is such a phenomenon as absolute chance. Thus, the chance which growth calls for is now seen to be absolute" (6.613). What he means by this is that irregular events are genuine violations of law, and that they and the appearance of novelty are not merely "that diversity in the universe which laws leave room for," as he held at one time (6.602). As we have seen, he accounts for the laws of nature by supposing them to be the results of evolution. This means that the laws are not absolute; they are not obeyed with perfect precision, though the tendency toward greater precision is operative. Hence there remains "an element of indeterminacy, spontaneity, or absolute chance in nature" (6.13).

The existence of absolute chance, he takes pains to point out, is not a chance event. Absolute chance and many of its characters are themselves general laws. In fact, in the original chaos the only uniformity there was, was the "general absence of any determinate law." And, as noted above, irregularity and diversity—being general and permanent conditions—are explained in terms of this "uniformity" (6.606).[57]

No further understanding of absolute chance is possible. It serves as an explanation of irregularity and diversity, but it itself cannot be explained by a more ultimate hypothesis. Peirce says that his conclusions regarding chance were made more secure by a careful re-examination of the function of chance in science and especially in the doctrine of evolution. But explanation even by evolution has a limit. It should be carried back as far as explanation is needed. "Being, and the uniformity in which being consists, require to be explained. The only thing that does not require it is non-existent spontaneity" (6.604). Absolute chance, therefore, is a proposed explanation of certain general characteristics of the universe; but it itself is beyond explaining. Nevertheless it is "not the mere creature of our ignorance. It is that diversity and variety of things and events which law does not prevent" (6.612).

Although chance is not completely open to understanding at present, there is some hope that in the future men will gain a better grasp of chance. If the road of inquiry is kept open, as it should be, scientists may some day be able to enlighten this common trait of nature. There is some kind of law there, Peirce conjectures, but it is beyond the capabilities of the present to determine.

An understanding of chance commensurate with the present state of human knowledge entails a fuller grasp of its evolutionary character and of the simultaneous growth of uniformity in the universe. Both law and chance are subject to growth. Evolution assures the growth of both intelligibility through law and of diversity through chance.[58] At first one may be inclined to think he perceives a contradiction here. If uniformity is becoming more and more common, should it not eliminate variety? The answer to the difficulty may lie in recalling that the evolution of the universe, as viewed by Peirce, has occurred in a manner not entirely unlike the development of the organic species as viewed by Darwin, Lamarck, and King. New species have developed in the organic world, with a resulting increase in the variety of the world. In a similar way the laws of nature have developed from indeterminacy, and with a parallel tendency toward originality.

Some of the new modes of action, developed out of this tendency, gradually acquire permanence as habits, and then evolve into laws. This does not mean that all have evolved from the first "flash." But it is more likely that there have been several distinct lines of flashes. It is not too relevant to argue about which of the various evolutionary theories comes closest to the facts; the important thing to emphasize is that, with the development of regularities in the universe, there is the ever present tendency toward novelty. Some of the novel events will progressively become stabilized into habits and regularities. Law and variety, then, are two of the main characteristics of the universe. Peirce, as was mentioned above, regards evolution as growth in the widest sense of the word. And growth is both diversification, or the increase of variety, and the development of law and regularity (1.174).

The tendency toward uniformity and law, then, is not a tendency toward homogeneity. In fact, in "A Guess at the Riddle," Peirce takes pains to show that there was no homogeneity, even at the indeterminate beginning of things. Variety cannot be explained by non-variety. Peirce continues the tradition begun by Thales and the Ionian philosophers, of inquiring about the ἀρχή, the beginning. In attempting to explain law in general, he turns to a consideration of how law has developed. Tracing the course of evolution back to the beginning, he asserts that, while the first is characterized by indeterminacy, this is still not the indeterminacy of homogeneity. Variety was already there, potentially and indefinitely.

> Indeterminacy is really a character of the first. But not the indeterminacy of homogeneity. The first is full of life and variety. Yet that variety is only potential; it is not definitely there. . . . [Variety comes] only by a principle of spontaneity, which is just that virtual variety that is the first [1.373].

The source from which the first "flashes" originate already has a tendency toward different kinds of "flashes." The indeterminacy of the source is a directed indeterminacy: it is full of potential variety.[59]

In summary: there are two tendencies in nature which explain the evolution of the cosmos. One is the habit-taking tendency which promotes the growth of law and regularity. But underneath it lies a *nisus* toward increased novelty. Once the latter *nisus* has begotten a new pattern, the habit-taking and law-forming tendency will take over.[60] As a result of these two tendencies, we have a universe in which there are ever increasing uniformities, and ever increasing varieties. Peirce thus explains the nature of law, the law of laws. This hypothesis concerning the habit-taking tendency of nature and the way it operates on chance events is adopted, he says,

> as the only possible escape from making the laws of nature monstrous arbitrary elements. We wish to make the laws themselves subject to law. For that purpose that law of laws must be a law capable of developing itself. Now the only conceivable law of which that is true is an evolutionary law. We therefore suppose that all law is the result of evolution, and to suppose this is to suppose it to be imperfect [6.91].

Because laws are developing from a condition of great indeterminacy and irregularity, we cannot expect them to be fully in control of nature. Particular laws, which physicists and others have formulated, are laws in process. They have not yet reached the stage of absolute perfection. The uniformities which they impose are not complete. Chance still roams the universe, restricting the absolute control of law, and introducing a magnificent variety into the cosmos.

d) The Element of Continuity—The evolution of the universe from chaos to law cannot be satisfactorily considered apart from continuity, just as continuity and evolution cannot be separated from the spontaneity of variety. A discussion of evolution and law must therefore be supplemented by a brief presentation of this indispensable element, continuity. Peirce calls his doctrine on continuity "Synechism," and insists that although chance is an important element of the universe, continuity is still more vital than chance, and therefore even more deserving of treatment.[61]

There are many places where Peirce asserts the importance of continuity. He maintains that it is not an exaggeration to say that continuity is the leading conception of science. "It enters into every fundamental and exact law of physics or of psychics that is known" (1.62). But its influence extends far beyond these two sciences. "It plays a great part in all scientific thought, and the greater the more scientific that thought is" (1.163).[62] It even goes beyond the particular idioscopic sciences and enters philosophy. Synechism is "that tendency of philosophical thought which insists upon the idea of continuity as of prime importance in philosophy and, in particular, upon the necessity of hypotheses involving true continuity" (6.169).

The importance of continuity can also be appreciated by understanding its extent. All things are characterized by continuity. "The doctrine of continuity is that *all things* . . . swim in continua" (1.171). Once the reality of continuity has been admitted, Peirce says, one can see many reasons for admitting the continuity of all things (1.170).[63]

Continuity is related to both chance and evolution. Evolution is the passage from the vague to the definite, from the undifferentiated to the differentiated, from irregularity to regularity (6.191). It is progress toward both variety and law.

Continuity functions in Peirce's description both of the ἀρχή and of the general process of evolution. At the earliest stirrings of evolutionary growth, out of the vague potentiality of the past, came a continuum of forms, not yet fully distinct. This early stage of evolution was a "contraction of the vagueness of that potentiality of everything in general, but of nothing in particular" (6.196). For example, the sense-qualities as we know them are the "relics of an ancient ruined continuum of qualities,"[64] characterized by considerably less differentiation and distinction at that early age than now. By an element of chance, or spontaneity, the general vagueness began to evolve into myriad definite qualities (6.197; 6.200).

> There is, therefore, every reason in logic why this here universe should be replete with accidental characters, for each of which, in its particularity, there is no other reason than that it is one of the ways in which the original vague potentiality has happened to get differentiated.
>
> But, for all that, it will be found that if we suppose the laws of nature to have been formed under the influence of a universal tendency of things to take habits, there are certain characters that those laws will necessarily possess [6.209].[65]

An accident, then, occurs in the original generality of the universe; the accident stays, a habit begins, and the accident "acquires some incipient staying quality, some tendency toward consistency" (6.204). This is the function of continuity.

The continuity of the universe is not peculiar to the original chaos. Variety, uniformity, and the passage from novel variety to uniformity characterize the universe which we experience (6.97). The variety observed is multiple; and the universe tends to stabilize the variety which it has achieved, by the formation of habits. This too is the function of continuity. Continuity characterizes any novel event which manages to survive, it stabilizes new forms, begotten by spontaneity, and develops them into habits. It makes them general, and open to our understanding. It keeps the universe from turning into a Heraclitean chaos of complete flux.

Chance occurrences become solidified and stabilized into habits by the generalizing tendency. A chance event, then, either in the original ἀρχή or in the evolving universe, rises spontaneously, and is new in its distinctive character. Its tendency to become a habit is derived from the directed potentiality from which it arose. In other words, its *continuity* comes from the continuity of the less evolved potency wherein it arose. The habit which develops is described as a "generalizing tendency, and as such a generalization, and as such a general, and as such a continuum or continuity" (6.204).

We may attempt a brief exegesis of this difficult text. From what we have already said, it is clear that, for Peirce, a habit is a generalizing tendency. That which develops in the direction of law by virtue of the habit-taking tendency of the universe becomes "a general," in the sense that the individual instance of such a thing or event is not radically singular. It is rather a member of a class of things, or events, and is therefore a symbol of its kind. Although it is the individual which acts on the knower and forces him to know, still the scientist is not particularly concerned about the individual in its individuality. He is more concerned about the kind of thing which the individual represents. The habit-taking, generalizing tendency of nature makes events repeat themselves in kind, and hence makes the individuals continuous with a class, and therefore knowable. Continuity, as we shall see, is a kind of generality.

Hence, though the origin of a new variety is a chance occurrence, it still arises within the original continuity inherent in potentiality. Spontaneity is not of itself continuous, but what arises spontaneously has a tendency toward continuing, because the original potentiality within which it arises is essentially continuous, or general. Continuity, therefore, is an important element in the development of the universe, since it gradually converts chance into law (6.204, 206).[66]

One passage in particular may be cited to tie together many of the themes which have been under consideration. It will also indicate how closely wrapped many of Peirce's most important teachings are.

Once you have embraced the principle of continuity no kind of explanation of things will satisfy you except that they *grew*. The infallibilist naturally thinks that everything always was substantially as it is now. Laws at any rate being absolute could not grow. They either always were, or they sprang instantaneously into being by a sudden fiat like the drill of a company of soldiers. This makes the laws of nature absolutely blind and inexplicable. Their why and wherefore can't be asked. This absolutely blocks the road of inquiry. The fallibilist won't do this. He asks may these *forces* of nature not be somehow amenable to reason? May they not have naturally grown up? After all, there is no reason to think they are absolute. If all things are continuous, the universe must be undergoing a continuous growth from non-existence to existence. There is no difficulty in conceiving existence as a matter of degree. The reality of things consists in their persistent forcing themselves upon our recognition. If a thing has no such persistence, it is a mere dream. Reality, then, is persistence, is regularity. In the original chaos, where there was no regularity, there was no existence. It was all a confused dream. This we may suppose was in the infinitely distant past. But as things are getting more regular, more persistent, they are getting less dreamy and more real.

Fallibilism will at least provide a big pigeon-hole for facts bearing on that theory [1.175].

Another approach to continuity can be made through the evolution of the organic species. There is a continuity of types from one generation to another. Evolution operates in such a way that types survive, not individuals. It is the *class* that evolution is concerned with. This continuity of the species "is precisely what the Darwinian theory accounts for. . . . It is to be remarked that the phrase 'survival of the fittest' in the formula of the principle does not mean the survival of the fittest individuals, but the survival of the fittest types" (1.397). Not entirely different from this is a statement which Peirce makes in his article in Baldwin's *Dictionary* on synechism. Although the example he uses is geometrical, the context is unlimited, since he has just mentioned the importance of continuity for philosophy. He then goes on to say: "A true continuum is something whose possibilities of determination no multitude of individuals can exhaust" (6.170). This agrees closely with what we have just said about individuals and types.

Relating this to the scientific method, continuity is of importance to the scientist, because what he investigates is law.

It is only so far as facts can be generalized that they can be understood; and the very reality, in his way [sc. the synechist's] of looking at the matter, is nothing else than the way in which facts must ultimately come to be understood. . . . The form under which alone anything can be understood is the form of generality, which is the same thing as continuity [6.173].

Continuity then is closely related to generality. The judgment based on observation of individuals, with which science begins, has an element of generality; the hypothesis, by which science progresses, classifies; and testing of the hypothesis is really an attempt to see whether or not the classification is correct. Generality is the heart of science.

From what has been said, it is easy to see how continuity is related to the scientist's attitude and to his work of inquiry. Since induction is knowledge of a class, inferred from the experience of members of that class, the fact that there is a gradually increasing conformity to class should direct the inquirer to place greater confidence in the inductive method. Chance variations, of course, will never be eliminated at any designated date in the future. But those chance variations which acquire adequate permanence will gradually become stabilized into law, and in this way they will become the subject matter for future scientific investigation. Chance events, which remain and endure, become solidified into types and subject to uniformity. In this way they become intelligible; they even *demand* investigation because of their novelty. It is the surprising event that stirs the curiosity of the scientist. And it is the continuous event that can be scientifically scrutinized.

What progress scientists have made in the past will be far surpassed by the progress of the future, provided we have men who are driven on by the genuine ἔρως to learn the truth. Nature is becoming more reasonable; and for this reason the scientific method will achieve increasingly better results.

But, although the uniformity of nature is always increasing with a corresponding decrease in chance, we cannot name the day when chance will have been completely eliminated. A knowledge of continuity helps us to gain a greater appreciation of fallibilism. As a controlling idea of the cosmos, continuity, the growth of chance into law, must necessarily entail a fallibilistic theory of knowledge.[67]

III. THE EVOLUTION AND CONTINUITY OF KNOWLEDGE

Evolution and continuity are characteristics not only of the object of scientific knowledge, but also of that knowledge itself. Mind and external reality, therefore, have a close affinity. The present section will deal with the evolution and continuity which characterize scientific knowledge, and in the following section I shall treat the close affinity of mind and reality.

a) *The Evolution of Knowledge*—The theory of evolution was seen to be a key doctrine in Peirce's description of the universe. It is likewise an important aspect of the development of *knowledge,* since the history of the development of the laws of nature reveals to some degree the characters of particular laws to the minds of scientists. It is obvious from what we have said that Peirce's views on evolution and on the laws of nature are closely entwined. And it will become clear that the theory of the evolution of the universe is closely allied to the teaching on the development of scientific knowledge.

Thought, like reality, is characterized by growth. It grows in individual minds, and in the community of minds. Peirce regards his philosophy as dependent both on his predecessors and on subsequent thinkers. Those who have gone before supply ideas and hypotheses, at least in a negative way. And future observers will help in the verification and evaluation of the hypotheses formed by the present generation of scientists.

> My philosophy may be described as the attempt of a physicist to make such conjecture as to the constitution of the universe as the methods of science may permit, with the aid of all that has been done by previous philosophers. . . . The best that can be done is to supply a hypothesis, not devoid of all likelihood, in the general line of growth of scientific ideas, and capable of being verified or refuted by future observers [1.7].

Similarly in his projected "History of Science" Peirce refers to the evolution of the history of science, both public and private. "The evolutionary theory in general throws great light upon history and especially upon the history of science—both its public history and the account of its development in an individual intellect" (1.103). The individual scientist grows and develops as his researches progress. And the beliefs which he accepts can be considered, in an evolutionary framework, as adjustive habits.[68] A similar growth characterizes the "public history" of science, as it progresses from one generation of scientists to another. The life of a single scientist or of a group of contemporaneous scientists is infinitesimally short in comparison with the span of nature. Scientists of the present depend on their predecessors and on their followers. "Science . . . looks upon this pursuit [of eternal verities], not as the work of one man's life, but as that of generation after generation, indefinitely" (5.589).[69]

The development of the scientific method itself from the proper motive—a topic that was considered in the second chapter—can be considered an instance of the evolutionary character of knowledge. "That which constitutes science, then, is not so much correct conclusions, as it is a correct method. But the method of science is itself a scientific result. It did not spring out of the brain of a beginner: it was a historic attainment and a scientific achievement" (6.428). Our predecessors have grown from a prolonged period of uncritical prescientific common-sensism to a scientific and pragmatic common-sensism. In both periods of history there have been indubitable beliefs, it is true, but through a gradual growth of cognitive self-control and deliberate, though genuine, inquiry, the original primitive beliefs have been checked by the refined steps of the scientific method. The transition in the history of the race from a primitive mode of life, when instinct was more influential, to our more advanced culture, in which instinct is subjected to deliberate self-control, parallels the growth in the history of knowledge from a more acritical acceptance of beliefs to the criticisms that the verification process imposes on the free and brilliant suggestions of instinct (5.442, 445, 511).[70]

Over and above the inevitable origin of the method, the scientific accomplishments of the method are also subject to evolutionary progress. A kind of Darwinian evolution occurs in the history of the sciences, for example, when one of the many suggested hypotheses is finally eliminated as impossible.

> Darwinian evolution undoubtedly does take place. We are studying over phenomena of which we have been unable to acquire any satisfactory account. Various tentative explanations recur to our minds from time to time, and at each occurrence are modified by omission, insertion, or change in the point of view, in an almost fortuitous way. Finally, one of these takes such an aspect that we are led to dismiss it as impossible. Then, all the energy of thought which had previously gone to the consideration of that becomes distributed among the other explanations, until finally one of them becomes greatly strengthened in our minds [1.107].

Scientific knowledge also advances in the Lamarckian manner. As investigations proceed and their results become known, science makes a continuous, though very gradual, progress toward the truth. Many of the results of ordinary research are insignificant, but, nevertheless, there is a movement toward the truth, no matter how imperceptible it may be (1.108).

Scientific knowledge, therefore, evolves according to both the Darwinian and the Lamarckian manner of development. But the main steps in the development of science have occurred by a process of leaps, according to the hypothesis which Clarence King devised to explain organic evolution. A new source of observation or a new way of reasoning about phenomena will lead to a sudden advance in scientific knowledge. A period of rapid growth of ideas will follow immediately upon such new approaches (1.109).[71]

Like nature, the evolution of science is necessarily characterized by continuity. There are leaps of knowledge, as there are leaps of nature; leaps in knowledge introduce revolutionary methods of observing or theorizing. The habit-taking function of nature also has its parallel in science, since some of the new methods and theories gain stability, prominence, and popularity by repeated use and extensive verification (6.613).

Although people who are acquainted with the results of science, but not with its method, tend to regard it as a completed process, incapable of further growth, scientists themselves regard science as a process, a living inquiry.[72] Its accepted propositions are only demi-cadences in the symphony of truth. The "results" of scientific inquiry are what they appeared "to Isaac Newton to be, a child's collection of pebbles gathered upon the beach—the vast ocean of Being lying there unsounded" (5.585). All the discoveries which the scientists have made, and the theories which they have devised and tested, are an insignificant achievement when compared with the vast areas of ignorance which still remain. Modern science is not "so very great a thing as to be commensurate with Nature and indeed to constitute of itself some account of the universe" (5.585). Reverence for the magnificence of nature, and humility before the meagerness of his knowledge should characterize the scientist's spirit. He must realize that his science is "altogether superficial and fragmentary" (1.119). Almost all relations of things other than those relative to the two narrow instincts of feeding and breeding have been left undeveloped and mixed with a strong blend of falsity (1.118). "Our science is altogether middle-sized and mediocre. Its insignificance compared with the universe cannot be exaggerated" (1.119; also 1.116f; 2.150; 5.65).

But the scientist must keep working and developing his field, confident in the efficacy of his method, and yet aware of the magnificence of nature, whose ways he seeks. The two characteristics—hope in the intelligibility of nature and in the capabilities of the human mind to understand nature, and reverent humility over the meager achievements of science as contrasted with the vastness of reality—are the corollaries to Peirce's first rule of reason.

> Upon this first, and in one sense this sole, rule of reason, that in order to learn you must desire to learn, and in so desiring not be satisfied with what you already incline to think, there follows one corollary which itself deserves to be inscribed upon every wall of the city of philosophy:
>
> Do not block the way of inquiry [1.135].

Neither sterile inert despair nor self-confident, complacent pride must be allowed to interfere with the march of knowledge. "Indeed, out of a contrite fallibilism, combined with a high faith in the reality of knowledge, and in intense desire to find things out, all my philosophy has always seemed to me to grow" (1.14).[73]

b) *Continuity of Knowledge, and Thirdness*—Peirce's article on synechism in Baldwin's *Dictionary* is a brief but comprehensive and accurate presentation of the importance of continuity in knowledge. "[Synechism is] that tendency of philosophical thought which insists upon the idea of continuity as of prime importance in philosophy and, in particular, upon the necessity of hypotheses involving true continuity" (6.169).[74] The same article explains two important prescriptions of Peircean synechism that are significant for scientific inquiry: first, an assertion of inexplicability must not be adopted as a hypothesis; second, understanding must involve generality, which is continuity.

A hypothesis is adopted to *explain* phenomena. Hence to adopt the hypothesis that phenomena are inexplicable is a self-stultifying process.[75] Such an assertion would not only be a useless hypothesis; it would attempt to close the way of inquiry and place a barrier across the path of scientific progress. An attitude of this sort is just as much against the fallible character of scientific knowledge as is the assertion that the final formulation of the truth has been reached. Fallibilism keeps the road of inquiry open to progress. It does not want science to cease, either from a presumptive boast of final certitude, or from the despairing suicide of final skepticism. "Inexplicabilities are not to be considered as possible explanations" (6.173).[76] Just as the spatial continuum has no ultimate non-spatial parts, so scientific understanding excludes ultimate inexplicabilities as explanatory hypotheses.

Moreover, no explanatory proposition can be formed by remaining with the individual as individual. Explanation must involve generality, which Peirce says is the same as, or very like, continuity. The synechist must generalize from what experience has forced on him, "especially since it is only so far as facts can be generalized that they can be understood" (6.173). The two tenets of synechism mentioned above are, therefore, closely related, since a hypothesis must explain, and an explanation, like any understanding, must involve generality, or continuity. "The form under which alone anything can be understood is the form of generality, which is the same thing as continuity" (6.173).

There is a close link between this view of continuity and Peircean pragmatism. The pragmatist treats general objects as real. The laws of nature are true, and therefore they represent the real. At the same time the laws of nature are general, since they are understood, and are a source of understanding. And to the synechist, "reality . . . is nothing else than the way in which facts must ultimately come to be understood" (6.173). This, of course, should be interpreted in the light of the understanding of reality given above and its relation to knowledge. The ultimacy here is not to be absolutely realized, as Peirce states; otherwise the synechist would be closing the road of inquiry, in contradiction to his principles.

A closer examination of Peirce's writings reveals that continuity and generality are not exactly the same. There is something special about continuity. "True continuity . . . is perfect generality elevated to the mode of conception of the Logic of Relations" (5.528).[77]

Obviously some acquaintance with the Peircean logic of relatives is required in order to understand how generality and continuity are connected.[78] The new logic of relatives is supposed to be able to deal with all sorts of inferences, and is not as confined as the more traditional logic was thought to be. The older logic, Peirce explains, is tied down because it considers only *genera* and *species,* i.e., classes, and "a *class* is a set of objects comprising all that stand to one another in a special relation of similarity" (4.5). But the new logic of relatives deals with systems, and a "*system* is a set of objects comprising all that stand to one another in a group of connected relations" (4.5). Furthermore, the scope of the new logic is very broad, since it regards "the form of relation in all its generality and in its different possible species" (4.5).

The main function of the logician is to classify arguments. But the classification done according to the old logic is based on a single set of relations resulting from the substitution of terms according to their logical breadth and depth.[79] However, in a mathematical proposition such as "A is greater than B," the subject is separated into two terms, A and B, the subject nominative and the object accusative respectively. "Is greater than" is the predicate (1.559). And in reasoning with such propositions, substitution resulting from the breadth and depth of terms is out of the question. This kind of substitution holds only for certain kinds of symbols, namely, terms constituting the fundamental units of a proposition. But Peirce remedies the limitations of the traditional logic by making the narrower relations of substitution special cases of the relations in mathematics, since these are more general, and hold between other types of symbols, as well as between non-symbols (4.5).

And so the logician who uses the logic of relatives will carry on his work by observing the patterns of relations which substitutions follow in reasoning. In this way he will be enabled to determine how the requirements of inference function in the thought process.

Since continuity in knowledge must be studied in connection with the logic of relatives, we have to discuss it as an element of the judgment. The new logic regards all predicating as relating.[80] This is a general inclusion of all predicates. This, however, is not the generality which Peirce links with continuity. His continuity goes far beyond the generality, or the all-inclusiveness, of regarding predication as relating.

Rather, the generality with which Peirce is concerned here is the generality which any predicate *asserts*. If with Peirce we look upon predicating as relating, we must still recognize that the predicate, the relation, is something general. "The predicate . . . is a word or phrase which will call up in the memory or imagination of the interpreter images of things such as he has seen or imagined and may see again. Thus 'gave' . . . conveys its meaning because the interpreter has had many experiences in which gifts were made" (5.542). "Gave" can be said of many individual actions, but of only one kind of action. Generality, as Peirce says, quoting Aristotle, "is *quod aptum natum est praedicari de pluribus*" (5.151).

A predicate, then, asserts something general. We have already spoken of the generality that is a necessary element of explanatory hypotheses. Generality extends to other kinds of judgment as well. Thirdness, or generality, is involved in the perceptual judgment, following the second of the cotary propositions[81] "that perceptual judgments contain general elements" (5.181). In fact "all ordinary judgments contain a predicate and . . . this predicate is general" (5.151). Even such an apparently singular judgment as "Tully is Cicero" really predicates the general relation of identity, as Peirce says. What is predicated here, as in all ordinary judgments, is both general and a relation. This seems to be the essential meaning of continuity in knowledge: a person in the operation of judging asserts a predicate, *a relation which is general* (5.150f).

Since judgment necessarily has a general element, reasoning too must involve generality.[82] The continuity of knowledge is the generality which is predicated, and the predicate is considered a relation, in the logic of relatives. This seems to be the meaning of a sentence from the last section of "What Pragmatism Is": "Continuity is an indispensable element of reality, and . . . is simply what generality becomes in the logic of relatives, and thus, like generality, and more than generality, is an affair of thought, and is the essence of thought" (5.436). There is, then, generality in reality; novelty becomes stabilized and gradually forms a class of things. It is by continuity that law and regularity develop in the universe. But continuity is also an element of thought, reflecting the generality of things.

In dealing with a theory of generality—or, as mentioned above, "thirdness"—Peirce is working within a discipline which he designates as phenomenology. This is a division of philosophy whose main work is the study of the categories of things. In addition to special categories, there are also three all-pervasive categories to which he gives the very vague names of firstness, secondness, and thirdness. Despite the vagueness of the names, his descriptions of these three are not at all vague.[83] As the main source of Peirce's treatment of the categories I shall use his lectures on pragmatism, a prolonged polemic against the nominalism which has plagued almost the whole history of philosophy as he views it; these lectures were delivered at Cambridge, Massachusetts, in the spring of 1903.

Firstness is the simplest character noted in every phenomenon present to the mind, and is merely the *presentness* of that phenomenon. "The present is just what it is regardless of the absent, regardless of past and future. . . . As they are in their presentness, each [quality of feeling] is sole and unique" (5.44). Hence the first category is quality of feeling or anything which is as it is regardless of all else.[84]

Peirce's treatment of the second category in the same lecture is quite lengthy. This is the category of struggle, or of resistance, of action and reaction. It is the simplest feature after presentness, which is common to all that comes before the mind. Whenever anything strikes the senses, there is the shock of action against the resistance of reaction; the surprise involved emphasizes the double consciousness of an ego and a non-ego struggling against each other. Secondness is the prominent characteristic of observation. The external world strikes upon the observer with some force, and shocks him into an awareness of its independence (5.45; 5.52f).[85]

It is in dealing with the category of thirdness that Peirce comes into direct conflict with the nominalists. He presents a rather clear picture of thirdness in the fourth lecture on pragmatism, in which he argues to the presence of this category in nature by discussing the knowledge he has that, if he releases a stone from his hand, it *will* fall to the floor. As Boler points out, Peirce's account of the reality of generals and his refutation of nominalism is based on his account of scientific prediction.[86] The knowledge that the stone will fall is true knowledge, and "if I *truly know* anything, that which I know must be real." It is absurd to call it a fiction. But how do we acquire such knowledge? "I know that this stone will fall if it is let go, because experience has convinced me that objects *of this kind always do fall*" (5.94f, emphasis added). The general proposition that solid bodies, unsupported and unimpeded, fall, is a representation. However, it is not a mere representation, as the nominalists say; it corresponds to a reality.[87] "The fact that I *know* that this stone will fall to the floor when I let it go . . . is the proof that the formula, or uniformity, as furnishing a safe basis for prediction is, or . . . *corresponds to,* a reality." In past experience, stones left unsupported and unimpeded have fallen, and this with overwhelming uniformity (5.96).

Such uniform experience opens the way to two hypotheses: 1.) the uniformity is due to mere chance, and gives no assurance at all that the next stone will fall; 2.) "the uniformity with which stones have fallen has been due to some *active general principle,* in which case it would be a strange coincidence that it should cease to act at the moment my prediction was based upon it." Our choice, then, is between a universe of thoroughgoing chance and a universe in which principles are really operative. The sane man, Peirce says, will choose the latter explanation, i.e., the doctrine of "scholastic realism" (5.100f).

A further understanding of the nature of thirdness is attained when we read that a general principle operative in the real world functions in the same way in which words produce physical effects. The action of words is merely logical; they act on thoughts, and "that thoughts act on the physical world and *conversely,* is one of the most familiar of facts." Because a general principle functions in the real world in the same way in which words produce physical effects, it is said to be a representation, a symbol. A general principle operative in nature is proposed to thought in the form of a law. But in itself a law is only a symbol; it is a general formula representing something in nature. The existing thing is an individual which reacts. It is not general; nor is it a representation. But the law which describes its activity is general, and, if it is a true law, then it corresponds to something in reality. "The general is essentially *predicative* and therefore of the nature of a representamen," involving an inexhaustible multitude (5.102f; 5.66).

The interaction between thought and things is difficult to understand. Peirce admits his inability to make a very promising guess how thought acts on things, and conversely. But at the end of the lecture he does dare to express an opinion—that "the universe is a vast representamen, a great symbol of God's purpose, working out its conclusions in living realities" (5.119). The universe is a huge demonstration, a process. For nature itself, the premises of the process are different from what they are for us.

The premises *for us* are our perceptual judgments. The predicate of a perceptual judgment, as we have seen, is a general term, and represents something in reality. The quality of the real thing, immediately presented in the perceptual judgment, is the same quality as is represented in that judgment, although the thing is not a representation. It is an individual which reacts. But both the thing and its representation in the perceptual judgment have the same "suchness."

On the other hand, "the premisses of Nature's own process are all the independent uncaused elements of facts that go to make up the variety of nature . . . which the Tychist supposes are continually receiving new accretions" (5.119). The "premisses" of nature's process form an argument when they are ordered by reasonableness—that is, when by virtue of the habit-taking tendency of nature (which Peirce could well regard as a premise, too) the spontaneous new qualities grow in regularity, persistence and intelligibility. They are ordered by nature's reasonableness, and become objects for human reason, which itself has a close affinity to nature.

All of this has a bearing on Peirce's antinominalistic position. Generality is operative in nature, not in the sense that real things are somehow universal rather than singular, but in the sense that what is represented in the predicate of a perceptual judgment in a general way actually exists in individual things.[88] Thirdness, in its full sense, is a "synonym for Representation," in the same way that a perceptual judgment represents reality. Hence, thirdness is something operative in nature (5.105).

Besides being operative in nature, thirdness is also directly perceived, and is not reasoned to. This is the theme of the last part of the lecture. In this section Peirce is treating some of the functions of pragmatism, particularly the satisfactory attitude which it should take toward the element of thirdness (5.206).[89] Pragmatism should help to render the idea of thirdness distinct. It is admittedly a difficult item to apprehend, and pragmatism should make it somewhat easier for us to grasp the idea of thirdness.

This position of Peirce's makes it rather difficult to agree with Arthur Burks, who maintains that Peirce cannot consistently hold both his pragmatic criterion of meaning and his scholastic realism. The former, Burks says, makes the latter meaningless, since the pragmatic criterion cannot detect any practical consequences distinguishing nominalism from realism. The counterfactuals dealt with by the realist, according to Burks, have the same practical consequences as the actuals which the nominalist discusses.[90] One can agree with Burks only at the risk of contradicting Peirce's statement: "Pragmaticism could hardly have entered a head that was not already convinced that there are real generals" (5.503). Realism and pragmatism are such highly prominent themes in Peirce that to assert that one eliminates the other is to condemn their author to intellectual death.

One might rather agree with Moore who holds that Peirce's "pragmatism grew out of his interest in [the nature of universals] and is, in the main, a reaffirmation of the position of Thomas Aquinas and Duns Scotus concerning the status of universals." [91]

However, to come to more immediate grips with Burks, it seems that he is making a double error in his understanding of the pragmatic maxim. First, he fails to use the pragmatic maxim as a criterion of *meaning* (as distinguished from, though certainly related to, the truth of statements).[92] The maxim guides the mind to an understanding of *what it means* to be hard, e.g., when the mind is presented with the proposition "all diamonds are hard." The pragmatic maxim might suggest that this proposition means "all diamonds, if submitted to the scratch test, would pass the test." Secondly, and similarly, Burks does not bring out the fact that Peirce is dealing with *conceived* action, and not necessarily with *actual* practical conduct.

Peirce himself wrote around 1905 in a letter to Mario Calderoni:

I myself went too far in the direction of nominalism when I said that it was a mere question of the convenience of speech whether we say that a diamond is hard when it is not pressed upon, or whether we say that it is soft until it is pressed upon. I *now* say that experiment will prove that the diamond is hard, as a positive fact. That is, it is a real fact that it *would* resist pressure, which amounts to extreme scholastic realism. I deny that pragmaticism as originally defined by me made the intellectual purport of symbols to consist in our conduct. On the contrary, I was most careful to say that it consists in our *concept* of what our conduct *would* be upon *conceivable* occasions [8.208].[93]

In Peirce's view the scientist knows now, i.e., predicts, that the stone will fall, if released—to employ the example given above. The nominalist, on the other hand, should abstain from prediction and affirm the stone's fall only after the event. What is at issue here is, as Boler points out, the consequence in pragmatic knowledge, not the consequent, understanding these terms as they are usually employed by logicians. After a series of actual events the scientist knows more than those actual events. "He has discovered a relation of events, and he can prove his extra knowledge by prediction." Although the observed events alone are actual, the genuine pragmatist holds "that some possibilities are real." [94] As was noted above, the real which is the object of the scientist's inquiry is more inclusive than the actual; in addition to the actual, the real also embraces the possible and the general (8.191).[95]

The would-be in Peirce's pragmatism is general, then, in the sense that it is not restricted to single actual events. Its reference ranges over past, present, future, and possible events. In addition the would-be also controls the events in some way. The diamond is, as Boler asserts following Peirce, "so disposed as to act in a certain way when certain conditions are realized." [96] Such a disposition or tendency Peirce describes as a habit, applying this description not only to men, but to all scientific objects (5.538; 2.664). It is the internal structure of a thing, in virtue of which it tends to act and be acted on in a definite way, not altogether unlike the schoolmen's nature, which relates a thing to other things in the cosmos.[97] Cognitive representation, then, manifests a relational structure of the known, and necessarily involves a virtual prediction.

Meaning, as was explained above, arises only in the perceptual judgment, where an individual is known as a member of a general class. And thirdness is meaning. While it is true that the hypothesis also classifies, and differently from the perceptual judgment which it is attempting to explain, the class to which the hypothesis assigns the individual must have first been known in some perceptual judgment. "Every general element of every hypothesis, however wild or sophisticated it may be, [is] given somewhere in perception" (5.186). This is an antinominalistic position, but it is even more forcefully directed against the attitude which would confine all knowledge of thirdness to inference.

Thirdness, then, for Peirce is directly perceived. This is the first of his three cotary propositions announced at the opening of the seventh lecture. The man who holds the cotary propositions "will have no difficulty with Thirdness . . . because he will hold that the conformity of action to general intentions is as much given in perception as is the element of action itself, which cannot really be mentally torn away from such general purposiveness" (5.212). Here again reference is made to the ability of the mind to grasp what is operative in nature. General purposive activity in nature is grasped by the mind, also in a general way. Individuals exist in nature, and act, and react. But their actions and reactions are either a part of a pattern of uniformity, or will gradually become such. Our perceptual judgments are not merely in a state of action and reaction with their object. They, like the object, go beyond secondness. Our judgments contain general elements which represent the general patterns of their objects. Our perceptual judgments contain meaning, which is always general, in the sense that it classifies objects in knowing them. What Thompson says on this question is quite helpful: "The process which starts out with a percept arising from reaction with a singular and ends in predicating that percept as of a subject something involving generality seems to reflect all the important elements of Peirce's philosophy."[98]

IV. THE AFFINITY OF MIND AND NATURE

From what has been said, it is rather clear that mind and reality are very closely linked. Reality is open to understanding, and there is nothing that cannot ultimately come to be known. Mind pursues reality, and the most effective pursuit is achieved by the method of the sciences. The success which science has had is due to the affinity between mind and nature. "Every single truth of science is due to the affinity of the human soul to the soul of the universe" (5.47). Man's knowledge of nature is not achieved by a purely deductive, rationalistic process; similarly nature is not rigidly rational, but is made plastic by the leaven of chance. A scientific knowledge of nature involves both induction and abduction, neither of which leads to an absolutely certain conclusion; it is a similar case with the spontaneous events of nature, and with its imperfect observance of law. The universe is like logic: it is not fully knowable by deductive necessary reason. It is known through abductive leaps, not unlike its own spontaneous events (2.750; 6.189; 6.218f).[99]

The success which scientists have enjoyed in selecting the correct hypotheses to explain nature results from the fact that the human mind is continuous with nature, and hence like nature.

The mind of man is strongly adapted to the comprehension of the world; at least, so far as this goes, that certain conceptions, highly important for such a comprehension, naturally arise in his mind; and, without such a tendency, the mind could never have had any development at all [6.417].

A theme which has already been treated can be recognized here: man's instinctive selection of the correct explanatory hypothesis from many possible suggested explanations of phenomena.[100]

After studying Peirce's views on evolution, continuity, reality, and the mind, we are in a better position to understand how scientists have been so successful in explaining nature. In the chapter on abduction a brief reference was made to the mind's continuity with the cosmos, and hence to its instinctive feel for the laws of the cosmos of which it is a part. The main elements of this theory are found in two lectures which his editors have brought together in a single chapter entitled by them "Methods for Attaining Truth." The first of these two lectures is the third of the series of "Detached Ideas on Vitally Important Topics," presented in 1898. The second is a selection from the eighth Lowell Lecture of 1903.

Science is a living process, of framing and testing hypotheses. And while the testing of the hypothesis is accomplished by a process rather loosely called induction, in which process science "simply surrenders itself to the force of facts," the mind finds that it must somehow go beyond facts in selecting the provisional explanatory position (5.589). In this leap toward an unobserved explanation, the mind calls "upon its inward sympathy with nature, its instinct for aid, just as we find Galileo at the dawn of modern science making his appeal to *il lume naturale*" (5.589). Science, then, progresses by virtue of the mind's relation to nature. Science is continually learning from nature, by way of the mind's instinct, and by way of nature's manifestation through observed facts. The value of facts to the mind consists only in this, "that they belong to Nature; and Nature is something great, and beautiful, and sacred, and eternal, and real—the object of its [science's] worship and its aspiration" (5.589).

A deeper understanding of the function of instinct in selecting a hypothesis for testing can be gotten from the second lecture. There a more ultimate reason for the scientist's success in choosing the correct hypothesis is given: "It is somehow more than a mere figure of speech to say that nature fecundates the mind of man with ideas which, when those ideas grow up, will resemble their father, Nature" (5.591).[101]

Later in the second lecture Peirce treats the instinctive selection of explanatory hypotheses, in a more obviously evolutionary framework. Not only have scientists had great success in ascertaining the laws of nature, as a result of the affinity of their minds to the universe, but it is precisely in view of this affinity that the human race has managed to *survive*. This affinity, then, is not a mere luxury for man: it is necessary for the continuation of the race. Were man not equipped with a mind adapted to his requirements, Peirce writes, he could not have acquired any knowledge, and would have become extinct within a generation. But as it is, man has been given certain instincts, "that is, certain natural beliefs that are true," relating mostly to forces and to the action of minds. Knowledge of the history of the universe, and particularly of the history of human knowledge, leads Peirce to infer abductively that the affinity of the human mind with nature is responsible both for the marvelous success of science, and even for the survival of man (5.603).

Certain uniformities, that is to say certain general ideas of action, prevail throughout the universe, and the reasoning mind is [it]self a product of this universe. These same laws are thus, by logical necessity, incorporated in his own being. . . . In this way, general considerations concerning the universe, strictly philosophical considerations, all but demonstrate that if the universe conforms, with any approach to accuracy, to certain highly pervasive laws, and if man's mind has been developed under the influence of those laws, it is to be expected that he should have a *natural light*, or *light of nature*, or *instinctive insight,* or genius, tending to make him guess those laws aright, or nearly aright. This conclusion is confirmed when we find that every species of animal is endowed with a similar genius. . . . The history of science, especially the early history of modern science, . . . completes the proof by showing how few were the guesses that men of surpassing genius had to make before they rightly guessed the laws of nature [5.603f].

Some of the main themes of Peircean thought are woven into this selection. In a sense it can serve as a summary of the present chapter, since it is impregnated with the evolutionary spirit, with continuity, with quick references to the regularity of nature. Mind is continuous with the rest of the cosmos. Hence by virtue of the habit-taking tendency of nature, mind must be characterized by the same general laws that are found in nature. Mind, as one with nature, and also as a knowing faculty, must have an instinctive feel for the ways of nature. This feel consists in ideas with which nature has fecundated its child, mind. The ideas are like seeds and, hence, like the rest of nature, must grow.

Evolution, that is, growth in the widest sense, belongs both to nature and to mind. The seeds of instinctive selection of explanatory hypotheses mature through scientific endeavor. Inquiry develops its own tools. Just as nature is continually evolving and moving in the direction of increasing knowability, by becoming more regular, more subject to law, so too the individual mind grows; if it engages in scientific inquiry, its *knowledge* of the cosmos increases gradually; but, like nature, mind also develops its *ability to know* more about the universe. It is not only knowledge that increases, but intelligence. The idea-seeds planted by nature in the mind continuous with nature mature under the stimulus of use, and the inquirer develops continually into a more and more effective pursuer of nature's ways.

All of this, however, must be contemplated with the corrective humility of fallibilism. In his "A Guess at The Riddle," Peirce remarks that "the whole history of thought shows that our instinctive beliefs, in their original condition, are so mixed up with error that they can never be trusted till they have been corrected by experience" (1.404). When the inquirer with astonishing success hits upon the correct explanation for observed events, he can attribute his success to instinct. However, he cannot be aware of his success until he has submitted his hypothesis to a rigid and detached process of verification, which, as we have seen at some length, is the testing and appraisal of the hypothesis through experience. But if experience finally justifies the hypothesis, the reflective investigator can attribute his original selection of the hypothesis to the continuity of his mind with the cosmos which he is studying. In choosing an explanation for testing, the inquirer is going on the hope that there is some affinity between his mind and nature. But he must be aware of the danger of error in such a choice, and must rely on observation to check the hypothesis and expose what error there may be (1.121).[102]

Chapter VI

SOME EVALUATIONS

IT IS NOT AN EASY TASK to evaluate the contribution that Peirce has made to philosophy and to the study of scientific method. The extent of his interests and the variety of his intellectual achievements leave the reader somewhat stunned at first. And even after long study the reader finds that he is still far from a complete comprehension of Peircean thought. Certain grand themes attain prominence, as is evident from the foregoing chapters, but their prominence in Peirce is no guarantee of their comprehension by the reader of Peirce.

During the almost four decades since the publication of the earlier volumes of his *Collected Papers,* Peirce has received some of the esteem he deserves. Authors have been generous in their praise of his stature. However, some have made vigorous efforts to get Peirce to defend their own positions, and in this way they have fallen back on the methods of tenacity and authority so clearly discredited by Peirce himself. Others, instead of using Peirce for their own defense, have made disinterested attempts to present Peirce's thought in a more detached fashion, hoping to understand Peirce as he intended himself to be understood. I have endeavored to present what I believe Peirce really thought about the method of the sciences, "without any sort of axe to grind" (1.44). It is in this final chapter that I may be permitted to evaluate Peirce's views from my own standpoint. There are certain outstanding features that deserve praise and there are some key shortcomings that will be criticized, perhaps inadequately.

Among the aspects of his thought which merit strong praise, I have selected two for rather lengthy treatment here: his Greek insistence on the primacy of theoretical knowledge, and his almost Teilhardian synthesis of evolutionary themes. My basic attitude toward both of these topics in Peirce is one of endorsement, but it must also be admitted that there are some defects in each that should be criticized.

I. GREEK EMPHASIS ON THEORY

Peirce was not only an outstanding philosopher but also a man well acquainted with the history of philosophy. His knowledge of history, going back to Plato, Aristotle, and other Greeks, contributed to the formation of his own personal philosophy. One obvious Greek attitude that he made his own was the dedication to theoretical knowledge.

In the texts presented in the second chapter it is clear that for Peirce the scientist is in search of knowledge for its own sake. But this is not just an historical fact, a summary of the motives of the generality of scientists. It is also a value judgment: that is what the scientist *must* search for, and the purity of his science is exactly proportional to the purity of his quest for the truth for its own sake.

Furthermore the search for truth for its own sake is a more admirable enterprise than the quest for practical, useful knowledge. This is an undeniable belief of Peirce's (1.671; 5.589; 8.142). But when the thinker begins to search in Peirce's writings for a philosophical underpinning of this value judgment, he runs into complexity.

Peirce did not remain content with the view that inquiry is undertaken from a motive of escaping the irritation of doubt and passing to the satisfaction of holding a settled opinion. Personal contentment is not the scientist's aim. He cannot accept the continuation and betterment of the human stock or the happiness of mankind and social efficiency as the goals of inquiry either, as he wrote in a review of Karl Pearson's *The Grammar of Science* (8.133–135).[1] Such a view, he writes, "is historically false, in that it does not accord with the predominant sentiment of scientific men; second, that it is bad ethics; and,

[1] The notes for this chapter begin on page 189.

third, . . . its propagation would retard the progress of science" (8.135). Peirce does not accuse Pearson of holding the "grotesque" opinion that scientists are motivated by the desire to strengthen the stability of society; but Pearson should have explained the motive that actually has inspired men of science. That motive Peirce himself describes in a lengthy paragraph that deserves quotation in full because of its richness:

> The man of science has received a deep impression of the majesty of truth, as that to which, sooner or later, every knee must bow. He has further found that his own mind is sufficiently akin to that truth, to enable him, on condition of submissive observation, to interpret it in some measure. As he gradually becomes better and better acquainted with the character of cosmical truth, and learns that human reason is its issue and can be brought step by step into accord with it, he conceives a passion for its fuller revelation. He is keenly aware of his own ignorance, and knows that personally he can make but small steps in discovery. Yet, small as they are, he deems them precious; and he hopes that by conscientiously pursuing the methods of science he may erect a foundation upon which his successors may climb higher. This, for him, is what makes life worth living and what makes the human race worth perpetuation. The very being of law, general truth, reason—call it what you will—consists in its expressing itself in a cosmos and in intellects which reflect it, and in doing this progressively; and that which makes progressive creation worth doing—so the researcher comes to feel—is precisely the reason, the law, the general truth for the sake of which it takes place [8.136].

The cosmos presents law, reason, general truth in a majestic way, for Peirce, and the man of science passionately endeavors to take small but precious steps in the discovery of that truth.[2] This description is proposed as a matter of historical or biographical fact, but it is the philosopher's task to say why, in ethical terms, it *should* be so.[3]

As Peirce explicitly asserts, what is at stake here is the determination of what is "desirable in itself without any ulterior reason." Though such motives as the pursuit of pleasure and the promotion of one's own way of life or one's creed can be discussed as desirable in themselves, it is still "furthering the realization of some ideal description of a state of things" that Peirce chooses in defending the theoretical character of scientific research (8.136*n*3; 8.140).

To look further in Peirce's writings for a philosophical justification of the superiority of theoretical knowledge over practical knowledge is a somewhat futile task, because when he discusses the question, he usually branches off either into a presentation of various other motives of human behavior, or into an epistemological investigation of what sort of science a knowledge of the good is. The latter is the more frequent course, and, though it is a worthwhile pursuit, it does not give the reader a satisfactory understanding of theory as an ultimate goal.

Peirce's approach to the justification of the value of theoretical knowledge is made through his logic and his value theory. Logic is not exclusively a formal study of knowledge, but a theory of knowledge in a very inclusive sense. His value theory is not a single science, it seems, but a complexus of phenomenology, ethics, and aesthetics. All of these are parts of philosophy, and so the theoretical defense of the value of theory is altogether a rather involved philosophical question. His most developed writings on this question were the products of his thinking in the late 1890s and the 1900s.[4]

Among these writings his "Why Study Logic?"—a long section of the projected "Minute Logic"—offers some insights into the context of the question of the value of scientific knowledge. In this work he makes it clear that value theory is not the same as ethics. Ethics deals with questions of aims, and not merely with questions of right and wrong: "The fundamental problem of ethics is not, therefore, What is right, but What am I prepared deliberately to accept as the statement of what I want to do, what am I to aim at, what am I after? To what is the force of my will to be directed?" (2.198). Ethics indicates the end of *life,* whereas logic, in the inclusive sense just mentioned, deals with the means of attaining the end of *thought.*[5] "It is, therefore, impossible to be thoroughly and rationally logical except upon an ethical basis" (2.198).[6]

But, since it is a part of logic to assert that the goal of scientific work is knowledge for its own sake, the justification of this goal as worthy of a man and as superior to other types of knowledge belongs to an ethical inquiry. Peirce recognizes this and regrets that he did not see it earlier in life.

But even ethics is of itself an unsatisfactory support of the superior value of theoretical knowledge. There is a more basic investigation that must be undertaken beyond ethics. This is aesthetics. Aesthetics is not exactly a theory of beauty, since such a theory "is but the product of this science" (2.199).

> Ethics asks to what end all effort shall be directed. That question obviously depends upon the question what it would be that, independently of the effort, we should like to experience. But in order to state the question of esthetics in its purity, we should eliminate from it, not merely all consideration of effort, but all consideration of action and reaction, including all consideration of our receiving pleasure, everything in short, belonging to the opposition of the *ego* and the *non-ego*. We have not in our language a word of the requisite generality [2.199].

Aesthetics attempts to uncover that one quality that is, καλός, a quality which he designates in another writing as the admirable in itself (1.611–615). As logic, therefore, depends on ethics, so ethics depends on aesthetics, the theory of the admirable in itself. "Esthetics, therefore, although I have terribly neglected it, appears to be possibly the first indispensable propedeutic to logic, and the logic of esthetics to be a distinct part of the science of logic that ought not to be omitted" (2.199).[7] But without pursuing the question of the truth, he immediately returns to a familiar theme: the justification of a method of inquiry—a logical question—should be framed in terms of its reliability in leading to the truth, or to an increasingly better and more accurate grasp of it (2.200).

Since "Why Study Logic?" has left the question of the admirableness of theoretical knowledge up in the air, we must turn to another work, which the editors have entitled "Ideals of Conduct." This is a draft of one of the Lowell lectures of 1903. After again acknowledging that the logician depends on the ethician and that the ethician depends on "the esthetician, whose business it is to say what is the state of things which is most admirable in itself regardless of any ulterior reason," he goes on to ask about that latter inquiry (1.611).

No particular quality of feeling can be considered admirable without ulterior reason. Rather, "the object admirable that is admirable *per se* must, no doubt, be general" (1.613). Peirce claims that the admirable in itself must be precisely known in a unitary ideal, and that turns out to be the development of reason, reason's governing individual events (1.615). This is the growth of reason, as opposed to a stationary situation; it is a process of development, an evolution, a continuum. "I do not see how one can have a more satisfying ideal of the admirable than the development of Reason so understood. The one thing whose admirableness is not due to an ulterior reason is Reason itself comprehended in all its fullness, so far as we can comprehend it" (1.615). Reason is what constitutes the admirable character of the cosmos. Moreover, this is a declaration of how we must evaluate a method of knowing: the ideal is to follow a method that will most effectively uncover the meaning of the universe. But does it come to immediate grips with the problem of philosophically grounding that same pursuit as admirable in itself?

In a sense it does, especially when one keeps in mind Peirce's attitude toward the contrast between a practical cognitive enterprise and a theoretical pursuit. A practical goal is likely to discolor the process of inquiry, inducing hasty belief for purposes of action; this is characteristic of seeking knowledge for the practical purposes of life, and not a reprehensible procedure. But the man who is motivated by the love of truth for its own sake will give only a careful and hesistant assent which is exactly proportional to the evidence manifested by nature. The admirable quality of this careful and hesitant assent is based on the continuity of the cosmos with the human mind. For science, "Nature is something great, and beautiful, and sacred, and eternal, and real—the object of its worship and aspiration" (5.589). And the human mind is in some way adapted to the apprehension of nature. But the intellectual grasping which is proportional to the evidence must be accomplished via a method which has been carefully weighed theoretically and controlled practically.

The pragmatic method of scientific inquiry is such a method, and has as its aim the expression of the cosmos in an explanatory fashion, and with careful control achieved in developing meaning through a knowledge of conceived consequences, expressed in conditionals. The admirableness of theory, then, consists in its being the most suitable way of uncovering cognitively—no matter how slightly—the manifestations of a cosmos evolving in the direction of increased lawfulness, developing more and more fully the embodiment of reason.

The combination of concrete reasonableness with the suitability of the pragmatic method to grasp it does indeed seem to be justified by

Peirce in his philosophy, and does seem to be within the reach of the pragmatic method as he understands it (though, perhaps not as some of his commentators have understood it). The beauty and magnificence of the cosmos are within the competence of the pragmatic method understood, as Peirce seems to understand it, in a fashion not excessively empirical. The admirable in itself and the admirable character of theoretical knowledge are within the ken of the rather broad interpretation of pragmatism which Peirce developed—a pragmatic method sufficiently flexible to include an understanding of scientific knowing and methodology. If Peirce's theory of knowledge—valid inasmuch as it is itself pragmatic—is to stand, then, there seems to be no reason, on the grounds of the requirements of the method, for excluding a pragmatic understanding of the admirable and of the admirableness of theoretical knowledge.

But what, then, has become of pragmatism? Has it become so inclusive as to be worthless in a scientific pursuit? Or is it a very general and yet adequate description of human knowing that should be applied in a proportional way to both scientific and philosophical problems? Peirce seems to tend to the latter understanding.

> The importance of the matter for pragmatism is obvious. For if the meaning of a symbol consists in *how* it might cause us to act, it is plain that this "how" cannot refer to the description of mechanical motions that it might cause, but must intend to refer to a description of the action as having this or that *aim*. In order to understand pragmatism, therefore, well enough to subject it to intelligent criticism, it is incumbent upon us to inquire what an ultimate aim, capable of being pursued in an indefinitely prolonged course of action, can be [5.135].

In view of this it seems that we are almost forced to recognize the value of the cosmos in terms of its being an object of scientific inquiry. In pragmatic terms the concrete reasonableness, the thirdness, of the cosmos means that it calls forth the action of assenting from us, that it deserves to be known for no other reason than the very knowing of it. Even if it be objected that such a conceived practical consequence is non-sensible and therefore non-pragmatic, the reply can be made that, if pragmatism is to stand as a method and theory of knowing, it must break free from its empirical shackles. If on purely empirical grounds knowledge becomes unknowable, how can any sort of theory of knowing, empirical, pragmatic, or what-have-you, be formed at all?

Peirce explicitly links his pragmatism with ethical and aesthetical ideals which transcend the sensibly verifiable.

And you . . . will see that since pragmaticism makes the purport to consist in a conditional proposition concerning conduct, a sufficiently deliberate consideration of that purport will reflect that the conditional conduct ought to be regulated by an ethical principle, which by further self-criticism may be made to accord with an esthetical ideal. For I cannot admit that any ideal can be too high for a duly transfigured esthetics. So, although I do not think that an esthetic valuation is essentially involved, *actualiter* (so to speak) in every intellectual purport, I do think that it is a *virtual* factor of a duly rationalized purport. That is to say, it really does belong to the purport, since conduct may depend upon its being appealed to [5.535].

The pragmatic method, then, does not exclude transempirical meaning. In fact, the method is regulated ultimately by aesthetics inasmuch as the conduct envisioned must accord with the admirable. In other words, grasped meaning, which is understanding, must be measured by the concrete reasonableness of the cosmos. And this is already a perfectly admirable human pursuit, apart from any admirableness which practical results (extra-cognitive elements) may add.

I think, then, that Peirce in his later years overcame the defects of certain excessively empirical expressions of the pragmatic method, found in some of the earlier works. Toward the end of his life he was working out, certainly in practice but also in theory to some extent, a pragmatic method, broad and unrestricted in scope—one which was adapted to transempirical meaning, to understandings that could not be checked merely by sensible phenomena. In this way it seems that he was no longer content with developing a methodology merely for the physical sciences. There are grounds for thinking that this later opinion represents a development of what was already in Peirce's thought from the beginning, though not so clearly articulated. Peirce, I think, was never an empiricist.[8]

What is involved in his defense of the admirableness of theoretical knowledge is the familiar Peircean theme of an increasingly more perfect double control: of chance by law in the cosmos, and of man's understanding through the community of scientific inquirers. The evolution of the cosmos and of scientific knowledge is a process of control.

> The pragmaticist does not make the *summum bonum* to consist in action, but makes it to consist in that process of evolution whereby the existent comes more and more to embody those generals which were just now said to be *destined*, which is what we strive to express in calling them *reasonable*. In its higher stages, evolution takes place more and more largely through self-control, and this gives the pragmaticist a sort of justification for making the rational purport to be general [5.433].

The *summum bonum* (an expression not too happily chosen) in the cosmos is for Peirce the development of thirdness, the control of law over chance.[9] And in thought, it is the process of using a method which has been critically justified and which is most suited, if applied correctly, to tracking down gradually and fallibly the secrets of the cosmos.[10]

Peirce's criticism of practical goals of knowledge is somewhat excessive but, it must be admitted in his defense, formed more in the tradition of the popular lecturer poking fun at the over-practical interests of his audience. Despite the excessive downgrading of "vitally important topics" and the interests of practical technological progress, he was altogether right in defending the purely theoretical goals of scientific pursuits. "True science is distinctively the study of useless things. For the useful things will get studied without the aid of scientific men. To employ these rare minds on such work is like running a steam engine by burning diamonds" (1.76). In a theoretical inquiry the human intelligence is operating with the freedom that it deserves. In such a process, knowledge, or the quest for knowledge, is not subordinated to a purpose that is outside itself, as it is in practical inquiry. It is not hampered by the needs of the immediately practical situation, but is allowed to adjust itself in keeping with the limits of a critically justified method to the evidence which the cosmos presents and which the inquirer finds.[11] Theoretical inquiry looks for intelligibility as an object to be possessed in understanding it, and does not aim at the service of a practical outcome. Pure knowledge is the goal of the scientist, and success in this endeavor is not possible on any terms other than the purity of his motivation.[12] For these reasons both science and philosophy must be free to pursue their goals without being put to the service of practical goals.

The true, then, is the intellect's goal apart from any practical justification. But even more, practical knowledge, in a very important sense, depends on theory. The practical judgment that *x* is useful for a need can ultimately be evaluated only in terms of a theoretical knowledge which is beyond the useful. It is in this sense that speculative knowledge is the source of all practical knowledge. And there can be no genuine human progress or human effectivity except insofar as the attempt to progress—even technologically—is based on a knowledge of the truth. The possession of truth undergirds the internal perfection of a man and his control over the cosmos. It is not so much that we put the truth to the service of progress, but rather that we gain freedom to progress by serving the truth.[13]

II. SYNTHESIS OF EVOLUTIONARY THEMES

The fifth chapter has already made it clear that Peirce understood evolution as one of the chief characteristics of the world. It is not restricted to the biological sphere, but extends to the whole cosmos and to the historical development of science. In proposing this synthetic, post-Darwinian view of evolution, Peirce was decades ahead of his time.

His stand on the development of law and regularity from chance, on the original "flashes" and the habit-taking tendency of things, is a cosmogonic inquiry, as Gallie points out.[14] A cosmogonic inquiry is eminently worthwhile, and its worth has been hailed by many philosophers of our own day. If it can be carried out critically, it may lead to an outstanding breakthrough in the cosmonomic inquiry itself. "Nomic" inquiry is the current movement of science, and it is accomplished largely through the steps already described in the third and fourth chapters of this book. But "nomic" inquiry, the search for explanations in terms of laws of the predictive type, carried out through tested hypotheses, stands to benefit from a "gonic" inquiry. This is true because a knowledge of the development of the cosmos should enable the scientist to know with far greater accuracy what explanations of the universe are more likely and what less likely. In addition, it proceeds in such a way as to destroy the old fixed world view of Ockham–Descartes–Hobbes–Newton, since it proposes nature as a process, and not as a fixed outlay of characters and objects to be explained by a fixed number of general laws. The latter world view barricades the road of inquiry.[15] What Peirce attempts to accomplish in his cosmogonic theory is to open the minds of man to the fruitfulness of the evolutionary view of the history of the world and of man's knowledge of the world. "Tell us how the laws of nature came about, and we may distinguish in some measure between laws that might and laws that could not have resulted from such a process of development" (1.408).

But whether hypothesis-and-verification is the proper method of a cosmogonic, as opposed to a cosmonomic, inquiry should be faced squarely.

As has already been mentioned in the fifth chapter, certain elements of Peirce's description of the habit-taking tendency of the world and of the "flashes" which grew into regular habits are to be regarded as figurative. But beneath the figurative language there is a strong commitment to an ontological growth of regularity and law. What must be questioned here is not the growth of the organic species or the changing character of the environment that occasions such growth. Rather it seems that in terms of the method to which he has committed himself he has overemphasized the parallel between knowledge and external reality. Within the limits of that method the historical development of knowledge from its primitive beginnings in men's minds to its present scientific perfection should not be taken as an archetype of the evolution of the cosmos from less to greater intelligibility. Peirce's own overhasty attempts at verifying the hypothesis of the growth from chance to law lead the reader to suspect that the hypothesis was never really studied as it should have been, and that, had it been so studied, it would have been proposed much less firmly.

His theory of the growth of reasonableness, it seems, may have resulted from an excessively constitutive use of logic.[16] The historical development of science is most obvious, but it cannot be taken as a model for the growth of the universe toward increased reasonableness. While Peirce makes frequent reference to the similarities between knowledge and the cosmos, it would be difficult to find an explicit defense of the use of the evolution of science as an archetype for the growth of reasonableness in the world. Nevertheless at a much more general level he does defend this procedure. For him metaphysics depends on logic, not merely in that it must use a method critically evaluated by logic, but also in that it must draw its principles from logic. "Metaphysics consists in the results of the absolute acceptance of logical principles not merely as regulatively valid, but as truths of being" (1.487). Logical processes are somewhat representative of the way things really are; we think in general terms and things really do belong to classes; the scientific mind naturally seeks explanations of observed reality and things really do have explanations; the gradual growth of law and reasonableness parallels the growth of knowledge. "Nature only appears intelligible so far as it appears rational, that is, so far as its processes are seen to be like processes of thought" (3.422).

Neither the method of hypothesis and verification nor that of the constitutive use of logic seems to be adequate for a cosmogonic inquiry. Peirce, as noted above, did make certain feeble attempts to justify his cosmogonic speculations by the method of hypothesis and verification, and the results are not at all impressive. As Goudge makes clear, the use of this method to test his hypothesis of flashes and the growth of the habit-taking tendency of the universe can lead to almost any prediction; it is for this reason not impressively successful. The deduction of consequents is not scientifically compelling.[17] In addition, as I pointed out above, the synthesis of the various evolutions, accomplished through the constitutive use of logic, seems to be out of step with the approved method, and to be more in line with an apriorism repeatedly discredited by Peirce himself.

If, then, the cosmogonic quest is worthwhile, as I think it is, both in itself and for the further progress of scientific inquiry in the more usual sense, can another method be employed?

Peirce's own warnings against blocking the road of inquiry seem quite inconsistent with his defenses of the method of hypothesis and verification as the only road. And in his own speculations, especially after 1900, he seems to be employing a method which is more metaphysical and even religious, in forming highly unified syntheses of knowledge which are very enlightening. But he never worked out the details of the method involved, and never engaged in a thoroughly critical discussion of this other method. For this reason Goudge and others have accused him of a basic inconsistency.

III. THE QUESTION OF METHOD

Peirce, then, both in his philosophical defense of the admirableness of scientific inquiry and in his cosmogonic proposals has to face the question of the method of knowing. A narrowly empirical understanding of pragmatism will not be able to defend the value of its own pursuit, though it seems that this value can be known, at least partially, through a pragmatism that breaks free from the excessive empiricism which some of Peirce's followers have emphasized. In a significant number of writings in which Peirce defends the value of theory in terms of ethics and aesthetics, he asserts sometimes explicitly and at other times implicitly that pragmatism is capable of grasping the worth of a theoretical inquiry. And in his cosmogonic proposals the reader gets the impression that the feeble attempts at verification are set forth with a certain embarrassment over the inadequacy of the method of hypothesis and verification to cope with such a quest.

In fact his attempts at metaphysics seem to be rather pathetic endeavors to account for philosophical attitudes to which he subscribed quite strongly, but for which he had no satisfactory method thematically worked out.[18] His handling of the questions of God's existence and the creation of the universe by God is a clear indication that he was a theist, and even a religious and moral person basically, but also that his knowledge-theory fell short in dealing with these important topics.[19]

It seems that what is called for both in the philosophy of Peirce and in our own Teilhardian, post-Darwinian age is an evolutionary philosophy that will be open to the evidences for evolution in the biological and earth sciences, and that will be able to synthesize these with a metaphysics carefully controlled and criticized that will show how in terms of theistic realism such a development may have come about. The elements of the synthesis have already been critically approached even by Peirce himself through the history of the sciences. And the attempt to form the synthesis with philosophical knowledge, especially with metaphysics, was made repeatedly by Peirce, though not with outstanding success.[20]

Present-day admirers of Peirce should feel themselves invited to keep the way of inquiry open, in the spirit of Peirce himself, by pursuing an evolutionary synthesis of philosophy and science which their master was unable to complete. For this task it is imperative that a method be followed which is proportionate to the insights sought, and which is therefore not a priori confined to hypothesis and empirical verification. In its metaphysical phase the method should be such as to achieve a knowledge of the sensible beings of our experience, initially in terms of that internal principle by which they are real, and then in terms of that transcendent Being, the Creator, who by efficiency and with liberality makes the cosmos be. The enterprise cannot stop at a philosophical acknowledgment of God's existence, however, but must push on to achieve a knowledge of the relations between the cosmos and the Creator, within the limits of philosophical investigation, understanding that the created sphere is a participation, an image of the uncreated Being, and reflects the Creator in some small way, especially by its being and its activity. The latter understanding—sc., of the active created sphere as a reflection of the active Creator—is, I think, essential to the formation of a theistic philosophy of evolution, and one that is altogether faithful to the philosophy of Peirce, though inadequately developed by him. A philosophical theology is all the richer for understanding the universe, not as an original outlay of fixed and permanent types from the Creator, but as endowed with an inner power by the Creator to develop itself from a less complete embodiment of perfection, through a process of evolution at many levels, to a more perfect image of the Creator. The process of evolution does not occur independently of the divine influence, but it nevertheless progresses in a manner commensurate with the beings which compose the cosmos acting according to their own natures, advancing the embodiment of perfection and reasonableness, without requiring a miraculous intervention of the Creator to produce greater variety and new types. It is altogether acceptable to assert that chance occurrences, resulting in a perfection greater than the created agents immediately involved but under the overarching providence of the Creator, may have led to the development of the universe as we find it. The role of the Creator in such conjectured events can be assessed by the philosopher working within the limits of his own discipline and aware of the unique perfection that the human person possesses, and consequently of the need of a special, though not miraculous, dependence which the human person and his form have on the

Creator. This does not rule out the possibility that the appearance of the first human beings may have been accomplished under divine Providence by events which were chance occurrences with respect to the created agents immediately involved, but altogether willed and intended by the Creator as the mechanism for bringing into being those agents who are the most astounding and outstanding reflections of the Creator within the cosmos.

From the slight eminence which the metaphysician can mount in his evolutionary synthesis, the role of final causality, advocated by Peirce himself, can be of significant help. Although Peirce discourages us from attempting to scrutinize the divine plan in the universe, it still seems a possible and worthwhile endeavor to uncover in the slight way that is open to a controlled and cautious metaphysics what God is about in His governing of the universe. Peirce himself has attempted this in proposing the growth of reasonableness. And in keeping with Peirce's own understanding of God as a benevolent being, the metaphysician can put forth the conclusion that the Creator is directing the universe, through a process of growth, to an increasing embodiment of being and goodness as sharings in the Infinite Goodness which He Himself is. In this process the Creator is cooperating with those things which He has created, and leading them to bring about, in their own sphere and by their own activity, a continually increasing embodiment of being and goodness. Since the appearance of man in the cosmos, the most obvious growth has been in the realm of knowledge, and of technology stemming from knowledge. It does not seem excessively cynical to say that, despite the basic human capacity for growing in virtue, even in the moral sphere of justice, prudence, and temperance, the growth has been disappointingly minimal. But the Creator, the author of freedom in men, is fully respectful of the free created agent and allows that agent freely to cooperate or freely to fail to cooperate within the necessarily social context of human living, with his endeavors to promote growth in all areas of human living. Our history has not been lacking in magnificent examples of such cooperation, but it must be openly admitted that this area of growth has been quite neglected.

The theistic metaphysician who is appreciative of Peirce's emphasis on evolution may find that Peirce himself has already supplied a key insight for the enterprise, even though it is inadequately developed:

the evolution of the universe is the working-out of a definite end, accomplished through love. The universe at all levels is acting through telic causation bringing to fulfillment in a developmental way the plan of the loving Creator, who is continually present to it. "In general, God is perpetually creating us, that is developing our real manhood, our spiritual reality" (6.507). Peirce's agapistic approach to growth may turn out to be very helpful in working out a synthetic philosophy of evolution, which will be faithful both to the riches which the biological and earth sciences offer and to those which the theistic metaphysician can supply.

The philosopher who attempts such a synthesis must like Peirce be imbued with the spirit of laboratory science, and not tied down to a mere "seminary" philosophy, which Peirce has criticized (1.3; 1.129). The philosophical training required is long and tedious. That man is only a beginner in philosophy "who has not been seriously, earnestly, and single-mindedly devoted to the study of it for more than six or eight years," and his ideas may be largely wrong (1.134). And the spirit in which the study of philosophy should be undertaken is "the spirit of joy in learning ourselves and in making others acquainted with the glories of God" (1.127).

What is most necessary in developing an evolutionary synthesis that will be genuinely philosophical is that the road of inquiry not be blocked by a declaration that one method is the exclusive way to the truth. Peirce deserves strong praise for advocating an open road, and for gradually progressing along that road toward an understanding of the cosmos, of the man who studies it, and of the value of that theoretical study. The progressive growth of concrete reasonableness in the cosmos and in intellects which reflect it is the basis of all worthwhile pursuits. For this reason, theorizing about method demands an openness of spirit both to the cosmos embodying reasonableness and to the mind discovering (and thereby embodying in its own way) that same reasonableness. This, I think, is what Peirce exemplifies and teaches.

What Dewey says prophetically may hold true for generations: "Peirce will always remain a philosopher's philosopher."[21] And Perry, echoing Dewey, puts it rather poetically:

Charles Peirce . . . stands like a lonely peak, its altitude increasing with distance. . . . He remains a philosopher's philosopher, belonging to no school, and having little in common with his American environment.[22]

Peirce was a man thoroughly dedicated to knowledge, a scientist, a philosopher, and a philosopher of science.

Appendix

THE BEGINNING OF PRAGMATISM AND 'PRAGMATISM'

PEIRCE CLAIMS TO HAVE USED THE WORD "PRAGMATISM" in philosophical conversations from the mid-'seventies on, to designate his theory of belief, and, although he explained the main elements of his pragmatic theory of meaning in the two articles published in the *Popular Science Monthly* in 1877 and 1878, he still did not dare to use the word "pragmatism" in print until 1902. He used it then only in response to a special request, in Baldwin's *Dictionary of Philosophy and Psychology,* under the heading "Pragmatism" (5.414*n*; 5.1–4). In preparing to write the articles for Baldwin, Peirce wrote to James on November 10, 1900: "Who originated the term pragmatism, I or you? Where did it first appear in print? What do you understand by it?" And on a postcard dated November 26, 1900 James replied: "You invented 'pragmatism' for which I gave you full credit in a lecture entitled 'Philosophical conceptions and practical results' of which I sent you 2 (unacknowledged) copies a couple of years ago" (8.253).

The lecture to which James refers was his famous paper delivered in 1898 at the University of California, wherein he presented his views of pragmatism. James' understanding of pragmatism was so different from Peirce's that the latter, to avoid ambiguity, devised a new term "pragmaticism" to describe his doctrine, in an article in *The Monist* in 1905. "The writer, finding his bantling 'pragmatism' so promoted, feels that it is time to kiss his child good-by and relinquish it to its higher destiny; while to serve the precise purpose of expressing the original definition, he begs to announce the birth of the word 'pragmaticism,' which is ugly enough to be safe from kidnappers" (5.414).

It is noteworthy that, in the brief carefully written article in Baldwin's *Dictionary,* Peirce quotes the pragmatic maxim verbatim from "How to Make Our Ideas Clear," and mentions that the article is the first published description of his theory of pragmatism (5.2f). Again, about 1905, Peirce wrote that the original statement of pragmatism, the last-mentioned article, was completed in September 1877 aboard a steamer, "a day or two before reaching Plymouth, nothing remaining to be done except to translate it into English" (5.526*n*). The article was first written in French (5.358*n*).

In 1905 Peirce acknowledged in *The Monist* that he invented the word "pragmatism," which he derived from Kant's *pragmatisch* to express a "relation to some definite human purpose" (5.412).

About 1906 Peirce wrote of the ancestry of the doctrine of pragmatism, of The Metaphysical Club, where pragmatism was born, and of Bain's definition of belief from which "pragmatism is scarce more than a corollary." In the same place he also makes mention of a little paper which he wrote for the members of the club, setting forth some of his opinions "that I had been urging all along under the name of pragmatism." The members responded so enthusiastically that he "was encouraged, some half dozen years later, on the invitation of the great publisher Mr. W. H. Appleton, to insert it, somewhat expanded, in the *Popular Science Monthly* for November, 1877 and January, 1878. . . . The same paper appeared the next year in a French redaction in the *Revue Philosophique* (Vol. VI, 1878, p. 553; Vol. VII, 1879, p. 39)" (5.12f).

Arthur W. Burks, editor of the seventh and eighth volumes of the *Collected Papers,* thinks it probable that some of the manuscripts forming 7.313–361 may have composed the little paper that Peirce describes above. Some of these manuscripts, as Burks reports, are dated 1873, and others were most likely written around 1872 or 1873. They contain some of the prominent themes of the articles published in the *Popular Science Monthly*—for example, the nature of doubt, belief, and investigation, the relation of belief to action, the need of genuine doubt as a condition of learning, some erroneous methods of settling opinion, and the importance of both observation and the pragmatic method of meaning.

Burks also notes that William James in a letter of November 24, 1872, to his brother Henry wrote: "Charles Peirce . . . read us an admirable introductory chapter to his book on logic the other day" (Perry, *Thought and Character*, I, 332 [7.313*n*1]).

Besides the manuscripts mentioned above, there are a few other foreshadowings of the doctrine of the mid-'seventies, but they are undeveloped and fragmentary in comparison with the two articles. See 5.238–242; 5.264–268; 8.16.

Again, in his famous "A Neglected Argument for the Reality of God," published in the *Hibbert Journal* in 1908, Peirce refers to the existence of The Metaphysical Club in Cambridge as the birthplace of the theory of pragmatism, and asserts that the doctrine can trace its origin, in some way, to Spinoza, Berkeley, Kant, and even back to Socrates (6.482; 6.490).

The influence of the English psychologist Alexander Bain on the origin of pragmatism has been described by Max Fisch ("Alexander Bain and the Genealogy of Pragmatism," *Journal of the History of Ideas,* XV [1954], 413–444). Murphey lists several reasons why Bain's ideas should have attracted Peirce in the early 'seventies: the doubt-belief-inquiry theory, the realistic response to Hume, and the evolutionary approach to belief as adjustive habits (Murphey, *Development,* pp. 160–163).

Arthur C. Lovejoy in his classic article "The Thirteen Pragmatisms" points out the various nuances in the understanding of pragmatism during the early years of the century. He does not, however, always identify their defenders (*The Journal of Philosophy, Psychology and Scientific Methods,* V [1908], 5–12 and 29–39; the article is reprinted in Arthur C. Lovejoy, *The Thirteen Pragmatisms and Other Essays* [Baltimore: The Johns Hopkins Press, 1963]).

BIBLIOGRAPHY OF MORE IMPORTANT WORKS REFERRED TO

I. PRIMARY SOURCES

Charles S. Peirce Papers. Houghton Library, Harvard University (Manuscripts).

Peirce, Charles S. *Chance, Love and Logic*. Edited with an introduction by Morris R. Cohen; with a supplementary essay on the pragmatism of Peirce by John Dewey. New York: Harcourt, Brace, & Company, 1923.

——. *Collected Papers of Charles Sanders Peirce*. Edited by Charles Hartshorne, Paul Weiss, and Arthur W. Burks. 8 vols. Cambridge: Harvard University Press, 1931–1935, 1958.

——. *Essays in the Philosophy of Science*. Edited by Vincent Tomas. New York: The Liberal Arts Press, 1957.

——. *Letters to Lady Welby*. Edited by Irwin C. Lieb. New Haven: Whitlock, 1953.

——. *Philosophical Writings of Peirce*. Edited by Justus Buchler. New York: Dover Publications, 1955.

——. *Values in a Universe of Chance*. Edited by Philip P. Wiener. Garden City: Doubleday & Company, 1958; repr. New York: Dover Publications, 1966.

II. SECONDARY SOURCES

1. *Books*

Blau, Joseph L. *Men and Movements in American Philosophy.* New York: Prentice-Hall, 1952.

Boler, John F. *Charles Peirce and Scholastic Realism.* Seattle: University of Washington Press, 1963.

Buchler, Justus. *Charles Peirce's Empiricism.* New York: Harcourt, Brace and Company; London: Kegan Paul, 1939.

Burks, Arthur W. "Charles Sanders Peirce, Introduction," *Classic American Philosophers.* Edited by Max H. Fisch. New York: Appleton-Century-Crofts, 1951.

Cohen, Morris R. *American Thought, A Critical Sketch.* Glencoe: The Free Press, 1954.

Feibleman, James. *An Introduction to Peirce's Philosophy.* New York: Harper & Brothers, 1946.

Fitzgerald, John J. *Peirce's Theory of Signs as Foundation for Pragmatism* (Studies in Philosophy, XI). The Hague: Mouton and Co., 1966.

Freeman, Eugene. *The Categories of Charles Peirce.* Chicago: The Open Court Publishing Company, 1934.

Gallie, W. B. *Peirce and Pragmatism.* Harmondsworth: Penguin Books, 1952.

Goudge, Thomas A. *The Thought of C. S. Peirce.* Toronto: University of Toronto Press, 1950.

Haas, William Paul, O.P. *The Conception of Law and the Unity of Peirce's Philosophy.* Fribourg, Switzerland: The University Press; Notre Dame: University of Notre Dame Press, 1964.

Knight, Thomas S. *Charles Peirce* (The Great American Thinkers Series). New York: Washington Square Press, 1965.

Moore, Edward C. *American Pragmatism: Peirce, James and Dewey.* New York: Columbia University Press, 1961.

Murphey, Murray G. *The Development of Peirce's Philosophy.* Cambridge: Harvard University Press, 1961.

Perry, Ralph Barton. *The Thought and Character of William James.* 2 vols. Boston: Little, Brown and Company, 1936.

Perspectives on Peirce: Critical Essays on Charles Sanders Peirce. Edited by Richard J. Bernstein. New Haven: Yale University Press, 1965.

Potter, Vincent G. *Charles S. Peirce on Norms and Ideals.* Amherst: University of Massachusetts Press, 1967.

Robin, Richard S. *Annotated Catalogue of the Papers of Charles S. Peirce.* Amherst: University of Massachusetts Press, 1967.

Studies in the Philosophy of Charles Sanders Peirce. Edited by Philip P. Wiener and Frederic H. Young. Cambridge: Harvard University Press, 1952.

Studies in the Philosophy of Charles Sanders Peirce. Edited by Edward C. Moore and Richard S. Robin. Amherst: University of Massachusetts Press, 1964.

Thompson, Manley. *The Pragmatic Philosophy of C. S. Peirce.* Chicago: University of Chicago Press, 1953.

Wennerberg, Hjalmar. *The Pragmatism of C. S. Peirce: An Analytic Study* (Library of Theoria, IX). Lund: C. W. K. Gleerup, 1962.

Wiener, Philip P. *Evolution and the Founders of Pragmatism.* Cambridge: Harvard University Press, 1949.

2. *Articles*

Braithwaite, R. B. Review of *Collected Papers of Charles Sanders Peirce,* Vols. I–IV. *Mind,* LXIII (1934), 487–511.

Britton, Karl. "Introduction to the Metaphysics and Theology of C. S. Peirce." *Ethics,* XLIX (1938–39), 435–465.

Buchler, Justus. "The Accidents of Peirce's System." *The Journal of Philosophy,* XXXVII (1940), 264–269.

Burks, Arthur W. "Peirce's Conception of Logic as a Normative Science." *The Philosophical Review,* LII (1934), 187–193.

——. "Peirce's Theory of Abduction." *Philosophy of Science,* XIII (1946), 301–306.

Burrell, David B., c.s.c. "C. S. Peirce: Pragmatism as a Theory of Judgment." *International Philosophical Quarterly,* V (1965), 521–540.

Davis, Ellery W. "Charles Peirce at Johns Hopkins." *The Mid-West Quarterly,* II (1914), 48–56.

Dewey, John. "Le Developpement du Pragmatisme Americain." *Revue de Metaphysique et de Morale,* XXIX (1922), 411–430.

——. Review of *Collected Papers of Charles Sanders Peirce,* Vols. I–VI. *The New Republic,* LXXXIX (1937), 415–416.

——. "The Pragmatism of Peirce." *The Journal of Philosophy, Psychology and Scientific Methods,* XIII (1916), 709–715.

Fairbanks, Matthew J. "C. S. Peirce and Positivism." *The Modern Schoolman,* XLI (1964), 323–337.

——. "Peirce's Debt to Hegel." *The New Scholasticism,* XXXVI (1962), 219–224.

Feuer, Lewis Samuel. Review of *Collected Papers of Charles Sanders Peirce,* Vol. VI. *Isis* XXVI (1936), 203–208.

Fisch, Max. "Alexander Bain and the Genealogy of Pragmatism." *Journal of the History of Ideas,* XV (1954), 413–444.

——. "Evolution in American Philosophy."*The Philosophical Review,* LVI (1947), 357–373.

Fitzgerald, John Joseph. "Peirce's 'How to Make Our Ideas Clear.'" *The New Scholasticism,* XXXIX (1965), 53–68.

Gallie, W. B. "The Metaphysics of C. S. Peirce." *Proceedings of the Aristotelian Society,* XLVII (1946–47), 27–62.

Goodwin, Robert P. "Charles Sanders Peirce: A Modern Scotist?" *The New Scholasticism,* XXXV (1961), 478–509.

Goudge, Thomas A. "Further Reflection on Peirce's Doctrine of the Given." *The Journal of Philosophy,* XXXIII (1936), 289–295.

——. "Peirce's Treatment of Induction." *Philosophy of Science,* VII (1940), 56–68.

——. "The Conflict of Naturalism and Transcendentalism in Peirce." *The Journal of Philosophy,* XLIV (1947), 365–375.

——. "The Views of Charles Peirce on the Given in Experience." *The Journal of Philosophy,* XXXII (1935), 533–545.

Hall, G. Stanley. "Philosophy in the United States." *Mind,* IV (1879), 89–105.

Hamblin, Frances Murphy. "A Comment on Peirce's 'Tychism.'" *The Journal of Philosophy,* XLII (1945), 378–383.

Hartshorne, Charles. "Charles Sanders Peirce's Metaphysics of Evolution." *New England Quarterly,* XIV (1941), 46–63.

Hill, W. H. "Peirce's Pragmatic Method." *Philosophy of Science,* VII (1940), 168–181.

Ladd-Franklin, Christine. "Charles S. Peirce at the Johns Hopkins." *The Journal of Philosophy, Psychology and Scientific Methods,* XIII (1916), 715–722.

Leonard, Henry S. "The Pragmatism and Scientific Metaphysics of C. S. Peirce." *Philosophy of Science,* IV (1937), 109–121.

Lovejoy, Arthur O. "The Thirteen Pragmatisms." *The Journal of Philosophy, Psychology and Scientific Methods,* V (1908), 5–12 and 29–39.

Madden, Edward H. "Chance and Counterfacts in Wright and Peirce." *The Review of Metaphysics,* IX (1956), 420–432.

Marra, William A. "The Five-sided Pragmatism of William James." *The Modern Schoolman,* XLI (1963), 45–61.

Moore, Edward C. "The Scholastic Realism of C. S. Peirce." *Philosophy and Phenomenological Research,* XII (1951–52), 406–417.

Murphree, Idus. "The Experimental Nature of Belief." *The Journal of Philosophy,* LX (1963), 309–317.

Nagel, Ernest. "Charles S. Peirce, Pioneer of Modern Empiricism." *Philosophy of Science,* VII (1940), 69–80.

——. "Charles Peirce's Guesses at the Riddle." *The Journal of Philosophy,* XXX (1933), 365–386.

Natanson, Maurice. "The Concept of the Given in Peirce and Mead." *The Modern Schoolman,* XXXII (1955), 143–157.

O'Connell, James. "C. S. Peirce's Conception of Philosophy." *The Downside Review,* LXXVII (1959), pp. 277–295.

——. "C. S. Peirce and the Problem of Knowledge." *Philosophical Studies,* VII (1957), 3–42.

Perry, R. R. "Is There a North American Philosophy?" *Philosophy and Phenomenological Research,* IX (1949), 356–369.

Roth, Robert J., S.J., "Is Peirce's Pragmatism Anti-Jamesian?" *International Philosophical Quarterly,* V (1965), 541–563.

Royce, Josiah, and Kernan, Fergus. "Charles Sanders Peirce." *The Journal of Philosophy, Psychology and Scientific Methods,* XIII (1916), 701–709.

Smith, James Ward. "Pragmatism, Realism, and Positivism in the United States." *Mind,* LXI (1952), 190–208.

Weiss, Paul. "Charles Sanders Peirce." *Sewanee Review,* L (1942), 184–192.

——. "Charles Sanders Peirce." *Dictionary of American Biography.* New York: Charles Scribner's Sons, (1934); XIV, 398–403.

——. "The Essence of Peirce's System." *The Journal of Philosophy,* XXXVII (1940), 253–264.

Wiener, Philip P. "Peirce's Metaphysical Club and the Genesis of Pragmatism." *Journal of the History of Ideas,* VII (1946), 218–233.

NOTES—CHAPTER I

1. Most of Peirce's writings have been published in the *Collected Papers of Charles Sanders Peirce*, edd. Charles Hartshorne, Paul Weiss, and Arthur W. Burks (8 vols.; Cambridge: Harvard University Press, 1931–1935 and 1958). The convention in citing from this edition is as follows: the number to the left of the decimal point designates the volume of the *Collected Papers*; the number to the right designates a numbered section in that volume. For example the reference (1.3) refers to the first volume, section 3. These references will occasionally be inserted in the main text.

2. See 6.604 and 1.3. As Wiener notes, "Charles S. Peirce made it his life work to analyze, as thoroughly as any single mind could, the basic logic and structure of the sciences" (*Values in a Universe of Chance*, ed. Philip P. Wiener [Garden City, N.Y.: Doubleday, 1958], p. xiii). This is a short collection of Peirce's writings including materials already published in the *Collected Papers* and elsewhere, as well as materials previously unpublished. In 1966 Dover Publications Inc. (New York) issued an unabridged republication of this collection, unaltered except for the title, *Charles S. Peirce: Selected Writings*, with the previous title as a subtitle. This book will hereafter be referred to as Wiener, *Values*.

3. For him logic embraced a study of the necessary and general conditions for the attainment of truth, and for its expression in thought-signs, as well as an inquiry into "laws of evolution of thought" and its communication from man to man (1.444).

4. Toward the end of his life, when considering the influence that ethics should have on logic, he wrote: "Life can have but one end. It is Ethics which defines that end. It is, therefore, impossible to be thoroughly and rationally logical except upon an ethical basis" (2.198).

5. W. B. Gallie, *Peirce and Pragmatism* (Harmondsworth: Penguin, 1952), inside cover.

6. *Values*, p. ix. Feibleman agrees that Peirce is America's greatest philosopher, and Young indicates why. Peirce, the latter writes, was possessed of "an intellect masculine in its boldness and sweep, vast in its learning, austere in its self-discipline, and comparable to that of a Leibniz in its combination of mathematical, logical, scientific, and metaphysical power" (James K. Feibleman, *An Introduction to Peirce's Philosophy Interpreted as a System* [New York: Harper, 1946], p. 4; Frederic H. Young, "Charles Sanders Peirce: 1839–1914," in *Studies in the Philosophy of Charles Sanders Peirce*, edd. Philip P. Wiener and Frederic H. Young [Cambridge: Harvard University Press, 1952], pp. 271f). Young notes that in letters written to him both F. S. C. Northrop and Charles Hartshorne compare Peirce to Leibniz. Alfred North Whitehead also wrote to Young that "Peirce was a very great man, with a variety of interests in each of which he made original contributions. The essence of his thought was originality in every subject that he taught. For this reason, none of the conventional labels apply to him. He conceived every topic in his own original way."

7. Morris R. Cohen, *American Thought: A Critical Sketch* (Glencoe: Free Press, 1954), p. 268.

8. Much of the biographical information which follows comes from the article on Charles Sanders Peirce by Paul Weiss in the *Dictionary of American Biography* (New York: Scribner's, 1934), XIV, 398–403.

9. Famous scientists and literary personalities were frequent visitors at Peirce's home. Among them can be named Agassiz, Asa Gray, Longfellow, Oliver Wendell Holmes, Ralph Waldo Emerson, and Margaret Fuller. Charles Peirce wrote in *The Monist* in 1892: "I may mention for the benefit of those who are curious in studying mental biographies, that I was born and reared in the neighborhood of Concord—I mean in Cambridge—at the time when Emerson, Hedge, and their friends were disseminating the ideas that they had caught from Schelling, and Schelling from Plotinus, from Boehm, or from God knows what minds stricken with the monstrous mysticism of the East. But the atmosphere of Cambridge held many an antiseptic against Concord transcendentalism; and I am not conscious of having contracted any of the virus" (6.102). See also *Charles S. Peirce's Letters to Lady Welby*, ed. Irwin C. Lieb (New Haven: Whitlock, 1953), p. 37.

About 1907 Peirce wrote of his father's "remarkable aesthetical discrimination," and of visitors to the family home in Cambridge during the years of his boyhood. See Charles S. Peirce Papers, Houghton Library, Harvard University, # 296 (this number is from Richard S. Robin, *Annotated Catalogue of the Papers of Charles S. Peirce* [Amherst: University of Massachusetts Press, 1967]).

10. Charles remained a theist throughout his life, though he became an Episcopalian in general religious orientation. Murray G. Murphey, *The Development of Peirce's Philosophy* (Cambridge: Harvard University Press, 1961), p. 15.

11. *Ibid.*, p. 17.

12. See Arthur W. Burks's general bibliography, *Collected Papers*, Vol. VIII, 260ff.

13. An excellent and well-known study of the thought of some of the members of the Metaphysical Club on the question of evolution and related topics has been written by Philip P. Weiner, *Evolution and the Founders of Pragmatism* (Cambridge: Harvard University Press, 1949). In this work Wiener expresses certain doubts about the accuracy of Peirce's claims and evidence for real existence of such a club in Cambridge, asking, for lack of evidence outside Peirce's own writings, whether the club might have been primarily a symbol in Peirce's imagination. Now, however, these doubts have been laid to rest by Max H. Fisch, who concludes from Peirce's own testimony and from that of others that there really was such a club (Max H. Fisch, "Was there a Metaphysical Club in Cambridge?" in *Studies in the Philosophy of Charles Sanders Peirce,* edd. Edward C. Moore and Richard S. Robin [second series; Amherst: University of Massachusetts Press, 1964], pp. 3–32. [In order to distinguish this collection of essays from the earlier collection with the same title, mentioned in note 6, the two will be referred to as *Studies* (first series) and *Studies* (second series).]).

Around 1907 Peirce wrote several accounts of the members of the Metaphysical Club. See Charles S. Peirce Papers, ## 319–322 and 324.

14. Gallie, *Peirce and Pragmatism*, p. 13.

15. See Ralph Barton Perry, *The Thought and Character of William James* (Boston: Little, Brown, 1936), vol. I, pp. 363, 538.

16. *Ibid.*, II, 117.

17. Peirce wrote in 1909 of his natural powers as being "rather below than

above mediocrity," but acknowledged his own habits of "self-criticism, persistence and logical analysis" (Charles S. Peirce Papers, ## 631 and 632).

18. The first six volumes (bound as three) were published again in 1960.

19. Murphey in his detailed study of Peirce's development shows that though Peirce was a system builder after the manner of Kant's architectonic theory of philosophy, he continually worked over parts of the system, improving the whole, reviewing and reformulating it in keeping with new insights. But the reformulations, since they keep as much of the preceding system as possible, should be regarded as revisions and not as distinct systems. *Development,* pp. 1ff.

20. Manley Thompson, *The Pragmatic Philosophy of C. S. Peirce* (Chicago: University of Chicago Press, 1953), p. xii.

21. Cohen, *American Thought,* p. 269.

22. *Ibid.,* p. 270.

23. Feibleman states it this way: "The reputation of a philosophy frequently owes as much to its random suggestiveness as to its complete and systematic form. Peirce's writings are systematic by implication only; but they continue to be immensely suggestive in every line. If the occasional insights which have been gleaned from Peirce have had so much effect, how much more valuable would be the full force of his whole philosophy when viewed in the round" (*An Introduction to Peirce's Philosophy,* p. 389).

NOTES—CHAPTER II

1. Wiener, *Values,* p. 227. See also 1.8, composed around 1897, where science is described as a pursuit of men "devoured by a desire to find things out."

2. That there is a *spirit* of inquiry is indicated by Peirce's repeated use of "emotive" language: impulse, burn to learn, Eros, desire, being seized, possessed by a passion to learn, devotion, animated. Such language for Peirce points out the scientist's aim (1.618; 7.605).

3. Wiener, *Values,* p. 228.

4. *Ibid.,* p. 267. This article is taken from the *Annual Report of the Smithsonian Institution for the Year ending June 30, 1900* (Washington, D.C., 1901), pp. 693–699, as Wiener notes.

5. *Ibid.,* p. 268.

6. At the beginning of the projected "History of Science," Peirce remarks that there are three classes of men. There are the men who create art, and for these nature is a picture. There are the men who regard nature as an opportunity for power and business. And finally there are the men of science who are "possessed by a passion to learn" (1.43).

7. See 5.589 for contrast of science with practice.

8. Peirce repeatedly emphasizes the dichotomy between scientific work and practical work, partially because of the widespread error of extolling the merit of doing things. In a brief work expressing his views on education, found in *Science* (April 20, 1900), pp. 620–622, as Wiener notes (*Values,* pp. 331f), Peirce reports the prevalent enthusiasm for activity, which has gained the ascendancy over knowledge, even in American colleges. He admits that in his youth even he made

the mistake of subordinating the conception to the act in his understanding of pragmatism. However, "subsequent experience of life has taught me that the only thing that is really desirable without a reason for being so, is to render ideas and things reasonable." In his emphasis on the theoretical, however, he does not want to deny that some of the sciences may, as a matter of fact, have sprung originally from practical arts, as geometry did from surveying (1.226). He also admits that historically science has made much progress as a result of the stimulus received from men of practice, looking for knowledge to guide their activities (7.52).

9. In his uncompleted "Minute Logic" Peirce describes how a man is transformed into a scientist. The transformation, he says, is usually sudden, and, when sudden, it consists in "their being seized with a great desire to learn the truth, and their going to work with all their might by a well-considered method to gratify that desire" (1.235). The primacy of motive and method are unmistakable here.

10. Thomas A. Goudge considers this contrast of theory and practice in Peirce characteristic of a transcendentalism, which Goudge opposes. (The presence of two main irreconcilable themes in Peirce—sc., naturalism and transcendentalism —is one of Goudge's favorite topics.) It may be that Peirce treats practical living with an unbecoming jocoseness, and even with obvious error in excluding reason from practice, and advocating an immoderate reliance on sentiment and instinct. But Goudge seems to weigh the balance on the opposite side, to the detriment of pure science. Thomas A. Goudge, *The Thought of C. S. Peirce* (Toronto: University of Toronto Press, 1950), p. 255. See also Thomas A. Goudge, "The Conflict of Naturalism and Transcendentalism in Peirce," *The Journal of Philosophy*, XLIV (1947), 366–368.

11. There is, however, a difficulty in this matter. In reading through Peirce, one comes upon certain passages which seem to deny the purely theoretical aim of science. In two separate works on the classification of the sciences we find mention of "practical science" (1.181 and 1.239). Is it true, then, that an inquiry undertaken for the sake of practical results can still be a genuine science?

A hint at the solution may be found in Peirce's understanding of the meaning of *branch*. Theoretical and practical are branches of science. *Branch* is a special term, dividing science according to its fundamental purpose. *Class*, *order*, and *family* are also special terms, dividing the branches and sub-branches according to other criteria. While pure science is an energetic pursuit of the truth only for the sake of knowing it, practice aims at doing things.

12. See also 1.640–642. Peirce claims to be an Aristotelian in that both he and Aristotle agree that theoretical science has "knowledge of theory as its ultimate end and aim" (1.618).

13. An undated manuscript, besides mentioning that science is the living pursuit of inquirers, also emphasizes the importance of the method and of the scientist's knowing "What justifies the belief, and just WHY and HOW the justification is sufficient" (7.49f).

14. In a letter to Lady Welby written in 1908, Peirce puts it very briefly: "Science consists in *inquiry, not* in 'doctrine'" (Wiener, *Values*, p. 402).

15. The Appendix contains some historical information on the beginning of both the doctrine and the word "pragmatism." The same appendix mentions the

change from "pragmatism" to "pragmaticism." I shall use the word "pragmaticist" as both a noun and an adjective, as the context requires.

16. Charles S. Peirce, "The Fixation of Belief," *Popular Science Monthly*, XII (1877), 1–15, and "How to Make Our Ideas Clear," *Ibid.*, 286–302. Both articles are also found in the *Collected Papers* (5.358–387 and 5.388–410).

17. The importance of these two articles can also be judged from their prominence in most expositions of Peirce's pragmatism, and their inclusion in all the selections from Peirce's writings which I have seen.

18. Wiener, *Values*, p. 230.

19. The editors of the *Collected Papers* have indicated numerous corrections made by Peirce; they have also pointed out that the two articles were meant to be included in two projected books that Peirce was working on in 1893, along with many clarifying notes written by him at that time. Again in 1903 Peirce undertook the work of revising the articles, and the editors have included the revisions in the notes. Finally in 1909 and 1910, as Burks states, Peirce was preparing a revision of the two articles, with the intention of publishing them together. Burks has given us the following words of Peirce, contained on page 1 of the 1909–1910 draft: "The main part of this Essay—the characterizations of Belief and of Doubt, the argument as to the effective aim of inquiry, the description of four methods directed toward that aim, with the criticisms of them, the discussion of the proper function of thinking, and the consequent maxim for attaining clear concepts,—reproduces almost verbatim a paper I read,—it must have been in 1872,—to a group of young men who used, at that time, to meet once a fortnight in Cambridge, Mass., under the name of 'The Metaphysical Club,'—a name chosen to alienate such as it would alienate" (7.313*n*1).

In addition to these corrections and revisions, there are numerous references back to the two articles, explicitly mentioning them, and quoting the pragmatic maxim either verbatim, or with a change of pronouns from the first to the second person. See the following, all written in 1903 or later: 5.17f, 28; 5.414–422; 5.438–442; 5.526–529; 5.563f; 6.485.

Hjalmar Wennerberg detects distinct earlier and later theories of belief and doubt in Peirce, but emphasizes that they "are not incompatible with each other but can be combined into a more general theory of belief and doubt" (Hjalmar Wennerberg, *The Pragmatism of C. S. Peirce: an Analytic Study*, Library of Theoria No. IX [Lund: Gleerup, 1962], p. 53).

20. See 5.372–375; 5.394; 5.510; 7.313–326.

21. The same dissatisfaction with certain ideas expressed in "The Fixation of Belief," is found again in an article published thirty years later. It is not true to say that because inquiry begins with doubt and ends with belief, truth amounts merely to a state of satisfaction, as the earlier work assumed. Scientific inquiry is more than a mere quest for mental satisfaction. "A Neglected Argument for the Reality of God," *Hibbert Journal*, VII (1908), 90–112. This work is found in the *Collected Papers* (6.452–493).

22. In the next chapter the four methods of fixing belief will be described and the superiority of the scientific method will be explained.

23. See also 6.3; 6.485.

24. There is an apparent inconsistency in Peirce's view on the extent of doubt.

On the one hand he excludes Descartes' universal methodic doubt with such vigor that he ends up with infallible, absolute truths. "There is much that you do not doubt, in the least. Now that which you do not at all doubt, you must and do regard as infallible, absolute truth" (5.416).

And yet, in quite another spirit he maintains that propositions which are here and now undoubted may later come under the scrutiny of doubt. This is a characteristic of all undoubted propositions (5.376*n*). In another place he asserts that "sure knowledge" is impossible, where sure knowledge means perfect knowledge that we have reached perfect knowledge on some point (4.63). "Perfect knowledge" is itself a technical term, meaning opinion which is so settled that no further inquiry *can* shake it. We cannot, then, be unshakably certain that we have attained unshakably certain knowledge. (The same view is expressed, in equivalent terms, in 5.514 and many other places.) There is, however, a "practically perfect belief," by which we treat some propositions as certain (4.64).

A solution of the apparently conflicting positions must take into account a fundamental maxim of all knowledge for Peirce: "Do not block the way of inquiry" (1.135). Now to maintain that there are ultimately indubitable beliefs blocks the way of inquiry, for Peirce. However, we must hold on to those beliefs that are actually not doubted. They can even be used as bases for demonstration, at least temporarily (5.376). For all practical purposes we are to leave these actually undoubted propositions alone: they *are to be treated as if* they were absolute and infallible, and they must not be submitted to any artificial, willful doubt. But, whenever we are impelled by some external circumstance to suspect the truth of propositions which we have believed up to now, then their mere seniority gives them no immunity from the careful probing of inquiry. So long as there is no reason for doubting them, they must be left alone; but when experience detects a weakness, then they should be submitted to doubt.

25. See also 2.192; 5.451.

26. The action of the man in doubt "is in imagination (or perhaps really) brought to a stop because he does not know whether (so to speak) the right hand road or the left hand road is the one that will bring him to his destination; and (to continue the figure of speech) he waits at the fork for an indication, and kicks his heels," as Peirce wrote about 1905 (5.510).

27. The habit-taking tendency of nature will be treated in Chapter V.

28. See also 5.371, 373, 387, 394.

29. Peirce frequently asserts that practical belief, since it is directed toward action, has nothing to do with science. Practical belief is a position that does not result from scientific reasoning. Rather it is an attitude of mind that is unaware of its own weakness, and that brashly disregards careful criticism. Peirce thinks that these defects are almost necessary for non-scientific belief, since this type of belief is meant for action. Action requires a certain brave and blind attitude of self-confidence, based largely on instinct and sentiment.

30. It is important to distinguish between Peirce's fake doubt and his feigned hesitancy. Fake doubt is Cartesian; it is opposed to the genuine doubt that should inaugurate a scientific inquiry, and is rejected by Peirce. But feigned hesitancy is the theoretical doubt which marks the beginning of a scientific investigation. It is a question concerning the constitution of the universe. Its answer will be presented

in terms of action, as here described—i.e., of imagined action. Only in this sense is scientific doubt feigned.

31. Justus Buchler, "What is the Pragmaticist Theory of Meaning?" in *Studies* (first series), p. 27.

32. This statement of Peirce's is open to serious objection. And it seems quite clear that Peirce himself later became aware of the shortcomings of the formulations of pragmatism in the two articles of 1877 and 1878. There are certain constants in Peirce's pragmatic theory of meaning, but there is also a considerable amount of development, and even of drastic revision. This is one of the main topics of Wennerberg's *The Pragmatism of C. S. Peirce*; see especially pp. 116 and 126ff.

According to some authors, although Peirce claims to be a scholastic realist and a follower of Scotus, his pragmatism sets him off from the latter, for it involves an identification of essence with behavior. For an elaboration of this, see Ralph J. Bastian, S.J., "The 'Scholastic' Realism of C. S. Peirce," *Philosophy and Phenomenological Research*, XIV (1953), 246–249, and Murphey, *Development*, pp. 154–163. However, as will be seen later, there is another interpretation, not devoid of likelihood, that in his later years Peirce developed a pragmatism closer to the understanding of the scholastic metaphysicians. See p. 136.

33. The importance of the conditional proposition is brought out in Peirce's "Issues of Pragmaticism," published in 1905, in which he writes as follows: "Pragmaticism makes the ultimate intellectual purport of what you please to consist in conceived conditional resolutions, or their substance; and therefore, the conditional propositions, with their hypothetical antecedents, in which such resolutions consist, being of the ultimate nature of meaning, must be capable of being true, that is, of expressing whatever there be which is such as the proposition expresses, independently of being thought to be so in any judgment, or being represented to be so in any other symbol of any man or men. But that amounts to saying that possibility is sometimes of a real kind" (5.453). The conditional aspect of pragmatism is also brought out in the two *Popular Science Monthly* articles of 1877 and 1878, as Murphey points out (*Development*, pp. 155–159).

34. In his later writings Peirce himself calls this rule a maxim.

35. Vincent G. Potter, S.J., *Charles S. Peirce on Norms and Ideals* (Amherst: University of Massachusetts Press, 1967), pp. 5 and 52ff. Fr. Potter's book examines in detail the categories, the normative sciences, pragmatism, and other dominant themes in Peirce, as elements of a unified philosophy. Chapter V of my book will present a similar position.

36. W. B. Gallie, *Peirce and Pragmatism*, p. 170.

37. Perry, *Thought and Character*, II, 424f. With regard to the *meaning* of concepts, it is interesting to read in a letter to William James, composed late in 1904, that Peirce disowns any quotation of his that may speak of "the meaning of a concept." The letter emphasizes the intellectual aspect of pragmatism. See Perry, *Thought and Character*, II, 432f. But in a letter to Mrs. Christine Ladd-Franklin, Peirce speaks of the pragmatic method and its reference to the *meaning* of *concepts*. "The meaning of a *concept* . . . lies in the manner in which it could *conceivably* modify purposive action, and *in this alone*" (Christine Ladd-Franklin, "Charles S. Peirce at the Johns Hopkins," *The Journal of Philosophy, Psychology*

and Scientific Methods, XIII [1916], 718). The same letter of Peirce contains his own summary of the origin of pragmatism, the friends and associates constituting the Metaphysical Club where the method was first crystallized, the articles proposing it, the appearance of the word, and many significant biographical facts. The same letter also gives very brief evaluations of the opinions of William James, Dewey, and Royce. *Ibid.,* pp. 719f.

This letter to Mrs. Franklin and paragraph 5.12 of the *Collected Papers* contain some of Peirce's main references to the origins of pragmatism.

38. One of the main points of difference between the pragmatism of Peirce and that of William James is their attitude toward particular actions. Peirce emphasized the *kind* of action involved (5.426), while James stressed the particular consequence. James spoke as follows in his California Union address of 1898: "The effective meaning of any philosophic proposition can always be brought down to some particular consequence, in our future practical experience, whether active or passive; the point lying rather in the fact that the experience must be *particular,* than in the fact that it must be active" (quotation [with emphasis added] in an article by John Dewey, "The Pragmatism of Peirce," *The Journal of Philosophy, Psychology and Scientific Methods,* XIII [1916], 710f). In another article Dewey mentions two misunderstandings of pragmatism—that pragmatism makes action the end of life, and that it subordinates thought and rational activity to the narrow purposes of interest and profit. "Le Developpement du Pragmatisme Americain," *Revue de Metaphysique et de Morale,* XXIX (1922), 413.

Perry describes the situation briefly: "The modern movement known as pragmatism is largely the result of James's misunderstanding of Peirce" (*Thought and Character,* II, 409). Robert Roth, however, has recently asked for a reconsideration of Perry's commonplace, by pointing out strong similarities between Peirce and James, without eliminating the differences. Roth asks whether James, instead of misunderstanding Peirce, might rather have extended certain of the latter's insights. Roth sees two dimensions in both thinkers: the scientific and the more inclusive non-scientific tradition that is open to vitally important matters (in the favorable sense) and to a knowledge of God's existence. But at the same time he admits a difference of emphasis in Peirce and James, because of their different temperaments (Robert J. Roth, S.J., "Is Peirce's Pragmatism Anti-Jamesian?" in *International Philosophical Quarterly,* V [1965], 541–563).

39. On the conditional and general aspect of pragmaticism, see also 6.485.

40. Thompson, *Pragmatic Philosophy,* pp. 203, 241ff, and Idus Murphree, "The Theme of Positivism in Peirce's Pragmatism," *Studies* (second series), pp. 236f.

41. W. B. Gallie, "Peirce's Pragmaticism," *Studies* (first series), p. 63.

NOTES—CHAPTER III

1. The main source of these views is "The Fixation of Belief." Peirce writes of the intent of this article as follows: "To describe the method of scientific investigation is the object of this series of papers. At present I have only room to notice some points of contrast between it and other methods of fixing belief" (5.385).

2. Peirce is even more forceful about the primacy of the scientific method over the other three, in a work which appeared in the *Popular Science Monthly* in 1878 as the last essay of the series "Illustrations of the Logic of Science," of which "The Fixation of Belief" and "How to Make Our Ideas Clear" were the first and second. In the last essay he asserts that the other three methods are of no value at all in the pursuit of knowledge. "Knowledge can only be furthered by the real desire for it, and . . . the methods of obstinacy, of authority, and every mode of trying to reach a foregone conclusion, are absolutely of no value" (2.635).

3. Wiener, *Values*, p. 326. The same view is expressed in the *Collected Papers* (4.530), though the context is more directly concerned with experiment.

4. Idus Murphree, "Peirce's Theory of Inquiry," *The Journal of Philosophy*, LVI (July 1959) 670. This article is a perceptive presentation of the themes of doubt–inquiry–belief, already considered.

5. Vincent Tomas gives a good brief summary of the scientific method in the introduction to his selections from Peirce's writings, *Essays in the Philosophy of Science* (New York: Liberal Arts Press, 1957), p. xiii.

6. Buchler gives a commendable explanation of what experience is for Peirce; I shall, however, not follow Buchler's divisions. Justus Buchler, *Charles Peirce's Empiricism* (New York: Harcourt, Brace, 1939), pp. 80–86.

7. The editors of the *Collected Papers* note that this lecture was entitled "Early Nominalism and Realism," from the series "Lectures on British Logicians." It was delivered at Harvard in 1869.

8. Peirce's reference is to William Whewell, *History of the Inductive Sciences, from the Earliest to the Present Time*. The intellectual character of experience is brought out quite sharply in the distinction which Peirce draws between perception and experience. Although it is probably true, as Peirce thinks, "that every element of experience is in the first place applied to an external object," experience still does not consist entirely in sense-perception (1.334f). The difference between experience and perception is explained briefly by Maurice Natanson, "The Concept of the Given in Peirce and Mead," *The Modern Schoolman*, XXXII (1955), 144f.

9. The book to which Peirce has reference is Ernst Mach, *Populär-wissenschaftliche Vorlesungen*. Sometimes the scientist would do well to substitute rational calculation for experiment. Peirce cites with contempt the example of the foolish experimenter who spent a month or more dropping a stick on the floor to ascertain experientially the value of pi with much less exactness than it could have been approximated by five minutes of calculation (4.69). Similarly ideal experimentation (which for Peirce seems to be the same as reasoning, or at least reasoning in regard to known possibilities) can sometimes supply a better answer than sensible experimentation. A chemist who hears from one assistant that fluorine is present in a majority of a given set of bottles, and from another assistant that oxygen is present in a majority of the same, and from both that fluorine and oxygen cannot exist together, knows apart from experimentation that there is an impossibility involved. It is impossible for both assistants to be right, as the head chemist knows, without testing the truth of their reports sensibly (3.527).

10. By "reason," I do not mean merely inference. In this context the term includes all types of intellectual activity and habits.

11. This process of experimentation, including reason, Peirce sometimes calls

"indagation," the tracking down of the constitution of the universe. It is not, however, a frequently used term.

12. For Peirce, therefore, observation seems to be a special kind of experience. While experience involves the forceful action of an independent object on the knower, observation seems to include an attitude of attentive studiousness on the observer's part. Experience is a forceful modification of our ways of thinking. But observation seems to be experience undertaken deliberately and with great attention and analysis. The citations on the last few and the next few pages document this interpretation.

13. Such a method, of course, Peirce claims to have followed in his own investigations.

14. For Peirce, percepts are initial data altogether within the order of thought. "I see an inkstand on the table: that is a percept. Moving my head, I get a different percept of the inkstand" (8.144; also 2.141). Percepts are not, however, the first impressions of sense. They are very fleeting thought-operations, not subject to the control of the will or to criticism. "Perceptual facts" are memorial records of percepts, and constitute the data from which inference begins. See Murphey, *Development*, p. 369.

15. This selection is taken from a brief note written by Peirce, "Pearson's Grammar of Science," *Popular Science Monthly*, LVIII (1900–1901), 301f. The book under discussion is Karl Pearson, *The Grammar of Science,* first published in 1892.

16. Peirce uses the example of the inkstand and the observer also in 8.153.

17. Goudge, surprisingly, makes use of this text to support his thesis that Peirce's naturalistic strain regards experience as noncognitive. For Goudge, the "brutality" of experience argues against its mental nature, despite the fact that, in the text just quoted, Peirce writes of the "brutal inroads of *ideas* from without" (1.321, emphasis added). According to Goudge, Peirce's naturalistic side takes experience as affective and "wholly non-cognitive," although Goudge is well aware of the "transcendental" view in Peirce that experience is cognitive. On this question the conjectured schizophrenia seems immoderate. Goudge, *The Thought of C. S. Peirce*, pp. 265–268. See also his articles in *The Journal of Philosophy*, XXXII (1935), 538; XXXIII (1936), 289; XLIV (1947), 366, 370f.

In fact, in a review of William James's *Principles of Psychology*, Peirce opposes the view, maintained also by Goudge's naturalistic sympathies, that "through feelings we become acquainted with things." This opinion, Peirce says, lies at the root of a large area of bad metaphysics. "On the contrary, the feelings are matters of indifference. . . . It is by the *reactions* of ourselves upon things and of their parts on one another that we become acquainted with things, as it seems to me" (Perry, *Thought and Character*, II, 107).

Regarding those commentators who see irreconcilable strains in Peirce, Burks has this to say: "It is fashionable today to conclude from the fact that Peirce's writings are fragmentary that his thought was likewise fragmentary. . . . But the lack of unity in his thought has been greatly overemphasized because of a failure to recognize three facts: first, that his logic is foundational to the rest of his philosophy, and hence that his three categories are basic in all his thought; second, that in a scientific spirit Peirce pursued the implications of different hypotheses (and as a consequence varied his terminology from paper to paper);

and third, that there was a temporal development in his thought" (Arthur W. Burks, "Peirce's Theory of Abduction," *Philosophy of Science,* XIII [1946], 301).

18. Although in this work I do not intend to go into the psychology of experience, except insofar as it is necessary for some understanding of the first moment of the scientific method, it should still be noted in passing that the existence of effort, or, as Peirce calls it, the oppositional aspect of experience, is known through inference (1.332–336).

19. Paragraph 5.539 also deals with some of the topics presented here. But 1.332–336 seem more adequate than 5.539, and were composed about three years later. In addition it should be mentioned that in 5.539 Peirce professes his agreement with the opinion of Thomas Reid on the direct perception of the world of material things. The same agreement with Reid is also mentioned in 5.56 and 6.95. Feibleman gives a helpful presentation of the influence of Reid on Peirce and on other nineteenth- and early-twentieth-century thinkers in *An Introduction to Peirce's Philosophy*, pp. 450ff.

20. In another work, also directed against Carus, but composed about ten years earlier, Peirce asserted that "being, and the uniformity in which being consists, require to be explained. The only thing that does not require it is non-existent spontaneity. This was soon seen to mean absolute chance" (6.604). Chance or irregularity he describes as "the absence of any coincidence," and asserts that such an event "calls for no explanation" (6.612). A surprising event—one which calls for explanation—is, accordingly, described as a coincidence.

Carus asserts that there is no need, in fact no possibility, of giving an account of facts. Peirce strongly disagrees and maintains that the existence of a fact demands an account (6.612). The role of chance will be treated in Chapter V.

21. For example, the different terms are used in the following sections: 1.354, 1.369, 2.774–791, 5.273, 6.144.

22. Paul Weiss sums up the importance of abduction for Peirce in words of high praise for this mental operation: "Under such titles as abduction, hypothesis, retroduction, and presumption, C. S. Peirce struggled over the years to lay bare the logic by which we get new ideas. He was, I think, more perceptive and bolder, and traced the problem into more crannies than anyone before or since. He took abduction to be of the very essence of pragmatism, saw that it was essential to history, and that it constituted the first stage of all inquiries. He insisted that it was a necessary part of perception, memory, and science. He thought it had a bearing on a proof of God, and that it was presupposed by all induction" (Paul Weiss, "The Logic of the Creative Process," *Studies* [first series], p. 166).

23. In the early days of the century poverty forced Peirce to give his time and talent to various jobs, like translating scientific papers for the Smithsonian Institution. Samuel P. Langley, secretary of the Smithsonian, took an interest in Peirce and helped him out of some financial difficulties. In the spring of 1901 Langley invited Peirce to write on the change in the meaning of "laws of nature" since Hume's day. Peirce replied with "Hume and the Laws of Nature," but did not satisfy Langley's request that he treat the change in the idea of laws of nature from Hume's time to Peirce's. Peirce disagreed with Langley's understanding of the history of the question, but wrote in reply another paper, "Hume on Miracles and Laws of Nature," later revised and re-entitled "The Laws of Nature and Hume's Argument against Miracles." These two works are dated June 1, 1901,

and September 5, 1901, respectively. Langley, because of his limited understanding of the question, was still unsatisfied, and neither of the works was published. (All this information is drawn from Wiener, *Values*, pp. 275–289. The composite text of the two last-mentioned articles is also given by Wiener, pp. 289–321. Wiener's article and the Peirce–Langley correspondence were originally published in the *Proceedings of the American Philosophical Society*, XCI [1947], 201–228.)

24. Wiener, *Values*, p. 320.

25. Vol. II, pp. 426–428.

26. In 1891 he wrote of the development of his ideas: "I hope my mind has not been stationary during all these [sixteen] years; yet there is little in those old articles which I now think positively erroneous. . . . My present views had, at that time, already begun to urge themselves on my mind; but they were not ripe for public avowal." He then goes on to give explicit approval of the ideas presented in two of the essays intended for republication in "Search for a Method" (6.609). Similarly in 1903 he wrote approvingly of his views of the three types of inference as explained in 1867 (5.144).

27. The article was published in the *Proceedings of the American Academy of Arts and Sciences*, VII (1867), 261–287.

28. This was published in the *Journal of Speculative Philosophy*, II (1868), 140–157.

29. Peirce presents his justification of the spelling of "premiss" and "premisses" in 2.582f.

30. A helpful example of classifying a particular man as a "mugwump" from characteristics learned from conversation with him, is given in 6.145.

31. The article appeared in the *Popular Science Monthly*, XIII (1878), 470–482.

32. Peirce regards as accidental the relation of the genera of arguments to the various figures of the syllogism. Induction and abduction must not be expected to result in necessary conclusions, as strictly syllogistic reasoning does. Thompson, *Pragmatic Philosophy*, pp. 97ff.

33. This article also notes the relevance of mathematical ratios, and hence of probability, to reasoning processes. It further proposes both induction and hypothesis as types of synthetic inference, which, as we shall see, is a way of understanding the introduction of new, and perhaps not directly observable, facts into scientific procedure (2.623, 641, 644).

34. The explanatory role of abduction is also mentioned but not emphasized earlier in the essay (2.707). "A Theory of Probable Inference" was originally published in *Studies in Logic, by Members of the Johns Hopkins University*, ed. C. S. Peirce (Boston: Little, Brown, 1883).

35. Arthur W. Burks presents some brief considerations on abduction as a process of reasoning, and as a distinct kind of argument from induction and deduction. When he confines his discussion to the difference between induction and abduction he too asserts that Peirce first regarded them both as *modes of argument* and later as *methods* in scientific inquiry.

The question then is to justify this latter view of abduction as a *reasoning* process. Is there a logic of discovery? According to Burks there is such a logic, since for Peirce reasoning is a deliberate and logically controlled process; it is the adoption of a conclusion because the man sees that the conclusion follows according to a leading principle which he approves. Abduction fulfills the requirement

(Arthur W. Burks, "Peirce's Theory of Abduction," *Philosophy of Science*, XIII [1946], 301–306).

36. Explanation consists in the reduction of a complex predicate to a simple predicate "from which the complex predicate follows on known principles," as he wrote in 1891 (6.612).

37. Note that in this passage the scientist reaches an explanatory hypothesis "at once." Later we will see that the scientific imagination devises an explanatory theory by a step that is sudden, free, and brilliant. It progresses by leaps. See p. 37.

38. The title of this paper is "On the Logic of Drawing History from Documents especially from Testimonies." Part of it is directed against Paul Carus. In another lengthy work also directed against Carus, but written about ten years earlier, Peirce repeats that the function of explanation is to show that the fact explained is a necessary or probable result of another fact (6.606).

39. In his famous article "A Neglected Argument for the Reality of God," Peirce summarizes these topics. Inquiry begins with a surprising event that the inquirer attempts to explain, by proposing a possible explanation, "by which I mean a syllogism exhibiting the surprising fact as necessarily consequent upon the circumstances of its occurrence together with the truth of the credible conjecture, as premisses" (6.469). The logical aspects of abduction, the surprising event, the conjecture as an explanation which renders the observed fact necessary, are important points of Peirce's basic teaching on abduction.

40. Peirce's long and somewhat exaggerated reply to Paul Carus, published in *The Monist* in 1893, should be consulted; *Collected Papers*, 6.588–618.

41. Selections from this undated paper are given in Wiener, *Values*, pp. 137–141.

42. A helpful article on Peirce's opposition to positivism is that of Matthew J. Fairbanks, "C. S. Peirce and Positivism," *The Modern Schoolman*, XLI (1964), 323–337. Fairbanks describes Peirce's rejection of the antimetaphysical bias of positivism, and includes some of Peirce's recommendations concerning the manner in which positivists might profit from a study of metaphysics.

43. The same view is expressed in 2.96: "An Abduction is Originary in respect to being the only kind of argument which starts a new idea."

44. An appeal to the continuity of the human mind with developing nature must be brought in also, in order to account for the success of abduction.

45. "The principal rule of presumption is that its conclusion should be such that definite consequences can be plentifully deduced from it of a kind which can be checked by observation" (2.786).

46. A major source of doctrine on economy in abduction is 7.218–223, a work composed about 1901.

47. Peirce's views on economy in research were developed in his minute experimental studies in physics and astronomy with the Coastal Survey in the eighteen-seventies. See his "Note on the Theory of the Economy of Research" (7.139–157).

48. In this same work, he also lists several rules for the economics of research (1.120–125). His work on Hume and the laws of nature expresses similar views. Wiener, *Values*, p. 302.

49. Apparently Peirce's views on instinct as based on the kinship of the human mind with the cosmos are themselves formed by a process of abduction. The openness of phenomena to rationalization is known by abduction. The affirmation of

the mind's kinship to the universe he calls a hypothesis, and asserts that this is the only explanation of the marvelous success that scientists have had in hitting on the correct hypothesis relatively early in the inquiry (7.219f).

50. It is to be noted, however, that besides this "scientific" instinct there is also a practical instinct that should guide men in everyday living, in certain cases even more reliably than reason. We are not dealing with practical intellect here (2.176f).

51. In these sections Peirce makes reference to Ockham's razor as a maxim of scientific procedure. For him the razor means that the inquirer should test the simpler explanation, the one with the fewest elements, first.

52. In at least one piece of writing composed in 1901 he seems to interpret simplicity as he did in 1908. But the interpretation is not emphatic: "We may, with great confidence follow the rule that that one of all admissible hypotheses which seems the simplest to the human mind ought to be taken up for examination first" (6.532).

53. Peirce's editors note (6.477) that Galileo's position is found in "Dialogues Concerning the Two Great Systems of the World," in *Mathematical Collections and Translations* of Thomas Salisbury, vol. 1, p. 301.

54. There are also some references to practical concerns in the section 6.496–500.

55. On this point, W. H. Hill has misjudged Peirce as having recourse to the a priori method of fixing belief. Hill represents Peirce as holding that man attains this knowledge of the universe by *checking* his beliefs, with "those insights upon which we can agree." Hill therefore interprets instinct (which Peirce proposes as a faculty for *selecting* hypotheses) as a kind of ultimate verification. "Peirce's 'Pragmatic' Method," *Philosophy of Science*, VII (1940), 180. See 6.530.

56. In addition to the perceptual indubitables, Peirce also considers as common-sense beliefs what Buchler calls the social indubitables such as the almost universal belief of the criminality of incest. Both the perceptual indubitables and the social indubitables can be described as primitive in some sense, at least inasmuch as they have not as yet been subjected to controlled criticism. Buchler, *Peirce's Empiricism,* pp. 59–61. See also Thompson, *Pragmatic Philosophy,* pp. 223f.

57. Peirce frequently refers to his own philosophy as "critical common-sensism." This, as Dewey points out, does not mean that it consists merely in a widely held body of opinion, but in ideas forced upon us by the world in which we live. Common sense is an affair of experience, but not of sensations exclusively, as most previous empiricists said. Again, with Dewey, Peirce's common-sensism is *critical,* since an uncritical acceptance of philosophical positions would block the way of inquiry. It is difficult, however, to accept Dewey's paraphrase as representative of the real Peirce: the opinions forced on us are "the ideas and beliefs that a man must hold in order to meet in his activities the urgent and imperative demands made upon him by his situation" (John Dewey, Review of *Collected Papers of Charles Sanders Peirce, The New Republic,* LXXXIX [1937], 415).

James O'Connell has explained quite competently the continuing presence of the common-sense indubitables in scientific work, as well as the function of the scientist in adjusting to these: "C. S. Peirce's Conception of Philosophy," *The Downside Review,* LXXVII (1959), 277–295.

58. As the editors of the *Collected Papers* note, Peirce was scheduled to give six lectures on pragmatism from March to May of 1903. But another written lecture,

entitled "Pragmatism—Lecture VII," was found in a notebook belonging to the same set of notebooks in which the other six lectures were found.

59. This is the third of his three "cotary propositions." Peirce informs the reader that the Latin *cos, cotis* means a whetstone; the three cotary propositions are supposed to put the edge on the pragmatic maxim. The form "cossal" is also used (5.180f).

60. The article was published in *The Monist,* and was entitled "Prolegomena to an Apology for Pragmaticism."

61. In the same sentence Peirce says that this is the only difference between the two.

62. Buchler holds the same, but I would hesitate to agree with him when he asserts that for Peirce the perceptual judgment is the conclusion of an inference. As Peirce says, the perceptual judgment is outside the field of rational control (5.181). In addition, Peirce frequently says that one of the distinguishing marks of inference is that it is subject to criticism and control. This would seem to deny Buchler's general statement that every synthetic proposition is a hypothesis (*Peirce's Empiricism,* pp. 39f, 135).

63. There are other examples of interpretation given by Peirce. We wake up at the hour we choose much more accurately than we could consciously guess; while preoccupied with study, we are oblivious of a clock striking the hours very audibly; proofreaders notice mistakes which the untrained eye, accustomed to correct spelling, will miss. Adjustment for interpreting the percept is a more relevant aspect of experience than the objective intensity of the percept.

64. Abductive inference and the perceptual judgment are seen to be both similar and dissimilar with regard to their interpretative character, in an illustration given by James O'Connell: a collection of dots on a page may in some cases very easily be recognized as the outline of a rabbit, while in other cases the observer may approach a group of points with the purpose of finding a rabbit's outline there, and may succeed only in view of this deliberately assumed attitude. The latter, O'Connell says, is more like the process of scientific abduction, while the former is more of an instance of the perceptual judgment (James O'Connell, S.M.A., "C. S. Peirce and the Problem of Knowledge," *Philosophical Studies,* VII [1957], 13–14).

65. This is a somewhat vague, though valuable, answer to the very important epistemological problem regarding the contributions that outside reality and the observer's constitution make to knowledge. James O'Connell understands Peirce correctly in saying that our knowledge is dependent on the nature of the external object known. The interpretative character both of explanatory hypotheses and of perceptual judgments O'Connell attributes to the "selective nature of our senses, and the general nature of our concepts, . . . our temperament, motives, and history, and . . . the actual situation at the moment of knowing" (*Ibid.,* p. 14). The subjectivity involved here is overcome by the verification process, which alone validates abductive conclusions, as O'Connell also points out, pp. 14f.

66. There is a genuine need for answering this question, since we cannot claim that Peirce did not really hold both these views. His position is too clearly put, and too frequently repeated, to allow us to deny either part.

67. There is evidence here of Peirce's opposition to nominalism, a theme which will be treated in Chapter V.

68. There is also an interesting analysis of the *form* of abductive inference, and of the way in which it is known. Peirce admits that he is venturing rather far in claiming that "every general *form* of putting concepts together is, in its elements, given in perception" (5.186). This is a difficult position to justify, more so since the position is general, including all forms of reasoning: deductive necessity, inductive probability, abductive expectability, the conception of inference itself. A formal conception originates when the reasoner perceives that one might conceivably reason in this way. "What can our first acquaintance with an inference, when it is not yet adopted, be but a perception of the world of ideas? In the first suggestion of it, the inference must be thought of as an inference, because when it is adopted there is always the thought that so one might reason in a whole class of cases. . . . The inference must, then, be thought of as an inference in the first suggestion of it" (5.194). In this way inference is known as inference. It becomes an object of thought, part of the *matter* of thought.

69. Murphey, *Development*, pp. 370f.

70. *Ibid.*, p. 372. Chisholm also brings out the central importance of the perceptual judgment for Peirce (Roderick M. Chisholm, "Fallibilism and Belief," *Studies* [first series], p. 104).

On perception as the starting point and testing ground of speculation, see also Richard J. Bernstein, "Peirce's Theory of Perception," *Studies* (second series), p. 184.

71. Wiener, *Values*, p. 283.

72. One formulation of the maxim is the following: "The maxim of pragmatism is that a conception can have no logical effect or import differing from that of a second conception except so far as, taken in connection with other conceptions and intentions, it might conceivably modify our practical conduct differently from that second conception" (5.196).

73. In the second chapter the intellectual emphasis of Peircean pragmaticism has already been noted.

74. Ernest Nagel, it seems, misses the stress which Peirce places on *conceived* action in the pragmatic maxim ("Charles S. Peirce, Pioneer of Modern Empiricism," *Philosophy of Science*, VII [1940], 73–76).

75. In confirmation of this interpretation, see also 4.447 and 5.412.

NOTES—CHAPTER IV

1. The book to which Peirce is referring is George Henry Lewes, *Aristotle: A Chapter from the History of Science* (London, 1864), as the editors note.

2. In the verification stage, the inquirer directs his attention to the hypothesis, rather than to the facts from which the hypothesis was generated. He studies out "what effect that hypothesis . . . must have in modifying our expectations in regard to future experience." Then he tests to see how the new expectations materialize (7.115). In the lecture quoted here, Peirce refers to the testing of the predictions as "quasi-experimentation," meaning by this word the operation of absolutizing the conditional propositions deduced from the hypothesis, and of noting how the matter turns out (7.115*n*).

3. Sections 2.755–772 are from a manuscript on induction and methodology, composed around 1905, and thought to be a draft of a section of "A Neglected Argument for the Reality of God," as mentioned in the general bibliography of Peirce's writings in the eighth volume of the *Collected Papers*, p. 298.

A considerable section (6.468–480) of the "Neglected Argument," published in 1908, is concerned with a presentation of scientific method. The following pages on deduction rely heavily on this work.

4. Peirce frequently uses the words "consequences" and "consequents" interchangeably. Boler, however, following the more usual understanding of the logicians, detects a difference between consequent (the observable result of provisionally accepting a hypothesis) and consequence (the nexus between the hypothesis and its consequent). I shall employ Boler's distinction in a later chapter where it will be quite helpful (p. 123), but for the most part I shall follow Peirce's policy of interchangeable usage, according to which "consequence" usually means "consequent" (John F. Boler, *Charles Peirce and Scholastic Realism* [Seattle: University of Washington Press, 1963], pp. 70, 97–99).

5. There are two difficulties that one meets in studying what the role of deduction is for Peirce in a scientific inquiry: 1.) in many places Peirce refers to the whole operation of verification as *induction,* without mentioning the word "deduction"; 2.) he frequently treats deductive inference apart from any relation to the scientific method. Later on in this chapter I shall explain somewhat more fully the different senses of induction for Peirce.

6. James Ward Smith wisely points out that the deductive stage of scientific inquiry is an application of pragmatism. In drawing observable consequences from his explanatory hypotheses, the scientific investigator is explicating the *meaning* of the predicate of the abductive proposition, in terms of observable consequences (James Ward Smith, "Pragmatism, Realism, and Positivism in the United States," *Mind*, LXI [1952], 191–192).

7. The proposition, then, that is deduced from the explanatory hypothesis is just as shaky as that hypothesis, up to the time of the actual testing. Nevertheless, deduction is for Peirce a real tool of progress in knowledge. The final evaluation of the hypothesis after the completion of the verification process is a real addition to knowledge, achieved partially through deduction. Furthermore, the verifiable propositions generated by deduction from the hypothesis are no more than virtually known before the deduction takes place. Peirce here goes beyond J. S. Mill in his estimate of deduction.

8. Virtual antecedence is best described by the illustration which Peirce gives (2.759). Suppose that an investigator, during the course of the deductive phase of scientific inquiry, finds to his surprise that the adopted hypothesis leads him to predict an event whose truth he already knows. He has not verified the prediction by testing it after deducing it from the hypothesis, in ignorance of the result. But just as soon as he sees that the hypothesis leads him to predict the event, he realizes that he already knows its truth from previous experience. May such an event be taken into consideration in evaluating the worth of the hypothesis? Peirce answers that if the predicted event has influenced the *formation* of the hypothesis, then it has performed its function in this inquiry, and may not be used again. If, however, the event has not been used in the generation of the hypothesis, then it not only *may* be considered in evaluating the hypothesis, but

must be so used. Such a prediction "virtually antecedes" the investigator's knowledge of it, since in this case it has been brought to his mind as an uncertain conclusion from an uncertain hypothesis (2.759). Hence its truth is "virtually unknown" (2.775), i.e., the prediction has been made only in virtue of a hypothesis, whose worth is as yet in doubt. See also 7.89f.

9. In a more compressed form: "Induction, is an Argument which sets out from a hypothesis, resulting from a previous Abduction, and from virtual predictions, drawn by Deduction, of the results of possible experiments, having performed the experiments, concludes that the hypothesis is true in the measure in which those predictions are verified, this conclusion, however, being held subject to probable modification to suit future experiments" (2.96).

10. Peirce makes it clear in this section that he does not understand experimentation in the narrow sense of varying the conditions of an experiment as much as one pleases. Such a method is accurate and easy, but the experimental method is rather putting a question to nature, and awaiting her reply.

11. Peirce uses the term "induction" to refer to different processes of reason, some more inclusive than others. There are four meanings which must be distinguished. 1.) In its most inclusive sense the term "induction" refers to all the stages of the scientific method. The method of the sciences is the inductive method. 2.) Peirce also uses the word to designate the process of verification; in this sense it includes the deductive phase. 3.) The term is also used by Peirce to designate that part of the verification process which occurs after experiential consequents have been deduced from the explanatory hypothesis. 4.) Its strictest meaning is the evaluation of a ratio. In this last sense, the inquirer concludes inductively that probably a given characteristic will be found in a whole class, in the same proportion as it has been found in a sample of that class. Toward the end of this chapter I will treat the fourth meaning of induction, in relation to the process described under the third meaning of induction. In the meantime, however, the word will be used mostly in the third sense; but the reader must be cautioned that the word is also used here both in the second sense and in the fourth sense, depending on the precise context.

The above quotation (5.170) is an example of the more inclusive meaning of induction, including deduction. In the text quoted, Peirce makes reference to the explanatory hypothesis (formed by abduction), to the predicting phase (a process of deduction, as he explicitly states), and to the testing operation which compares the theory with observed facts. The last step is induction, in its more restricted meaning.

12. For information on this work, see note 3, above.

13. The book was published by Little, Brown and Co., Boston, in 1883. Peirce intended to republish the article as Essay XIV of the projected "Search for A Method." Like the other essays of this projected book, "A Theory of Probable Inference" follows an approach somewhat like that of formal logic, as has already been mentioned, p. 34.

14. Both these requirements are mentioned and briefly explained in Peirce's projected "History of Science" (1.93–95).

15. Predesignation could have been considered under the heading of deduction, since strictly it is by a process of deduction that the predesignation actually occurs. However, it is better to consider it here, since Peirce usually considers predesigna-

tion under induction, and since the reasons for predesignation can be more fully appreciated here.

16. Peirce gives the example of a man doing biographical research who notes the ages at death of the first five poets listed in a biographical dictionary. After long contemplation of the five numbers, he finds several characteristics that they have in common, e.g., "the first digit [of each of the ages] raised to the power indicated by the second, and then divided by three, leaves a remainder of *one*." And yet, he says, "there is not the smallest reason to believe that the next poet's age would possess these characters" (2.738). The results of not predesignating the character sought for are most fallacious, and disastrous to science.

Another example of faulty induction, based on failure to predesignate, is found in an article by Peirce in Baldwin's *Dictionary*. This passage also brings out the importance of random sampling as the basis of induction. "Thus Macaulay, in his essay on the inductive philosophy, collects a number of instances of Irish whigs—which we may suppose constitute a random sample, as they ought, since they are to be used as the basis of an induction. By the exercise of ingenuity and patience, the writer succeeds in finding a character which they all possess, that of carrying middle names; whereupon he seems to think that an unobjectionable induction would be that all Irish whigs have middle names. But he has violated the rule, based on the theory of probabilities, that the character for which the samples are to be used as inductive instances must be specified independently of the result of the examination. Upon the same principle only those consequents of a hypothesis support the truth of the hypothesis which were predicted, or, at least, in no way influenced the character of the hypothesis" (2.790).

17. Peirce in one text admits the possibility under certain conditions of a successful test without the predesignation of the character. If striking characters are discovered in a large sample without being predesignated, we may infer inductively that the striking characters belong to the whole class. Again, if the objects being examined possess a large number of characters in common with some familiar object, the inductive inference may be drawn that the two classes of objects are practically identical. An inductive inference without predesignation, however, is less reliable than the same inference in which the character sought for has been predesignated (2.740).

18. This teaching is the same as that found in the Johns Hopkins *Studies*, although the latter was published almost twenty years before the articles in Baldwin's *Dictionary*.

19. Again in the article on "Probable Inference," in Baldwin's *Dictionary*, Peirce repeats the same instructions for induction. The investigator asks how often certain conditions will be followed by results of a predesignated character. Then, after a number of instances, he infers that about the same ratio will hold true of the whole class, as he has found in the instances examined (2.784). See also 2.661.

20. "Presume" is a misleading word. At the end of the chapter we shall see that such a "presumption" is not a postulate. It is a reasoned position concerning the trustworthiness of the testing procedure.

21. This double restriction is also mentioned in 2.720, 2.733, and other places. In the rest of this chapter I shall discuss probability *passim*, but without any attempt to treat it with the adequacy which Peirce's views on the subject deserve. The respect, which Peirce's work on probability deserves, is brought out by

Goudge, who, however, is not in complete agreement with Peirce. "What impresses me most about his discussions [on probability] is their sensitiveness to the manifold aspects of this difficult subject. They are particularly valuable, also, because they seek to formulate a doctrine of probability that is in harmony with the practice of the empirical sciences, to ground the doctrine in objective fact, and to state it in such a way that subsequent refinement has been not only possible but fruitful. The recent development of the frequency theory by men like von Mises and Reichenbach has stemmed in large measure from Peirce's pioneering" (*The Thought of C. S. Peirce*, pp. 171f).

It is difficult to agree with the opinion of Chisholm that Peirce's theory of inquiry can be suitably described without reference to his positions on probability and induction (Roderick M. Chisholm, "Fallibilism and Belief," *Studies* [first series], p. 95).

22. Quantitative induction, one of several types of induction, will be explained in the next section of this chapter.

23. Wiener, *Values*, pp. 289f.

24. I have used the word "subject-class" in order to avoid ambiguity. The testable consequences of an explanatory hypothesis are, of course, proposed as hypothetical assertions. "If such-and-such an explanation is true, then the members of class A should be marked by the character X." The inquirer then chooses at random certain members of class A, and tests them to see whether they actually are marked by the character X. He must, in fact, choose A's—sc., members of the subject-class—for testing.

25. This paragraph is taken from his article "The Probability of Induction," published in 1878 in the *Popular Science Monthly*, and intended for republication in 1893 in the projected "Search for a Method."

26. This same position is again emphasized in a work written about 1905 (2.763 and 2.766).

27. The "Third Stage" is, of course, the process of induction, which tests the consequences drawn by deduction from the hypothesis.

28. For Peirce, the probability of the ratio with which induction deals is concerned with the future, as Goudge points out. A projection into the future of a ratio gained from past experience is quite shaky, and is subject to continual modification as new instances of the class under investigation turn up (*The Thought of C. S. Peirce*, pp. 169f).

29. As Davis says, "If science lead us astray, more science will set us straight" (Ellery W. Davis, "Charles Peirce at Johns Hopkins," *The Mid-West Quarterly*, II [1914], 49). This is a brief article presenting several of the major themes of Peirce's work. The article was published in October, 1914, about six months after Peirce's death, although no mention of his death is made.

30. Braithwaite judges it of some importance that Peirce is not defending the validity of any particular induction. A particular induction in Braithwaite's opinion is valid, not in itself, but only as a member of a class of reasonings valid because of their method. What Peirce is justifying, therefore, is the method (R. B. Braithwaite, Review of *Collected Papers of Charles Sanders Peirce*, Vols. 1–4, *Mind*, XLII [1934], 508). That Braithwaite has interpreted Peirce correctly becomes more evident by reading a short section from the seventh of the Lowell Lectures of 1903: "Suppose we define Inductive reasoning as that reasoning whose

conclusion is justified not by there being any necessity of its being true or approximately true but by its being the result of a method which if steadily persisted in must bring the reasoner to the truth of the matter or must cause his conclusion in its changes to converge to the truth as its limit" (7.110). This is more than a mere supposition; it is a real assertion.

31. E.g., 5.575f.

32. As Murphree says, "what we fix upon is a method, not a set of unchanging beliefs" (Idus Murphree, "Peirce's Theory of Inquiry," *The Journal of Philosophy*, LVI [July 1959], 670).

33. This is a position held by Peirce late in life; the articles cited were written or published after 1900.

34. Madden criticizes Peirce's position on the "long run" corrective function of induction, but he does not take into consideration this second aspect of prolonged testing and the contribution that it makes to progress in knowledge (Edward H. Madden, "Peirce on Probability," *Studies* [second series], pp. 122–140).

35. Recall a selection, which I have already quoted (p. 64), which asserts that the investigator may judge that the hypothesis "ought to receive a definite modification in the light of the new experiments, . . . or whether finally, that while not true it probably presents some analogy to the truth, and that the results of the induction may help to suggest a better hypothesis" (2.759).

36. P. 74, and the paragraphs cited there: 2.781; 5.145; 6.474, among others. The seventh Lowell Lecture of 1903 presents the same view of induction (7.110).

37. See pp. 67–69.

38. See also 2.750, where a similar position is upheld. There are, however, places in Peirce's writings where he seems to assert that a process of induction *presumes* that all members of a class will have all the characters common to the known members (5.272). This early writing, "Some Consequences of Four Incapacities," was published in 1868 at a time when Peirce, while interested in statistical reasoning, tended to consider inductive inference as an inversion of deductive inference. The same position is found in his work of 1867, "On the Natural Classification of Arguments" (2.515). Both works were intended for republication in 1893 in "Search for a Method," even though by that time Peirce seems to have rejected any dependence of induction on such presumptions (2.750; 6.39–42).

NOTES—CHAPTER V

1. In this chapter I am going counter to the advice of Justus Buchler who maintains that to attempt to associate Peircean fallibilism with Peircean metaphysical evolutionism leads to a misunderstanding of fallibilism. Buchler warns that, in general, interpreting Peirce's individual theories primarily in the light of his whole scheme leads to vicious consequences. Buchler's exegetical principle seems unreasonable ("The Accidents of Peirce's System," *The Journal of Philosophy*, XXXVII [1940], 265).

Weiss, on the other hand, maintains that the main prima facie inconsistencies in Peirce can be reconciled ("The Essence of Peirce's System," *Ibid.*, p. 261). This approach to interpretation is more moderate.

2. Gallie, *Peirce and Pragmatism*, pp. 39f.

3. According to Goudge, Peirce attributes the validity of induction to the regularity of the universe which induction, if continued long enough, will discover. The regularity, however, Goudge says, is *postulated* by Peirce (*The Thought of C. S. Peirce*, pp. 189–193). A later section of this chapter may lead one to think that the orderly character of the universe is not a postulate.

4. It is not absolutely certain how far Peirce intended his fallibilism to extend. In one piece of writing he confines fallibilism to a knowledge of *fact,* asserting that one may well accept the multiplication table as certain, while in another place the multiplication table does not enjoy any immunity from fallibilism. According to the latter place there is only one absolutely certain judgment: "If I must make any exception, let it be that the assertion that every assertion but this is fallible, is the only one that is absolutely infallible" (2.75; also 1.149).

5. Ernest Nagel, "Charles Peirce's Guesses at the Riddle," *The Journal of Philosophy,* XXX (1933), 381.

6. Justus Buchler, *Peirce's Empiricism*, pp. 54–61.

7. *Ibid.,* p. 59; see also 5.451 and 5.514.

8. Buchler, *Peirce's Empiricism*, p. 65; Goudge, *The Thought of C. S. Peirce*, pp. 30–34.

9. Peirce, though he does not reject the possibility of revelation, still finds many weak spots in a person's maintaining that he comprehends a proposition which he is certain has been revealed. Similarly, innate judgments, direct experience, and memory are known sources of error. Hence there is no way of reaching perfect certitude or exactitude (1.143–146).

10. In the chapter on abduction I have already mentioned the mind's instinctive scent for truthful hypotheses along the lines of mechanics and psychics. These two instincts have been influential because they are necessary for the survival of the individual and for the propagation of the species. In an evolutionary spirit, Peirce compares man's facility at guessing the truth with the instincts of animals which guide their activities of feeding and breeding. By "psychics" he seems to mean a discipline which has some knowledge of what occurs in people's minds, how they react to certain situations, what their needs and desires are.

11. The "biographical" approach to fallibilism is found in a fragment which his editors have used as a preface to the first volume of the *Collected Papers.*

12. The book reviewed was Alexander Campbell Fraser's *The Works of George Berkeley, D.D., formerly Bishop of Cloyne: Including many of his Writings hitherto Unpublished,* four volumes (Oxford: Clarendon Press, 1871); the review appeared in *The North American Review*, CXIII (October 1871), 449–472. It is presented in the *Collected Papers,* 8.7–38.

13. The article is "Issues of Pragmaticism," *The Monist,* XV (1905), 481–499; also *Collected Papers,* 5.438–463.

14. Gallie, *Peirce and Pragmatism,* p. 61.

15. *Ibid.,* pp. 61f; see also Buchler, *Peirce's Empiricism,* p. x.

16. By "laws of perception," Peirce may mean the general truths about perception, i.e., those characteristics that we are considering here. In perception, outside reality forces itself on us, and if we investigate it with the intention of learning the truth, we will inevitably be forced to attain some knowledge of it. We must, of course, recognize its cognizability and its public character.

17. "The real is that which insists upon forcing its way to recognition as something *other* than the mind's creation" (1.325). The outer world, when it presents itself to thought, does so with force and compulsion (5.474).

18. In this article, entitled "Truth and Falsity and Error," Peirce writes that a statement can be perfectly true only if it admits its own inaccuracy and imperfection (5.565, 567). The emphasis on the fallible character of knowledge is obvious here. See also note 4, *supra.*

19. In a letter to William James composed in 1904, Peirce states that one cannot believe what one pleases. "As for people who say that pragmatism means believing anything one pleases, my answer to that . . . is, in brief, that if one could believe what one pleased that would be true. But the fact is that one cannot. I wish I had Royce's text where he asks how the mere pragmatist can feel it a duty to think truly, for he was present at my lecture where I showed that pragmatism (*my* pragmatism) makes logic a mere special case of ethics" (Perry, *Thought and Character,* II, 433).

20. The same view is presented also in 2.153, 4.432, 5.525, 6.328, and other places. It is also found in his review of Fraser's work on Berkeley (8.12) and in the letter to Lady Welby, in *Charles S. Peirce's Letters to Lady Welby,* ed. Lieb, pp. 38f, and in Wiener, *Values,* pp. 419f.

21. In a work "Why Study Logic?" Peirce repeats this theme of the independence of facts from what individuals have thought them to be (2.173). However, reality for Peirce includes generals and possibles besides facts. A diamond, for instance, which was consumed without ever being subjected to pressure would still be hard. Pragmaticism insists upon the reality of certain possibilities (5.453, 457).

22. This was written as a sequel to "Questions Concerning Certain Faculties claimed for Man." Both of these anti-Cartesian and anti-Kantian articles touch on the theme: "We have no conception of the absolutely incognizable" (5.265). Hence, "whatever is meant by any term as 'the real' is cognizable" (5.310). Throughout this section, I shall also make frequent use of "How to Make Our Ideas Clear," published in the *Popular Science Monthly* in 1878.

23. Peirce may consider this position Cartesian in the sense that for Descartes we have no initial certainty about the external world; certainty comes only after knowing the self first. For Peirce, however, as well as for William James, self-consciousness is suspect. "It appears, therefore, that there is no reason for supposing a power of introspection; and, consequently, the only way of investigating a psychological question is by inference from external facts" (5.249). "Self-consciousness may easily be the result of inference" (5.237). For Peirce the method of intuitive introspection is not primary as it is for Descartes.

24. The knowability of reality is the theme of the last section of "Some Consequences," in which Peirce insists that whatever is real is knowable. There is no thing which is not related to the mind, as knowable by the mind. However, "things which are relative to the mind doubtless are, apart from that relation" (5.311). In other words, although all reality is related to the individual mind, it has not been generated by that mind.

25. "One man's experience is nothing, if it stands alone. If he sees what others cannot, we call it hallucination. It is not 'my' experience, but 'our' experience that has to be thought of; and this 'us' has indefinite possibilities" (5.402*n*2; also 5.384). "The objective final opinion is independent of the thoughts of any parti-

cular men, but is not independent of thought *in general*" (7.336). According to Joseph L. Blau, Peirce is partially responsible for the emphasis which Josiah Royce puts on the role of the community. Knowledge becomes a kind of social process, related to the community of minds (Joseph L. Blau, *Men and Movements in American Philosophy* [New York: Prentice-Hall, 1952], p. 215). Among Royce's many works, his Gifford Lectures, entitled *The World and the Individual* (2 vols.; New York: Macmillan, 1899 and 1901), and his *The Problem of Christianity* (2 vols.; New York: Macmillan, 1914) are perhaps the most noteworthy for this stress.

26. This is the sense of Peirce's own personal habit of examining the opinions of others before assenting to a conclusion in his own mind. As mentioned above, he used to give special consideration to views inconsistent with his own, attempting to place himself in the point of view of his opponents (6.181). The same emphasis on the social character of science is brought out in his "The Ethics of Terminology," where he says: "The progress of science cannot go far except by collaboration; or, to speak more accurately, no mind can take one step without the aid of other minds" (2.220).

27. For a more lengthy presentation of this pragmatic description of the real, and of the weaknesses of such a description, see Edward C. Moore, *American Pragmatism: Peirce, James and Dewey* (New York: Columbia University Press, 1961), pp. 69–73. Vincent Potter's excellent book throws helpful light on this topic: *Charles S. Peirce on Norms and Ideals,* pp. 62–65.

28. Buchler's presentation of this matter is excellent: *Peirce's Empiricism,* pp. 73f and 145–149. Murphey places greater emphasis on the questions of the actual future agreement of investigators and the reality of other minds than I do (*Development,* pp. 141–147, 165–171, and 302f). See also Manley A. Thompson, Jr., "The Paradox of Peirce's Realism," *Studies* (first series), pp. 137 and 139, and *Pragmatic Philosophy,* pp. 177f, where the uncertainty of the indefinite continuation of inquiry is proposed as an additional ground of fallibilism.

Haas is in substantial agreement with the interpretation I have given when he explains that the dependence of the real on the community is a *notional* dependence, and that the community in this context is a possible condition of knowledge in general (William Paul Haas, O.P., *The Conception of Law and the Unity of Peirce's Philosophy* [Fribourg, Switzerland: The University Press; Notre Dame: The University of Notre Dame Press, 1964], pp. 114f).

John E. Smith also holds that Peirce's theory of the real is pragmatistic. Peirce, according to Smith, was attempting to combine elements of realism, idealism and pragmatism in presenting his theory of the real. While not denying the combination, I would hesitate to agree that Peirce's presentation of thirdness is as idealistic as Smith says it is (John E. Smith, "Community and Reality," in *Perspectives on Peirce: Critical Essays on Charles Sanders Peirce,* ed. Richard J. Bernstein [New Haven: Yale University Press, 1965] pp. 92–119).

29. In this connection see 7.336, quoted in note 25.

30. It is important to note here that the community of scientists form more than a *jury* deciding that certain opinions are right, and others wrong. The community of scientists are also *workers*, achieving more and more accurate formulations of the truth by virtue of their solidarity and cooperation. "It is quite true that the

success of modern science largely depends upon a certain solidarity among investigators" (2.166). The community, of course, includes not only contemporaneous workers, but the men of the past on whose accomplishments current theories are built. See 7.51.

31. *Charles S. Peirce's Letters to Lady Welby*, ed. Lieb, p. 26; also in Wiener, *Values*, p. 398.

32. Thompson considers cosmic evolution the central theme of Peirce's metaphysics, and rightly bases the fallible character of knowledge on such a general evolution (*Pragmatic Philosophy*, pp. 264f).

33. Philip Wiener summarizes the fields in which Peirce judged evolution operative: "(1) intellectual history, especially the history of science; (2) the logic of the sciences, especially that of probable induction; (3) the metaphysics of history and of science" (*Evolution*, p. 86). Royce and Kernan are right in asserting that Peircean evolution applies to the development of the laws of nature, but their exclusion of its application to the development of the bodies in the universe is open to question (Josiah Royce and Fergus Kernan, "Charles Sanders Peirce," *The Journal of Philosophy, Psychology and Scientific Methods,* XIII [1916], 703).

Goudge, too, gives a rather good summary of evolution, emphasizing its generality. "Peirce was convinced the empirical evidence obliged the metaphysician to recognize (*a*) that change or becoming is a primary aspect of reality; (*b*) that the most important form of change is development or growth; (*c*) that growth cannot be understood in purely mechanical terms; (*d*) that it is a unidirectional process involving 'creativity' or the 'emergence of novelty'; and (*e*) that the facts entitle us to extend the category of evolution, thus conceived, beyond the domain of the biological to the interpretation of physical, social, and historical phenomena" (*The Thought of C. S. Peirce*, p. 229).

34. In the present text he does not mention King by name, but merely refers to a "third" theory. That he is thinking of King is evident, however, from 6.17 where he again lists the same theories and designates the third theory as King's. King's dates are 1842–1901. Like Peirce, he was a field worker in geology, particularly along the 40th parallel, and in Southern California and Arizona. In 1877 he published *Catastrophism and the Evolution of Environment.* He has two other works, *Systematic Geology* and *Mountaineering in the Sierra Nevada.* A biography of this colorful, but little known, American is now available: Thurman Wilkins, *Clarence King: A Biography* (New York: Macmillan, 1958).

35. Peirce maintains that the three types of evolution are distinct, though no sharp line of demarcation can be drawn between them (6.306). He gives some treatment of Darwin's and Lamarck's theories and their backgrounds in his article called "Evolutionary Love" (6.296–305).

36. Furthermore, "these three modes of organic evolution have their parallels in other departments of evolution" (1.105). For example, the revisions that have taken place in weights and measures could have occurred in a way resembling Darwinian evolution in organic species or in a manner more like Lamarck's or King's explanations. Agassiz was also a defender of the cataclysmic mode of evolution, as Wiener notes. Peirce was a student and admirer of Agassiz. *Evolution,* p. 77.

37. As Peirce warns, however, the scientist must not attempt to make any prog-

ress without painstaking work, or without careful regard for the work of his predecessors. This is a severe limitation, almost a denial, of cataclysmic progress in science (2.157).

I shall discuss the mind's evolution later. Here I am interested in showing that, for Peirce, evolution is not tied down to the development of the organic species. Rather it extends downward to the changes in the environment, and upward to the progress of knowledge.

38. A text confirming the generality of evolution can be found in the first section of his "A Guess at the Riddle," where he says that the evolutionist will hold that "the whole universe is approaching in the infinitely distant future a state having a general character different from that toward which we look back in the infinitely distant past" (1.362). See note 41.

39. In another place (6.336) Peirce defines existence as "that mode of being which consists in the resultant genuine dyadic relation of a strict individual with all the other such individuals of the same universe." The strength of this dyadic relation between individuals and knowing beings becomes stronger as the world evolves.

40. In an article in *The Monist* (I [1891], 161–176) entitled "The Architecture of Theories," Peirce makes reference both to the general character of evolution, and to the direction in which the universe is evolving—sc., toward an increase of law and regularity. He says that evolution accounts for the laws of nature and for uniformity *in general* without restricting it to organic species. The discrepancy between our predictions may be due either to errors of observation, or to "the imperfect cogency of the law itself, to a certain swerving of the facts from any definite formula" (6.13). In the same context he asserts that the Darwinian principle (of accidental variations in reproduction and of the destruction of weaker breeds) is capable of great generalization. Similarly, King's process of sudden leaps resulting from external forces "certainly has been the chief factor in the evolution of *institutions* as in that of *ideas*; and cannot possibly be refused a very prominent place in the process of evolution of *the universe in general*" (6.16f, emphasis added). Some of these themes will be developed later.

41. The material for the next several pages comes from Peirce's projected "A Guess at the Riddle," composed about 1890, in which he presents a moderately full treatment of the evolution of the universe toward law and regularity. In general this proposed book is a treatise on the triadic character of the world. The section most relevant to our interest is the last of the completed divisions, entitled "The Triad in Physics" (1.400–416). The title of the projected work derives from Emerson's poem "The Sphinx," whose riddle is concerned with the ultimate nature of the universe. The editors of the *Collected Papers* note that one of the drafts of this work is headed "Notes for a Book, to be entitled 'A Guess at the Riddle,' with a Vignette of the Sphynx below the Title."

42. Idioscopy or the idioscopic sciences are those sciences which depend on *special* ways of observing, and are distinguished from philosophy, a coenoscopic science, which makes use of the data of everyday life. Both words are used by Bentham.

43. Although uniformity in some sense is an obvious character of the universe, the pragmaticist will refuse to allow uniformity in Mill's sense to substitute for law. Uniformity, it is true, might be perfectly realized in a short series of past

events, Peirce admits; but law is "essentially a character of an indefinite future, and . . . only requires an approach to uniformity in a decided majority of cases" (8.192).

44. This article was published in *The Monist,* XV (1905), 161–181.

45. This fits in with Peirce's antinominalistic views.

46. Rather clear accounts of Peirce's views on these topics are given by the following: Karl Britton, "Introduction to the Metaphysics and Theology of C. S. Peirce," *Ethics,* XLIX (1938–39), 446–448; Frances Murphy Hamblin, "A Comment on Peirce's 'Tychism'," *The Journal of Philosophy,* XLII (1945), 378–383; Josiah Royce and Fergus Kernan, "Charles Sanders Peirce," *The Journal of Philosophy, Psychology and Scientific Methods,* XIII (1916), 703–706.

47. The same idea is brought out in the sixth Lowell Lecture: "The hypothesis suggested by the present writer is that all laws are results of evolution; that underlying all other laws is the only tendency which can grow by its own virtue, the tendency of all things to take habits. Now . . . this same tendency is the one sole fundamental law of mind" (6.101). See also 6.58 and 6.64.

48. Because these views are proposed as hypotheses according to the approved method of the sciences, and because of Peirce's insistence on the necessity of this method, it is difficult to agree with Eugene Freeman who asserts that Peirce's metaphysics is rationalistic (Eugene Freeman, *The Categories of Charles Peirce* [Chicago: Open Court Publishing Co., 1934], pp. 1–6, *et passim*).

49. It is interesting to note that, in the seventh lecture on pragmatism, Peirce compares an abductive suggestion to a flash. "The abductive suggestion comes to us like a flash. . . . The idea of putting together what we had never before dreamed of putting together . . . flashes the new suggestion before our contemplation" (5.181). See also 2.755 where he says that retroductive inferences are like chance variations.

50. Physical scientists must not think that theorizing at such a general level is of little importance to them. High theorizing of the above type may well save the special scientists some fifty years of work. Peirce asserts that at the time of writing the theory of the molecular construction of matter had advanced as far as indications allowed. Further progress could be made only by hypothesis and verification. But the possible hypotheses were innumerable, and none enjoyed more antecedent probability than another. Framing and testing so many possible hypotheses would take half a century or more. However, if the chemist or physicist knew how the laws of nature developed, he might be able to distinguish with some accuracy between laws that might, and laws that could not, have resulted from this process of development (1.408). A knowledge of the history of the development of laws might lead one to an accurate conjecture about the individual laws themselves. Such a highly generalized knowledge might prove very economical in enabling the special scientist to select the correct explanatory hypothesis rather early in the inquiry. "Tell us how the laws of nature came about, and we may distinguish in some measure between laws that might and laws that could not have resulted from such a process of development" (1.408).

51. Gallie is quite critical of Peirce's proposals about the origin of the universe. For Gallie, Peircean cosmogony is outside the competence of the pragmatic, scientific method. Metaphysical statements, such as Peirce's views on the ἀρχή, are vague and hopelessly beyond the clarifying power of the pragmatic method.

Peirce's explanations cannot be made to generate empirically testable concepts (Gallie, *Peirce and Pragmatism,* pp. 179–180).

52. Peirce calls his doctrine on chance "tychism," from the Greek word for chance, τύχη, as he himself notes. At the beginning of an article for *The Monist,* II (1892), 533–599, he gives a brief autobiographical sketch of his views on tychism (6.102).

53. In this section, as in many others, Peirce is writing against the doctrine of mechanistic necessitarianism. See 6.60, 6.588, 6.553–556, where Spencer and Carus are special targets of Peirce's criticism. Both Spencer's popularity in America and the opposition of Spencer from Peirce, William James, and Chauncey Wright are brought out in an article by Max H. Fisch, "Evolution in American Philosophy" (*The Philosophical Review,* LVI [1947], 357–373). Hartshorne regards Peirce as one of the leading figures in turning philosophical minds away from the opinion that the laws of nature are absolute and immutable. Determinism, according to Hartshorne, was at its height from 1670 to 1870 (Charles Hartshorne, "Charles Sanders Peirce's Metaphysics of Evolution," *The New England Quarterly,* XIV [1941], 50).

As Haas points out, although Peirce regards chance as an *explanation* of law, he nowhere considers it a *cause* of order. In fact, as will be seen later, chance itself cannot be explained apart from law.

Thomas S. Knight makes the opposition to mechanistic determinism the principal theme of his presentation of Peirce's tychism: *Charles Peirce,* The Great American Thinkers Series (New York: Washington Square Press, 1965), pp. 148ff.

54. In the rejoinder, Peirce lists four arguments for believing in chance. Most of the comments on the arguments are cast in an antimechanistic mold. My restriction of the arguments to two is in no sense a betrayal of Peirce.

55. This of course, does not deny the regularity of things, as the same text indicates.

56. As Weiss says, the meaning of variety is explainable, though not its occurrences (Paul Weiss, "The Essence of Peirce's System," *The Journal of Philosophy,* XXXVII [1940], 255).

57. At this point Peirce inserts a footnote stating that he admits the absolute truth of this proposition, because it relates to the Absolute. This is an aspect of fallibilism that was never developed.

58. In the sixth Lowell Lecture Peirce describes several opinions on the amounts of law and variety in the universe. His own view is presented rather briefly and echoes some of the ideas expressed in "A Guess at the Riddle." The lecture, however, was composed about thirteen years after the "Guess." In the lecture, he says that the uniformities of the universe are never absolutely exact, and that "the variety of the universe is forever increasing" (6.91).

59. In the rudimentary nothingness, Peirce says, there is no variety. But there is what he calls "an indefinite specificability, which is nothing but a tendency to the diversification of the nothing, while leaving it as nothing as it was before" (6.612).

In a paragraph in "The Logic of Events," Peirce states that, before the universe existed, the initial condition was a state of "just nothing" (6.215). But a few lines later he makes it clear that this was not the nothing of negation. "It is the germinal nothing, in which the whole universe is involved or foreshadowed. As such, it is absolutely undefined and unlimited possibility—boundless possibility. There is no compulsion and no law. It is boundless freedom. So of *potential* being there was in that initial state no lack" (6.217).

60. That is, the habit-taking tendency is responsible for those new patterns which last. Not every thing or every event formed by chance gets stabilized and brought to the perfection of law. Some chance events, in evolutionary terms, are not fit to survive. They may deviate so far from a firmly established habit of nature that they must necessarily perish without developing. Nature is a reasonable structure, in which uniformity, law, and regularity are continually increasing. Not just any chance event can be repeated and developed into the status of habit.

61. "Synechism" derives from the Greek word for continuity, *συνέχεια*. The formation of such derivatives is a familiar Peircean practice; cf. tychism, agapism, anancasm.

62. This short paragraph points out the importance of continuity for mathematics, for science, and for philosophy. It also mentions a connection between continuity and fallibilism. Fallibilism cannot be fully appreciated apart from continuity. Similarly when pointing out the nexus between continuity and thirdness, he asserts that "no conception yet discovered is higher [than True Continuity]" (5.67).

63. Another indication of the importance of continuity for Peirce is the lengthy section on "Synechism and Agapism," as the editors entitle it, in the sixth volume of the *Collected Papers*. This section, as well as many others, makes repeated reference to continuity. Fairbanks, in opposition to writers like Russell, Reichenbach, and others who praise Peirce and damn Hegel, offers documentary proof of Peirce's debt to Hegel in the area of continuity (Matthew J. Fairbanks, "Peirce's Debt to Hegel," *The New Scholasticism*, XXXVI [1962], 219–224).

64. In the context of this selection, Peirce speaks of the world as evolving from Platonic forms. This interesting aspect of Peirce is somewhat beyond the scope of this work. See 6.189–209.

65. Not only this paragraph but the whole section from which we have been working is set forth as a *hypothesis*. This is evident from the frequent repetition of certain words: suppose, assume, if, presumably.

66. Peirce does not seem to have examined the problem of the efficient causality operative in the universe. His interest in the evolution of the cosmos seems to have been limited to a conjectured description of what chance and regularity were like in the early days of the world.

67. For further study on these topics, see 1.163; 1.171f; 1.409; 5.4; 5.436; 6.13; 6.610; Wiener, *Values*, pp. 300f. The doctrine of continuity is also closely related to other prominent themes in Peirce. "This doctrine [of continuity] gives room for explanations of many facts which without it are absolutely and hopelessly inexplicable; and further . . . it carries along with it the following doctrines: first, a logical realism of the most pronounced type; second, objective idealism; third, tychism, with its consequent thorough-going evolutionism. We also notice that the doctrine presents no hindrances to spiritual influences, such as some philosophies are felt to do" (6.163).

68. See Murphey, *Development*, pp. 163 and 324.

69. This is an aspect of the social character of scientific inquiry.

70. See Thompson, *Pragmatic Philosophy*, p. 241.

71. Peirce illustrates the various kinds of evolution of men's ways of thinking about the world, in a lecture on the history of science (Wiener, *Values,* pp. 257–260).

72. In the second chapter I mentioned that the inquiry has a question–answer format. The evolutionary character of this format is brought out in a brief paragraph on logic, sc. the theory of scientific knowing. "Looking upon the course of logic as a whole we see that it proceeds from the question to the answer—from the vague to the definite. And so likewise all the evolution we know of proceeds from the vague to the definite" (6.191).

73. Peirce repeatedly emphasizes this theme of the growth of science. As a pursuit of living men, rather than as a systematized knowledge, it must live its own life, and hence grow (1.232). The desire to learn must be a permanent character of the scientist's life. Such a desire will direct him to the best method, and will assure the continual self-corrective growth of his pursuit of nature, as noted above (5.582).

74. See also 6.173.

75. It is worth noting here that the hypothesis of spontaneous chance was adopted by Peirce in order to save the universe from inexplicability. To classify an irregular occurrence as a member of a general class of irregularities is in a sense to render it open to understanding (1.156–166).

76. However, even the synechist must admit an element of the ultimate and inexplicable. Experience forces this on him. But clearly this admission must not be allowed as an explanation for anything (6.172).

77. "Continuity is shown by the logic of relations to be nothing but a higher type of that which we know as generality. It is relational generality" (6.190). "Continuity is simply what generality becomes in the logic of relatives" (5.436). "True generality is, in fact, nothing but a rudimentary form of true continuity. Continuity is nothing but perfect generality of a law of relationship" (6.172).

78. Peirce gives the credit to Augustus De Morgan for his first interest in the logic of relatives (1.562, 564). Furthermore, he states elsewhere that it is impossible to understand continuity apart from a knowledge of the logic of relations (Wiener, *Values,* p. 261).

79. The basis of our treatment of the logic of relatives is found in Thompson, and in the citations from Peirce which he lists: *Pragmatic Philosophy,* pp. 15 and 273.

The breadth of a term is its "extension," sc., the objects to which it can be applied; its depth is its "comprehension," sc., what the term attributes to the objects.

80. The new logic "regards the form of relation in all its generality and in its different possible species" (4.5).

81. With regard to the cotary propositions, see Chapter III, note 59.

82. All necessary reasoning, Peirce says, is mathematical, and therefore diagrammatic. Although the diagram is a special case, it is still a representation of something general and the reasoner is supposed to see that what is true of this particular diagram "will be so in any case" (5.148).

83. In 1905 Peirce wrote to William James congratulating him for the clarity achieved in a paper written in French. James replied immediately with a warm "tu quoque" letter: "Your encouragement to me to become a French classic both

gratifies and amuses. *I* will if *you* will,—we shall both be clearer, no doubt. Try putting your first, seconds, thirds into the Gallic tongue and see if you don't make more converts!" (Perry, *Thought and Character,* II, 433–435). It should be noted that Peirce had already written a very clear letter to James on the categories two years previously, in English (8.264–269). Another helpful letter on the categories was written to Lady Welby in October 1904 (*Charles S. Peirce's Letters to Lady Welby,* ed. Lieb, pp. 7–14, and *Collected Papers,* 8.327–341).

84. Richard J. Bernstein has written a helpful explanation of the categories, and of the importance of firstness: "Peirce's Theory of Perception," *Studies* (second series), pp. 165–189.

85. This doctrine of immediate perception, Peirce says, is defended by Kant and Reid, and denied by Descartes, Leibniz, and other idealists, all of whom have cut themselves off from the possibility of ever knowing a relation (5.56).

86. Boler, *Peirce and Scholastic Realism,* pp. 109–112.

87. The heart of Peircean realism is brought out again toward the end of "Some Consequences of Four Incapacities," where he affirms the real existence of generals; what is represented in a true representation is real. What the word "man" means is real. The nominalist, on the other hand, although he admits that "man" is applicable to something, still holds that there is a hidden incognizable reality beneath that something (5.312).

88. Peirce's review of Fraser's *Berkeley* is, among other things, a decided commitment to realism. The following is a sample: "If, therefore, it is asked whether the universal is in things, the answer is, that the nature which in the mind is universal, and is not in itself singular, exists in things. It is the very same nature which in the mind is universal and *in re* is singular; for if it were not, in knowing anything of a universal we should be knowing nothing of things, but only of our own thoughts, and our opinion would not be converted from true to false by a change in things. This nature is actually indeterminate only so far as it is in the mind. But to say that an object is in the mind is only a metaphorical way of saying that it stands to the intellect in the relation of known to knower. The truth is, therefore, that that real nature which exists *in re,* apart from all action of the intellect, though in itself, apart from its relations, it be singular, yet is actually universal as it exists in relation to the mind. But this universal only differs from the singular in the manner of its being conceived (*formaliter*), but not in the manner of its existence (*realiter*)" (8.18).

89. Eugene Freeman expresses the link between pragmatism and thirdness when he writes that pragmatism "is a *theory of meaning* developed from the logical implications of the category of thirdness. As a matter of fact, it is the category of thirdness, expanded into logic" (*The Categories of Charles Peirce,* p. 41).

Somewhat similarly, John J. Fitzgerald has linked Peirce's theory of signs with his pragmatism. Neither theory was orginally constructed with the other explicitly in view, Fitzgerald maintains, but the emergence of the central role of habit as the ultimate logical interpretant of signs can be taken as a theoretical underpinning of pragmatism. Both are concerned with meaning and both necessarily involve the category of thirdness. In scientific inquiry pragmatic meaning establishes a habit of expectation in the inquirer, which is the logical interpretant of the signs involved (John J. Fitzgerald, *Peirce's Theory of Signs as Foundation for Pragmatism* [The Hague: Mouton, 1966], especially pp. 158–176).

90. Arthur W. Burks, "Charles Sanders Peirce: Introduction," *Classic American Philosophers,* ed. Max H. Fisch (New York: Appleton-Century-Crofts, 1951), pp. 48–52.

91. Edward C. Moore, "The Scholastic Realism of C. S. Peirce," *Philosophy and Phenomenological Research,* XII (1951), 406. This interpretation of Peirce parallels closely Peirce's own words quoted above (5.503).

92. The pragmatic theory of meaning is for Peirce the criterion of admissibility of hypotheses preliminary to their verification, but their proposal is clearly intended as a step toward a knowledge of the truth of things to be expressed in statements which may also be pragmatically formed. See p. 20.

93. Madden, too, takes issue explicitly with Burks in this matter, asserting that Burks's conclusion seems impetuous (Edward H. Madden, "Chance and Counterfactuals in Wright and Peirce," *The Review of Metaphysics,* IX [1956], 431).

Morton White, too, although he does not mention Burks, presents a "counterfactual" interpretation of Peirce's pragmatism, i.e., an "if–would" criterion of meaning (hypotheticalism). The "if" clause expresses a human action (operationalism), and the "then–would" clause expresses something subject to experience (experientialism) (Morton White, *The Age of Analysis, 20th Century Philosophers* [New York: New American Library, 1955], p. 141).

Weiss, too, points out that "the heart of the pragmatic maxim lies in its interpretation of the meaning of concepts as involving a reference . . . to the rational or general," using 5.3 and 5.491 as evidence (Paul Weiss, "The Essence of Peirce's System," *The Journal of Philosophy,* XXXVII [1940], 259).

Finally, Burks would find it difficult to reconcile his interpretation with a work on logic composed around 1873 (7.340 and 341), and with two works published after 1900 (5.3 and 5.457).

94. Boler, *Peirce and Scholastic Realism,* p. 111. See also Haas, *Conception of Law,* pp. 89–92, and 135–138.

95. See note 21.

96. Boler, *Peirce and Scholastic Realism,* p. 101. See also Potter, *Charles S. Peirce on Norms and Ideals,* pp. 94–102.

97. See Robert P. Goodwin, "Charles Sanders Peirce: A Modern Scotist?" in *The New Scholasticism,* XXXV (1961), 478–509, and Haas, *Conception of Law,* pp. 129–131.

98. Thompson, *Pragmatic Philosophy,* p. 207. Peirce considers himself an "Aristotelian of the scholastic wing, approaching Scotism, but going much further in the direction of scholastic realism" (5.77*n*).

99. Murphey brings this out when he writes that the law of habit formation in the universe is "essentially a form of ampliative inference, and illustrates Peirce's thesis that the universe creates order by the use of the same logical processes which we employ to discover that order" (*Development,* p. 405).

100. Peirce infers the existence of such an instinct by a process of abduction. Instinct explains the obvious success which scientists have had in tracking down the laws of nature. Science has been successful in selecting the right hypothesis, in numerous instances. However, as we have seen above, science is still very middle-sized in relation to the vastness of nature. It is only a handful of pebbles, while the cosmos is a vast ocean. If the mind were not somehow in tune with nature, there would be nothing like the progress which science has actually

made. Hence, the existence of instinct is proposed as a hypothesis to explain the notable success that science has enjoyed in selecting the correct explanatory hypotheses.

Peirce cautions his reader, however, that instinct cannot adequately account for the success which science has enjoyed. It is a partial explanation, but there is most likely some other element, still unknown. "Such an hypothesis naturally suggests itself, but it must be admitted that it does not seem sufficient to account for the extraordinary accuracy with which these conceptions apply to the phenomena of Nature, and it is probable that there is some secret here which remains to be discovered" (6.418).

101. A similar view is brought out in "The Laws of Nature and Hume's Argument Against Miracles," in a section in which Peirce explains the foreknowledge involved in a law of nature. The mind of man can attain such foreknowledge, he says, because "there is an energizing reasonableness that shapes phenomena in some sense, and . . . this same working reasonableness has molded the reason of man into something like its own image." The fact that man has achieved a "foreknowing generalization of observation," as Peirce defines a law of nature in this context, proves, he says, that there is such an energizing reasonableness as he describes (Wiener, *Values,* p. 291).

102. In a later work, intended as part of the proposed "Minute Logic," Peirce again points out the parallel between the evolution of nature and the growth of scientific knowledge. Both experience and the explanatory guess have their equivalents in the development of nature. We come to a knowledge of the laws of nature, Peirce says, by guessing them out bit by bit, and checking our guess by experimentation, and revising them to accord with the experience gained (2.86). And according to the theory of natural selection, nature performs similar experiments on a stock of plants or animals, to adapt it to its slowly changing environment. Furthermore, "a stock in some degree out of adjustment to its environment immediately begins to sport, and that not wildly but in ways having some sort of relation to the change needed. Still more remarkable is the fact that a man before whom a scientific problem is placed immediately begins to make guesses, not wildly remote from the true guess" (2.86). See also Wiener, *Evolution,* pp. 91f, and "Peirce's Evolutionary Interpretations of the History of Science," *Studies* (first series), pp. 151f.

NOTES—CHAPTER VI

1. The review was published in the *Popular Science Monthly,* LVIII (1901), 296–306.

2. The same is also expressed in another short piece of writing, presumably a partial draft of the review, which the editor has placed as a footnote to the above-quoted paragraph.

3. Richard S. Robin also points out the connection between Peirce's discussion of inquiry and his theory of the normative sciences in "Peirce's Doctrine of the Normative Sciences," *Studies* (second series), p. 275.

4. In 5.111, 5.129, and 2.197f he mentions the late development of his interest in ethics and aesthetics.

5. See also 1.578f.

6. The relation between logic and ethics is also brought out in a book review published in *The Nation* in 1901 (8.158 with note), and in a letter dated 1902 to Mrs. Christine Ladd-Franklin, quoted in the *Journal of Philosophy, Psychology and Scientific Methods,* XIII (1916), 717.

7. For a similar understanding of the three normative sciences, logic, ethics, and aesthetics, and of pre-normative phenomenology, see 5.34–37 and 5.120–136. Both of these works were written in 1903. On aesthetics as the study of the admirable in itself, see Potter, *Charles S. Peirce on Norms and Ideals,* pp. 34–51.

8. John J. Fitzgerald thinks that even the rather early essay "How to Make Our Ideas Clear" is not as stoical in its defense of phenomenalism as it seems at first sight ("Peirce's 'How to Make Our Ideas Clear'," *The New Scholasticism,* XXXIX [1965], 53–68). There is, of course, in Peirce's later writings much more ample evidence of the openness of the pragmatic method to transempirical meaning, as Fitzgerald indicates throughout his book, *Peirce's Theory of Signs as Foundation for Pragmatism,* especially pp. 94–105.

9. As Goudge explains, "the *summum bonum* . . . pronounced by esthetics to be most admirable in itself, and further accepted by ethics as the ultimate goal for action, is the promotion of 'concrete reasonableness'" (*The Thought of C. S. Peirce,* p. 305).

Richard J. Bernstein has explained well the centrality of the theme of the growth of concrete reasonableness in Peirce's philosophy. "We have come to the very coping stone of Peirce's thought—the ultimate ideal of self-control—the complete commitment to the growth of concrete reasonableness as the *summum bonum.* We have tried to show one path that weaves through an apparent disarray of ideas and themes to this culmination. What initially appears to be confused, chaotic, and even inconsistent, turns out upon analysis systematic, coherent, and powerful. . . . In delineating the connections between the concepts of action, conduct, habit, criticism, community, and control, we have come to the central theme of rationality as self-control, a self-control manifested in a hierarchy of normative sciences where our ultimate ideal, our final end, the *summum bonum,* is the continued growth of concrete reasonableness" ("Action, Conduct, and Self-Control," in *Perspectives on Peirce: Critical Essays on Charles Sanders Peirce,* p. 89).

10. Thompson develops the theme, found in Peirce, of the evolution from primitive man via self-control to the modern scientist, paralleling the evolution from knowledge for use to knowledge for itself (*Pragmatic Philosophy,* pp. 223–227).

11. Idus Murphree, commenting on Peirce's insistence that science is theoretical rather than practical, writes: "Peirce's theme here is the old and familiar one of opposition to restrictions placed on inquiry, restrictions that would block inquiry at the outset if the topics to be investigated had to be those set for the sciences by engineers and deans of men" ("Peirce: The Experimental Nature of Belief," *The Journal of Philosophy,* LX [1963], 314).

12. A philosopher of the 1960s and 1970s can, however, rightfully insist that

the human problems of our contemporaries must influence the choice of questions to be pursued theoretically.

13. These are themes developed by Maritain, Gilson, Pieper, Lonergan, and others.

14. Gallie, *Peirce and Pragmatism,* pp. 237f.

15. *Ibid.*

16. Wiener, *Evolution,* p. 93.

17. Goudge, *The Thought of C. S. Peirce,* p. 286; Wiener, *Evolution,* p. 95. W. Donald Oliver also asserts that the roles of continuity and chance do not account for *this* world. He sees a possibility of accounting for this world through the medium of agapasm advocated by Peirce, but not quite in the same way that Peirce proposed it ("The Final Cause and Agapasm in Peirce's Philosophy," *Studies* [second series], pp. 289–303).

18. Paul Weiss, "Charles Sanders Peirce," *Sewanee Review,* L (1942), 189. It is the opinion of Henry S. Leonard that Peirce has actually made use of other methods besides the pragmatic in his metaphysics, particularly as found in the sixth volume of the *Collected Papers* (Henry S. Leonard, "The Pragmatism and Scientific Metaphysics of C. S. Peirce," *Philosophy of Science,* IV [1937], 119).

Robert J. Roth, S.J., has also pointed to a significant area of Peirce's thought which is outside the scientific tradition: "Is Peirce's Pragmatism Anti-Jamesian?" in *International Philosophical Quarterly,* V (1965), 541–563.

19. In 1905 Peirce explicitly dissociated pragmaticism from any denial of the Absolute, or from an interpretation that would make action the *summum bonum.* He wrote: ". . . I am one of those who say 'We believe in God, the Father Almighty, Maker of heaven and earth and of all things visible and *invisible*' where the invisible things, I take it, are Love, Beauty, Truth, the Principle of Contradiction, Time, etc. Clearly I can have but the vaguest analogical notion of the Maker of such things, and Pragmaticism, I am sure, does not require that all my beliefs should be definite" (Charles S. Peirce Papers, # 284).

20. Nynfa Bosco has shown that though Peirce rejected a type of dogmatic metaphysics, he was altogether in favor of developing a "scientific" metaphysics, i.e., one that was public, capable of verification and progress, and guided by those who were well trained in its method. It must not be scientistic or positivistic in intent ("Peirce and Metaphysics," *Studies* [second series], pp. 345–358).

21. John Dewey, Review of *Collected Papers of Charles Sanders Peirce,* Vols. 1–6, *The New Republic,* LXXXIX (1937), 415.

22. R. B. Perry, "Is There a North American Philosophy?" in *Philosophy and Phenomenological Research,* IX (1949), 367.

INDEX